A BIBLIOGRAPHY OF MUSEUM STUDIES

This comprehensive guide to the full range of published material on museums and collections will be invaluable to both students and museum professionals.

The 4,254 references are systematically arranged in sections dealing with, among other topics, collections management, communication and exhibitions, museum education, material culture, the museums profession and museums management.

Compiled from the unparalleled research and teaching resources of the Department of Museum Studies at the University of Leicester, this redeveloped, revised and expanded edition of a long-established and widely respected departmental publication is an essential resource for everyone studying or working in museums and trying to come to grips with a large, growing and widely dispersed literature. Whether you are developing a disaster plan or a visitor survey, entering the profession or compiling a national museums budget, it will be your only effective guide to the relevant contemporary literature.

A Bibliography of Museum Studies

Compiled and Edited by

SIMON J. KNELL
Department of Museum Studies
University of Leicester

Ashgate

Aldershot • Brookfield USA • Singapore • Sydney

Previously published by the Department of Museum Studies, University of Leicester, as the *Bibliography for Museum Studies Training*. Tenth edition, 1991, entitled *Museum Studies Bibliography*.

This 11th edition published 1994 by

Ashgate Publishing Limited
Gower House
Croft Road
Aldershot,Hampshire
GU11 3HR
Great Britain

Ashgate Publishing Company
Old Post Road
Brookfield
Vermont 05036
USA

Reprinted 1998

British Library Cataloguing in Publication Data

Bibliography of Museum Studies.-11Rev.ed
I. Knell, Simon J.
016.069

ISBN 1 85928 061 7

Library of Congress Cataloging-in-Publication Data

Knell, Simon J.
    A bibliography of museum studies / Simon J. Knell
    p. ; cm
    Includes index
    ISBN 1-85928-061-7
    1. Museums--Bibliography. I. Title.
Z5052.K64 1994
[AM5]   94-8279
            CIP

Printed in Great Britain by Biddles Limited,
Guildford and King's Lynn

Contents

Preface

A Bibliography of Museum Studies aims to provide a bibliographic source of reference for those engaged in museum training and research, as well as those museum workers, and others, who simply wish to access the contemporary literature on museums. First published by the Department of Museum Studies as the *Bibliography for Museum Studies Training*, it reached its tenth edition in 1991 under the title *Museum Studies Bibliography*. For this, the first Scolar edition, the content has been completely revised and re-organised, and references are now systematically arranged into subject-based sections. An author index has also been added. Many sections in this edition have been greatly expanded and older references have been retained where it is felt that they give historical context to modern developments or still remain relevant to contemporary practice.

Museum studies now embraces a large body of research and no authoritative bibliography can be the product of a single worker. This bibliography reflects its many years of evolution and embodies the results of teaching and research by all the Department's staff. I would like to thank the present team - Professor Susan Pearce, Dr Eilean Hooper-Greenhill, Gaynor Kavanagh, Kevin Moore and Janet Owen - for freely providing lists of references currently used by them, and also former members of staff, particularly Anne Fahy, Geoffrey Lewis, and Geoffrey Stansfield, who have contributed considerably to the development of this work.

The Department of Museum Studies has long maintained an interest in gathering together bibliographical information and publications relating to museums and collections. Much of this information now forms the basis of the Department's Museum Documentation Centre which is currently being developed as a new research facility. In this objective we gratefully acknowledge the assistance of the Museums & Galleries Commission.

I welcome comments and suggestions on the content of this bibliography.

Simon Knell
Department of Museum Studies
University of Leicester
105 Princess Road East
Leicester LE1 7LG
England

1 Museum Context

1.1 Museums - An Introduction

Ambrose, T.M. (1993) *Managing New Museums: A Guide to Good Practice*, HMSO/Scottish Museums Council.

Ambrose, T.M. (ed.) (1987) *Education in Museums; Museums in Education*, HMSO/Scottish Museums Council.

Ambrose, T.M. (ed.) (1988) *Working with Museums*, HMSO/Scottish Museums Council.

Ambrose, T.M. (ed.) (1991) *Money, Money, Money and Museums*, HMSO/Scottish Museums Council.

Ambrose, T.M. & Paine, C. (1993) *Museum Basics*, Routledge, London.

Ambrose, T.M. & Runyard, S. (eds.) (1991) *Forward Planning*, Routledge, London.

American Association of Museums (1992) *Excellence and Equity: Education and the Public Dimension of Museums*, American Association of Museums, Washington DC.

Annis, S. (1987) The museum as a staging ground for symbolic action, *Museum*, 38(3), 168-171.

Arnold, K. (1993) Mysterious museums and curious curators, *Museums Journal*, 93(8), 20-21.

Cannizzo, J. (1987) How sweet it is: cultural politics in Barbados, *Muse*, Winter, 22-27.

Edson, G. & Dean, D. (1994) *The Handbook for Museums*, Routledge, London.

Falk, J. & Dierking, L. (1992) *The Museum Experience*, Whaleback Books, Washington.

Goode, G.B. (1895) The principles of museum administration, *Museums Association Conference Proceedings*, 69-79.

Greene, J.P. (1989) Museums for the year 2000: a case for continuous revolution, *Museums Journal*, 88(4), 179-180.

Hebditch, M. (1991) Essential values, *Museums Journal*, 91(11), 29-31.

Hooper-Greenhill, E. (1992) *Museums and the Shaping of Knowledge*, Routledge, London.

Hudson, K. (1987) *Museums of Influence: The Pioneers of the Last 200 Years*, Cambridge University Press, Cambridge.

Hudson, K. & Nichols, A. (1989) *Cambridge Guide to the Museums of Britain and Ireland*, Cambridge University Press, Cambridge.

Hudson, K. & Nichols, A. (1991) *Cambridge Guide to the Museums of Europe*, Cambridge University Press, Cambridge.

International Council of Museums (1990) *ICOM (International Council of Museums) Statutes and Code of Professional Ethics*, ICOM.

Jenkins, P. (1993) Museum futures, *Museums Journal*, 19(7), 22-23.

Karp, I., Kreamer, C. M. & Lavine, S. D. (eds.) (1992) *Museums and Communities: Debating Public Culture*, Smithsonian Institution Press, Washington DC.

Karp, I. & Lavine, S.D. (eds.) (1991) *Exhibiting Cultures, the Poetics and Politics of Museum Display*, Smithsonian Institution Press, Washington DC.

Kavanagh, G. (ed.) (1991) *Museum Languages: Objects and Texts*, Leicester University Press, Leicester, London and New York.

Kavanagh, G. (ed.) (1991) *The Museums Profession: Internal and External Relations*, Leicester University Press, Leicester, London and New York.

Lewis, G.D. (1987) Museums, *Encyclopaedia Britannica*, 15th edition, Chicago, 478-490.

Lewis, J. (1990) *Art, Culture and Enterprise: The Politics of Art and the Cultural Industries*, Routledge, London.

Lord, G.D. & Lord, B. (eds.) (1991) *The Manual of Museum Planning*, Museum of Science and Industry, Manchester and HMSO, London.

Lumley, R., (ed.) (1988) *The Museum Time Machine*, Methuen/Routledge, London.

Montaner, J.M. (1990) *New Museums*, Architectural & Design Press.

O'Neill, M. (1991) Museums and their communities, in Lord, G., D & Lord, B. (eds.), *The Manual of Museum Planning*, Museum of Science and Industry, Manchester and HMSO, London, 19-34.

O'Neill, M. (1992) Piero della Francesca and the trainspotters, *A New Head of Steam: Industrial History in the Museum*, Scottish Museums Council, 33-36.

Pearce, S.M. (1993) Making up is hard to do, *Museums Journal*, 93(12), 25-27.

Pearce, S.M. (ed.) (1988) *Museum Studies in Material Culture*, Leicester University Press, Leicester, London and New York.

Pearce, S.M. (ed.) (1991) *Museum Economics and the Community*, New Research in Museum Studies, Vol. 2, Athlone, London.

Pearce, S.M. (ed.) (1994) *Museums and Europe*, New Research in Museum Studies, Vol. 3, Athlone, London.

Pearce, S.M. (ed.) (1994) *Museums and the Appropriation of Culture*, New Research in Museum Studies, Vol. 4, Athlone, London.

Postman, N. (1990) Museum as dialogue, *Museum News*, 69(5), 55-58.

Riviere, G.H. (1989) *La Muséologie*, Paris.

Roberts, J. (1990) *Postmodernism, Politics and Art*, Manchester University Press, Manchester.

Sande, T. A. (1992) Museums, museums, museums, *Museum Management & Curatorship*, 11, 185-192.

Thompson, J.M.A. *et al.* **(eds.)** (1992) *Manual of Curatorship: A Guide to Museum Practice*, Museums Association/Butterworths, London.

Vergo, P. (ed.) (1989) *The New Museology*, Reaktion Books, London.

Weil, S.E. (1985) *Beauty and the Beasts: On Museums, Art, the Law, and the Market*, Smithsonian Institution Press, Washington DC.

Weil, S.E. (1990) *Rethinking the Museum and Other and Meditations*, Smithsonian Institution Press, Washington DC.

1.2 Museums UK

Anderson, R.G.W. (1990) *A New Museum for Scotland*, National Museums of Scotland, Edinburgh.

Attenborough, R. (1985) *Arts and Disabled People*, Carnegie UK Trust and the Centre for Environment for the Handicapped.

Audit Commission (1991) *Local Authorities, Entertainment and the Arts*, HMSO, London.

Audit Commission (1991) *The Road to Wigan Pier? Managing Local Authority Museums and Art Galleries*, HMSO, London.

Boylan, P.J. (1993) Survey highlights staff cuts in 50% of local authority museums, *Museums Journal*, 93(11), 14-15.

Durant, J. (ed.) (1992) *Museums and the Public Understanding of Science*, Science Museum in Association with the Committee on the Public Understanding of Science, London.

Feber, S. (1992) Is big boring?, *Museums Journal*, 92(12), 34-36.

Fiest, A. & Hutchinson, R. (1989) Museums, *Cultural Trends 4*, Policy Studies Institute, London.

Fiest, A. & Hutchinson, R. (1990) Funding the arts in seven western countries, *Cultural Trends 5*, Policy Studies Institute, London.

Fleming, D., Paine, C. & Rhodes, J. (eds.) (1992) *Social History in Museums: A Manual of Curatorship*, HMSO, London.

Fowler, P. (1992) *The Past in Contemporary Society*, Routledge, London.

Harvey, B. (1987) *Visiting the National Portrait Gallery: A Report of a Survey of Visitors to the National Portrait Gallery*, Office of Population Censuses and Surveys, Social Survey Division, HMSO.

Heady, P. (1984) *Visiting Museums: A Report of a Survey of Visitors to the Victoria & Albert, Science and National Railway Museums for the Office of Arts and Libraries*, Office of Population Censuses and Surveys, HMSO, London.

Hebditch, M. (1992) Museums and the contract culture, *Museums Journal*, 92(12), 32-34.

Hewison, R. (1987) *The Heritage Industry*, Methuen, London.

Hewison, R. (1990) *Future Tense: A New Art for the Nineties*, Methuen, London.

Horne, D. (1984) *The Great Museum*, Pluto Press, London & Sidney.

House of Commons Education, Science and Arts Committee (1990) *Should Museums Charge? Some Case Studies*, HMSO, London.

Hudson, K. (1990) *1992: Prayer or Promise?*, Museums & Galleries Commission, HMSO, London.

Institution of Professionals, Managers & Specialists (1989) *Britain's Heritage - IPMS Policy*, Chapter 4, IPMS, London.

Kavanagh, G. (1987) Are museums for keeps, *International Council of Museums International Committee for Museology (ICOFOM) Study Series 2*.

Kavanagh, G. (1990) *History Curatorship*, Leicester University Press, Leicester, London and New York.

Kavanagh, G. (ed.) (1991) *Museum Languages: Objects and Texts*, Leicester University Press, Leicester, London and New York.

Kavanagh, G. (ed.) (1991) *The Museums Profession: Internal and External Relations*, Leicester University Press, Leicester, London and New York.

Knell, S.J. & Taylor, M.A. (1989) *Geology and the Local Museum*, HMSO, London.

Lewis, G.D. (1989) *For Instruction and Recreation: A Centenary History of the Museums Association*, Quiller Press, London.

Lord, B., Lord, G.D. & Nicks, J. (1989) *The Cost of Collecting: Collection Management in UK Museums*, HMSO, London.

Lumley, R. (ed.) (1988) *The Museum Time Machine*, Methuen/Routledge, London.

Merriman, N. (1991) *Beyond the Glass Case: The Past, Heritage and the Public in Britain*, Leicester University Press, Leicester, London and New York.

Middleton, V. (1990) *New Visions for Independent Museums in the UK*, Association of Independent Museums, West Sussex.

Minihan, J. (1977) *The Nationalisation of Culture: The Development of State Subsidy of the Arts in Britain*, Hamish Hamilton, London.

Museums Association (1993) *A National Strategy for Museums*, Museums Association, London.

Museums & Galleries Commission (1988) *The National Museums*, HMSO, London.

Museums & Galleries Commission (1991) *Local Authorities and Museums*, HMSO, London.

Museums & Galleries Commission (1991) *Local Authority Museums: Report by a Working Party*, HMSO, London.

Museums & Galleries Commission (1992) *Museums Matter*, MGC, London.

Museums & Galleries Commission (1994) *Registration Scheme for Museums & Galleries in the UK, Second Phase*, Museum & Galleries Commission, London.

Museums & Galleries Commission (annual) *Annual Report*, MGC, London.

Myerscough, J. (1988) *The Economic Importance of the Arts in Britain*, Policy Studies Institute, London.

National Audit Office (1988) *Management of the Collections of the English National Museums and Galleries*, HMSO, London.

National Audit Office (1993) *Department of National Heritage, National Museums and Galleries: Quality of Service to the Public*, HMSO, London.

Office of Arts & Libraries (1991) *Report on the Development of Performance Indicators for the National Museums and Galleries*, OAL, London.

Office of Arts & Libraries (1991) *Volunteers in Museums and Heritage Organisations: Policy and Planning and Management*, HMSO, London.

Pearce, S.M. (1989) *Archaeology Curatorship*, Leicester University Press, Leicester, London and New York.

Prince, D.R. & Higgins-McLoughlin, B. (1987) *Museums UK: The Findings of the Museums Data-Base Project*, Museums Association, London.

Runyard, S. (1993) *Museums and Tourism*, Museums & Galleries Commission.

Stansfield, G. (ed.) (1994) *Manual of Natural History Curatorship*, HMSO, London.

Swann Report (1985) *Education for All: Summary of the Swann Report on the Education of Ethnic Minority Children*, The Runneymede Trust.

Tate, S. (1989) *Palaces of Discovery: The Changing World of Britain's Museums*, Quiller Press, London.

Thompson, J. (1993) Contractual obligations, *Museums Journal*, 93(6), 25-26.

Thompson, J.M.A. et al. (eds.) (1992) *Manual of Curatorship: A Guide to Museum Practice*, Museums Association/Butterworths, London.

Touche Ross (1989) *Museum Funding and Services: The Visitor's Perspective*, Touche Ross, London.

United Kingdom Institute for Conservation (1989) *The Survey: Conservation Facilities in Museums and Galleries*, UKIC, London.

Vergo, P. (ed.) (1989) *The New Museology*, Reaktion Books, London.

Warhurst, A. (1986) A triple crisis in university museums, *Museums Journal*, 86(3), 137-140.

Warhurst, A. (1992) Higher concerns, *Museums Journal*, 92, 27-31.

Woroncow, B. (1992) Public palaces or private places?, *Museums Journal*, 92(12), 27-29.

1.3 Museums Western Europe

Biddulph, F. (1990) Spotlight on David, *Museums Journal*, 90(1), 25.
Boylan, P. J. (1993) Cross-community curatorial competences, *Museums Journal*, 93(1), 26-29.
Carlsson, G. & Ågren, P.-U. (1982) *Utställningsspråk: Om Utställningar för Upplevelse och Kunskap*, Prisma, Riksutställningar, Stockholm.
Clifford, T. (1989) Le Grand Louvre, *Museums Journal*, 89(8), 18-22.
Davies, F. (1993) Postcard from Moscow, *Museums Journal*, 93(12), 19.
Davies, I. (1990) Only a step away (Northern France), *Museums Journal*, 90(8), 19.
Grunfeld, J.-F. (1989) *SIME- blowing the museum trumpet*, 17 August.
Hebditch, M. (1990) Community concerns, *Museums Journal*, 90(5), 35-38.
Hebditch, M. (1993) Facing the future, *Museums Journal*, 93(1), 30-34.
Hudson, K. (1990) *1992: Prayer or Promise?*, HMSO for MGC.
Janes, D. (1993) Uniting a divided past (Berlin), *Museums Journal*, 93(10), 23-25.
Kay, A. (1990) The wind of change (Bulgaria), *Museums Journal*, 90(6), 23.
Miles, R. & Zavala, L. (1993) *Towards the Museum of the Future: New European Perspectives*, Routledge, London.
Murdin, L. (1993) Community co-operation, *Museums Journal*, 93(1), 21-25.
Pearce, S.M. (ed.) (1994) *Museums and Europe*, New Research in Museum Studies, Vol. 3, Athlone, London.
Rosander, G. (ed.) (1980) *Today for Tomorrow: Museum Documentation of Contemporary Society in Sweden by Acquisition of Objects*, SAMDOK, Stockholm.
Stavenow-Hidemark, E. (1985) *Home Thoughts from Abroad: An Evaluation of the SAMDOK Homes Pool*, Nordiska Museet/SAMDOK, Stockholm.
Trustram, M. (1991) History from below (Germany), *Museums Journal*, 91(3), 19.
Walsh, A. (1991) Russian Revolutions, *Museums Journal*, 91(11), 18-19.
Wright, P. (1989) Museums and the French state, *Museums Journal*, 89(8), 23-31.
Wright, P. (1990) Shedding responsibilities (Holland), *Museums Journal*, 90(5), 24-33.

Wright, P. (1991) Inside Italy, *Museums Journal*, 91(6), 25-36.
Wright, P. (1992) States of the nation (Spain), *Museums Journal*, 92(6), 25-33.

1.4 Museums America

American Association for State and Local History (1991) Documentation Practices in Historical Collections. A Report from the Common Agenda, *History News,* 46(1), Technical Leaflet.
African-American Museums Association (1988) *Profile of Black Museums*, American Association for State and Local History (AASLH), Nashville, Tennessee.
American Association of Museums (1984) *Museums for a New Century*, American Association of Museums, Washington DC.
American Association of Museums (1992) *Data Report from the 1989 National Museum Survey*, American Association of Museums, Washington DC.
American Association of Museums (1992) *Excellence and Equity: Education and the Public Dimension of Museums*, American Association of Museums, Washington DC.
American Association of Museums (1993) *Museums Count*, American Association of Museums, Washington DC.
Ballinger, C. (1993) Culture clash (Mexico), *Museums Journal*, 93(8), 25-32.
Benson, S. *et al.* (1986) *Presenting the Past: Essays on History and the Public*, Temple University Press.
Blatti, J. (ed.) (1987) *Past Meets Present: Essays about Historic Interpretation and Public Audiences*, Smithsonian Institution Press, Washington DC.
Dickenson, J. (1992) Leaving the past behind (Brazil), *Museums Journal*, 92(3), 32-34.
George, G. (1990) *Visiting History: Arguments over Museums and Historic Sites*, American Association of Museums, Washington DC.
Hall, P. & Seemann, C. (ed.) (1987) *Folklife and Museums: Selected Readings*, American Association for State and Local History (AASLH), Nashville, Tennessee.
Karp, I., Kreamer, C. M. & Lavine, S. D. (eds.) (1992) *Museums and Communities: Debating Public Culture*, Smithsonian Institution Press, Washington DC.
Karp, I. & Lavine, S.D. (1991) *Exhibiting Cultures: The Poetics and*

Politics of Museum Display, Smithsonian Institution Press, Washington DC.

Leon, W. & Rosenzweig, R. (eds.) (1989) *History Museums in the United States: A Critical Assessment*, University of Illinois Press, Urbana and Chicago.

Quimby, I.M.G. (1978) *Material Culture and the Study of American Life*, Norton, New York.

Schlereth, T.J. (1980) *Artifacts and the American Past*, American Association for State and Local History (AASLH), Nashville, Tennessee.

Schlereth, T.J. (ed.) (1982) *Material Culture Studies in America*, American Association for State and Local History (AASLH), Nashville, Tennessee.

Wallace, M. (1981) Visiting the past: history museums in the United States, *Radical History Review*, 25, 63-96.

Wallace, M. (1987) Industrial museums and the history of deindustrialisation, *The Public Historian*, 9 (1), 9-19.

Wallace, M. (1987) The politics of public history, in J. Blatti (ed.), *Past Meets Present: Essays about Historic Interpretation and Public Audiences*, Smithsonian Institution Press, Washington DC.

Wallace, M. (1989) The future of history museums, *History News*, 44 (4), 5-33.

2 Collection Studies & Museum History

2.1 General

Abercrombie, N. (1982) *Cultural Policy in the United Kingdom*, UNESCO, Paris.

Adam, T.R. (1937) *The Civic Value of Museums*, New York.

Adam, T.R. (1939) *The Museum and Popular Culture*, New York.

Alexander, E.P. (1979) *Museums in Motion*, American Association for State and Local History (AASLH), Nashville, Tennessee.

Alexander, E.P. (1983) *Museum Masters:Their Museums and Their Influence*, American Association for State and Local History (AASLH), Nashville, Tennessee.

Alsop, J. (1982) *The Rare Art Traditions: A History of Collecting and its linked Phenomena*, Harper & Row, New York.

American Association of Museums (1984) *Museums for a New Century*, American Association of Museums, Washington DC.

Anderson, J. & Black, G.F. (1888) Reports on local museums in Scotland obtained through Dr R.H. Gunnings jubilee gift to the Society, *Proceedings of the Society of Antiquaries of Scotland*, 10(NS), 331-422.

Aristides, N. (1988) Calm and uncollected, *American Scholar*, 57(3), 327-336.

Ashmolean Museum (1986) *Patronage and collecting in the seventeenth century: Earl of Arundel*, Ashmolean Museum, Oxford.

Baekeland, F. (1988) Psychological aspects of art collecting, *Psychiatry*, 44, 45-59.

Bazin, G. (1967) *The Museum Age*, Brussels.

Bedini, S.A. (1965) The evolution of science museums, *Technology and Culture*, 6, 1-29.

Belk, R. (1988) Possessions and the extended self, *Journal of Consumer Research*, 15, 139-168.

Belk, R. & Wallendorf, M. (1992) Of mice and men: gender identity in collecting, in Ames, K. & Martinez, K. (eds.), *Material Culture of Gender/Gender of Material Culture*, University of Michigan Research Press, Ann Arbor, 1-18.

Belk, R., Wallendorf, M. & Sherry, J. (1989) The sacred and profane in consumer behaviour: theodicy on the odyssey, *Journal of Consumer Reseach*, 16, 1-38.

Belk, R., Wallendorf, M., Sherry, J. & Holbrook, M. (1990) Collecting in a consumer culture, *Highways and Buyways*, Association of Consumer Research, Utah.

Belk, R., Wallendorf, M., Sherry, J., Holbrook, M. & Roberts, S. (1988) Collectors and collecting, *Advances in consumer research*, 15, 548-553.

Bell. W.J. *et al.* (1967) *A Cabinet of Curiosities: Five Episodes in the Evolution of American Museums,*, University Press of Virginia, Charlottesville.

Bradler, R. (1990) *The Passage of Arms*, Cambridge University Press.

Brandt, A. (1983) The temple of nature - what really is the function of a great museum, *Connoisseur*, 213(855), 85-95.

Brawne, M. (1965) *The New Museum*, Architectural Press, London.

Brears, P.C.D. (1984) Temples of the Muses: the Yorkshire philosophical societies, *Museums Journal*, 84(1), 3-19.

Brears, P.C.D. (1989) *Of Curiosity and Rare Things: The Story of Leeds City Museums*, Friends of Leeds City Museums.

Brears, P.C.D. & Davies, S. (1989) *Treasures for the People:The Story of Museums and Galleries in Yorkshire and Humberside*, Yorkshire and Humberside Museums Council, Leeds.

British Association for the Advancement of Science (1887) *Report of the British Association for the Advancement of Science 1887*, 97-130.

British Association for the Advancement of Science (1888) *Report of the British Association for the Advancement of Science 1888*, 124-32.

British Association for the Advancement of Science (1920) *Report of the British Association for the Advancement of Science 1920*, 267-80.

Burcaw, G.E. (1983) *Introduction to Museum Work*, American Association for State and Local History (AASLH), Nashville, Tennessee.

Carey, F. (1991) *Collecting for the twentieth century*, British Museum, London.

Carlisle, E., Countess of (1988) *A History of the Commission*, Museums & Galleries Commission, London.

Caygill, M. (1992) *The Story of the British Museum*, 2nd edition, British Museum Publications,London.

Chapman, W. (1985) Arranging Ethnology in Stocking, G. (ed.), *Objects and Others: Essays on Museums and Material Culture*, History of Anthropology, Vol. 3, University of Wisconsin Press, 15-54.

Chapman, W. (1991) Like a game of dominoes: Augustus Pitt Rivers and the typological museum idea, in Pearce, S. (ed.), *Museum Economics and the Community*, New Research in Museum Studies, Vol. 2, Athlone, London, 135-176.

Clifford, J. (1988) *The Predicament of Culture: Twentieth Century Ethnography, Literature and Art*, Harvard University Press, Cambridge, Mass..

Clifford, T. (1982) The historical approach to the display of paintings, *International J. of Museum Management and Curatorship*, 1, 93-106.

Coleman, L.V. (1939) *The Museum in America*, American Association of Museums, Washington DC.

Colvin, C. & Cast, L. (1898) *The History of the Society of Dilettanti.*

Cossons, N. (1983) The new museum movement in the United Kingdom, *Museum*, 35(2), 83-89.

Danet, B. & Katriel, T. (1989) No two alike: play and aesthetics in collecting, *Play and Culture*, 2, 253-277.

Davies, G. (ed.) (1991) Plaster and marble: the classical and neo-classical portrait bust, *Journal of History of Collections*, 3(2).

Davies, S. (1985) Collecting and recalling the twentieth century, *Museums Journal*, 85(1), 27-29.

Durbin, G. (1984) *The Past Displayed: History of the Norwich Museums*, Norfolk County Museum Service,Norwich.

Findler, P. (1989) The museum: its classical etymology and its renaissance genealogy, *Journal of History of Collections*, 1, 59-78.

Finlay, I. (1977) *Priceless Heritage: The Future of Museums*, Faber & Faber, London.

Flower, Sir W.H. (1898) *Essays on Museums and Other Subjects*, MacMillan, London.

Foster, R. (1981) Standards of performance - the larger provincial museums and galleries, *Museums Journal*, 81(3) supplement, 7-9.

Foster, R. (1983) The large provincial museums and art galleries in the UK administered by local authorities, *Museums Journal*, 83(1), 15-19.

Fyfe, G. & Law, J. (eds.) (1988) *Picturing Power*, Sociological Review Monograph 35, Routledge.

Gibson, M. & Wright, S. (eds.) (1988) *Joseph Meyer of Liverpool 1803-1886*, Society of Antiquaries and National Museums and Galleries on Merseyside, London and Liverpool.

Gilman, B. (1918) *Museum Ideals of Purpose and Method*, Cambridge, Massachusetts.

Greenaway, F. (1983) National museums, *Museums Journal*, 83(1), 7-12.

Greene, J.P. (1983) Independent and working museums in Britain, *Museums Journal*, 83(1), 25-28.

Greenhalgh, P. (1988) *Ephemeral Vistas:The Expositions Universelles, Great Exhibitions and World Fairs 1851-1939*, Manchester University Press, Manchester.

Greenwood, T. (1888) *Museums and Art Galleries*, Simpkin Marshall, London.

Gutfleisch, B. & Menzhausen, J. (1989) How a Kunstkammer should be formed, *Journal of History of Collections*, 1, 3-32.

Hancock, E.G. (1980) One of those dreadful combats - a surviving display from William Bullock's London Museum, 1807-1818, *Museums Journal*, 74(4), 172-175.

Harris, P. (1980) A historical perspective on museum advocacy, *Museum*

News, 59(3), 61-86.

Harrison, M. (1967) *Changing Museums*, Longman, London.

Herman, F. (1972) *The English as Collectors*, Chatto and Windus, London.

Hewison, R. (1987) *The Heritage Industry*, Methuen, London.

Hewison, R. (1990) *Future Tense: A New Art for the Nineties*, Methuen, London.

Hodder, I. (1986) *Reading the Past*, Cambridge University Press.

Hoetink, H. (1982) The evolution of the art market and collecting in Holland, *International J. of Museum Management and Curatorship*, 1, 107-18.

Hooper-Greenhill, E. (1989) Museums in the disciplinary society, in Pearce, S.M. (ed.), *Museum Studies in Material Culture*, Leicester University Press, Leicester, London and New York, 63-70.

Howarth, E. & Platnauer, H.M. (1911) *Directory of Museums in Great Britian & Ireland... with a Section on Indian and Colonial Museums*, Museums Association, London.

Howie, F.M.P. (1986) Conserving and mounting fossils: a historical review;, *Curator*, 29 (1), 5-24.

Hudson, K. (1977) *Museums for the 1980s: A World Survey of Trends*, MacMillan, London.

Hudson, K. (1987) *Museums of Influence: The Pioneers of the Last 200 Years*, Cambridge University Press.

Huth, H. (1967) Museums and galleries, *Encyclopaedia Britannica*, 14th edition, Benton, Chicago, 1037-1053.

Impey, O. & MacGregor, A. (eds) (1985) *The Origins of Museums: The Cabinets of Curiosities in Sixteenth and Seventeenth Century Europe*, Oxford University Press.

Jones, M. (1990) *Fake? The Art of Deception*, British Museum, London.

Karp, I. & Lavine, S.D. (eds.) (1991) *Exhibiting Cultures: The Poetics and Politics of Museum Display,* Smithsonian Institution Press, Washington DC.

Katz, H. & Katz, M. (1965) *Museums USA - A History and Guide*, Doubleday, New York.

Kavanagh, G. (1988) Museum as memorial: the origins of the Imperial War Museum, *Journal of Contemporary History*, 23, 77-97.

Kavanagh, G. (1988) The First World War and its implications for education on British museums, *History of Education*, 17, 163-176.

Kenyon, F.G. (1927) *Museums and National Life*, Oxford.

Kenyon, F.G. (1930) *Libraries and Museums*, London.

Key, A. (1973) *Beyond Four Walls*, McClelland & Stewart, Toronto.

Knell, S.J. (1991) The responsible collector, *Geology Today*, 7(3), 106-110.

Lee, S.E. (ed.) (1975) *On Understanding Art Museums*, American Assembly, Columbia University.

Lewis, G.D. (1948) *Directory of Museums and Art Galleries in the British*

Isles, Museums Association, London.

Lewis, G.D. (1989) *For Instruction and Recreation: A Centenary History of the Museums Association*, Quiller Press, London.

Lewis, G.D. (1992) Museums and their precursors: a brief world survey, in Thompson, J.M.A. *et al. (eds.), Manual of Curatorship: A Guide to Museum Practice*, 5-21.

Lowe, E.E. (1928) *A Report on American Museum Work*, Carnegie United Kingdom Trust, Edinburgh.

Markham, S.F. (1938) *A Report on the Museums and Art Galleries of the British Isles*, Carnegie United Kingdom Trust, Dumfermline.

Michelsen, P. (1966) The origin and aim of the Open Air Museum, *Dansk Folkenmuseum and Frilandmuseet: History and Activities*, Nationalmuseet, Copenhagen, Denmark, 226-43.

Miers, Sir H.A. (1928) *A Report on the Public Museums of the British Isles*, Carnegie United Kingdom Trust, Edinburgh.

Minihan, J. (1977) *The Nationalization of Culture: The Development of State Subsidies to the Arts in Great Britain*, Hamish Hamilton, London.

Mullens, W.H. (1915) Some museums of old London, *Museums Journal*, 15(4), 123-29.

Mullens, W.H. (1915) Some museums of old London, *Museums Journal*, 15(5), 162-73.

Mullens, W.H. (1917) Some museums of old London, *Museums Journal*, 17(4), 51-6.

Mullens, W.H. (1917) Some museums of old London, *Museums Journal*, 17(9), 132-137.

Mullens, W.H. (1917) Some museums of old London, *Museums Journal*, 17(12), 180-187.

Murray, D. (1904) *Museums: Their History and Their Use*, (3 volumes), J. MacLehose & Sons, Glasgow.

Museums Association (1945) *Museums Journal*, 45(3), 33-45.

Neickel, C.F. (1727) *Museographia*, M. Hubert, Leipzig.

Nicholson, J. (1983) Tinsel, Terracotta or Tantric: Representing Reality Museums in Carruthers, A. (ed.)Bias in Museums, *Museum Professionals Group (MPG) Transactions*, 22, 26-31.

Nochlin, L. (1972) Museums and radicals: a history of emergencies, in O'Doherty. B. (ed.), *Museums in Crisis*, George Braziller, New York, 11-40.

O'Doherty, B. (ed.) (1972) *Museums in Crisis*, George Braziller, New York.

Outhwaite, L. (1967) *Museums and the Future*, Institute of Public Administration, New York.

Ovenell, R.F. (1986) *The Ashmolean Museum 1683-1894*, Oxford.

Paine, C. (1983) Local museums, *Museums Journal*, 83(1), 21-24.

Pearce, S.M. (1992) *Museums, Objects and Collections: A Cultural Study*, Leicester University Press, Leicester, London and New York.

Pearce, S.M. (ed.) (1991) Collecting Reconsidered in Kavanagh, G. (ed.), *Museum Languages: Objects and Texts*, Leicester University Press, Leicester, London and New York, 135-154.

Pearson, N. (1982) *The State and the Visual Arts*, Open University Press, Milton Keynes.

Peponis, J. & Hedin, J. (nd) The layout of themes in the Natural History Museum, *9h*, 2(3), 21-25.

Pevsner, N. (1940) *Academies of Art, Past and Present*, Cambridge University Press.

Pomian, K. (1990) *Collectors and Curiosities: Paris and Venice, 1500-1800*, Polity Press, Cambridge.

Price, D. (1989) John Woodward and a surviving British geological collection of the early eighteenth century, *Journal of History of Collections*, 1, 79-85.

Redcliffe-Maud, Lord (1976) *Support for the Arts in England & Wales*, Calouste Gulbenkian Foundation, London.

Ripley, S. (1970) *The Sacred Grove: Museums and Their Evolution*, Gollanz, New York.

Ritterbuch, P.C. (1985) Art and science as influences on the early development of natural history collections, in Cohen, D.M. & Cressey, R.F. (eds.), *Natural history collectors: past; present; future - Proceedings of Biological Society of Washington*, 82, 561-78.

Royal Commission on National Museums and Galleries (1928) *Interim Report*, HMSO, London.

Royal Commission on National Museums and Galleries (1929) *Final Report 1 & 2*, HMSO, London.

Royal Society of Arts (1949) *Museums in Modern Life*, London.

Schultz, E. (1990) Notes on the history of collecting and of museums in the light of selected literature of the sixteenth to the eighteenth century, *Journal of History of Collections*, 2(2), 205-218.

Seling, H. (1967) The genesis of the museum, *Architectural Review*, 141, 103-14.

Sheets-Pyensen, S. (1989) *Cathedrals of Science: The Development of Colonial Natural History Museums During the Late Nineteenth Century*, McGill-Queens University Press, Montreal.

Sherman, D.J. (1989) *Worthy Monuments: Art Museums and Politics of Culture in 19th Century France*, Cambridge, Massachusetts.

Singleton, R. (1981) A multitude of museums - some personal reflections, *Museums Journal*, 81(2), 111-13.

Stewart, S. (1984) *On Longing: Narratives of the Miniature, the Gigantic, the Souvenir and the Collections*, John Hopkins, Baltimore.

Stocking, G.W. (ed.) (1985) *Objects and Others: Essays on Museums and Material Culture*, History of Anthropology, Vol. 3, University of Wisconsin Press.

Taborsky, E. (1982) The socio-structural role of the museum, *International J. of Museum Management and Curatorship*, 1(4), 339-45.

Tate, S. (1989) *Palaces of Discovery: The Changing World of Britain's Museums*, Quiller Press, London.

Taylor, F.H. (1948) *The Taste of Angels*, Little, Brown & Co., Boston.

Teather, J.L. (1983) *Museology and Its Traditions: The British Experience 1845-1945*, unpublished PhD thesis, Department of Museum Studies, University of Leicester.

Thompson, M. (1979) *Rubbish Theory: the Creation and Destruction of Value*, Oxford University Press.

Trevor-Roper, H. (1976) *Princes and Artists*, Thames & Hudson, London.

Von Holst, N. (1967) *Creators, Collectors and Connoisseurs*, Thames & Hudson, London.

Wallace, M. (1981) Visiting the past: history museums in the United States, *Radical History Review*, 25, 63-96.

Weil, S.E. (1983) *Beauty and the Beasts*, Smithsonian Institution Press, Washington DC.

Whitehead, P.J.S. (1970) Museums in the history of zoology part 1, *Museums Journal*, 70(2), 50-57.

Whitehead, P.J.S. (1971) Museums in the history of zoology part 2, *Museums Journal*, 70(4), 155-60.

Wittlin, A. (1949) *The Museum: Its History and Its Tasks in Education*, London.

Wittlin, A. (1970) *Museums: In Search of a Usable Future*, Massachusetts institute of Technology Press, Cambridge, Massachusetts.

Witty, P. (1931) Sex differences: collecting interests, *Journal of Educational Psychology*, 22, 221-228.

2.2 Britain

Ackland, H.W. & Ruskin, J. (1893) *The Oxford Museums*, George Allen.

Alexander, J. & Binski, P. (1987) *The Age of Chivalry*, Royal Academy of Arts.

Allan, D.A. *et al.* (1954) *The Royal Scottish Museum1854-1954*, R. & R. Clark,Edinburgh.

Anderson, R.G.W. (1978) *The Playfair Collection and the Teaching of Chemistry At the University of Edinburgh,1713-1858*, Royal Scottish Museum, Edinburgh.

Anon. (1957) *The Science Museum: The First Hundred Years*, HMSO, London.

Barker,. W.R. (1906) *The British Museum and Art Galler the Development of the Institution During a Hundred and Thirty-Four Years1772-1906*, J.W. Arrowsmith, Bristol.

Bassett, D.A. (1982-4) *The Making of a National Museum, Parts I - III*, Honourable Society of Cymmrodorion.

Bell, A.S. (ed.) (1981) *The Scottish Antiquarian Tradition: Essays to mark the Bicentenary of the Society of Antiquaries of Scotland 1780-1980*, J. Donald, Edinburgh.

Blackwood, B. (1974) *The Origin and Development of the Pitt Rivers Museum*, Pitt Rivers Museum, Oxford.

Blair, J.A. (ed.) (1973) *100 Years of Dundee Museums and Art Galleries 1873-1973*, Dundee Museums & Art Galleries.

Boulton, W. (1930) *The Romance of the British Museum*, London.

Bowden, M. (1984) *General Pitt Rivers*, Salisbury and South Wiltshire Museum.

Bowley, J.M.E. (1902) History of Sunderland Museum, *Museums Journal*, 2(6), 175-77.

Brears, P.C.D. (1980) Kirk of the castle, *Museums Journal*, 80(2), 90-92.

Brears, P.C.D. (1989) *Curiosities and Rare Things*, Leeds City Museums.

Brears, P. & Davies, S. (1989) *Treasures for the People*, Yorkshire and Humberside Museums Council.

British Museum (Natural History) (1981) *Nature Stored, Nature Studied*, Butler & Tanner, London, 8-38.

Brooks, E. St J. (1954) *Sir Hans Sloane*, Blatchworth Press.

Bury, H. (1909) Walter Percy Sladen, *Transactions Linnean Society of London*, 12(5), xi-xxii.

Caldwell, D.H. (ed.) (1982) *Angels, Nobels and Unicorns: Art and Patronage in Medieval Scotland*, National Museum of Antiquities of Scotland, Edinburgh.

Caygill, M. (1981) *The Story of the British Museum*, British Museum, London.

Clubb, J.A. (1922) The Public Museums of Liverpool, *Museums Journal*, 21(8), 164-66.

Cocks, A.S. (1977) *The Townley Marbles in Westminster and Bloomsbury*, British Museum Yearbook 2, 34-78.

Cocks, A.S. (1980) *The Victoria & Albert Museum: The Making of the Collection*, Windward, London.

Cook, B. (1985) *The Townley Marbles*, British Museum, London.

Cranstone, B.A.L. & Seidenburg, S. (1984) *The General's Gift: The Pitt Rivers Museum... 1884-1984*, Oxford.

Crook, J.M. (1972) *The British Museum*, Penguin Press, London.

Curtis, W.H. (1955) *The Curtis Museum, Alton, Hampshire: The First Hundred Years of a Small Museum*, Curtis Museum, Alton.

Daniel, S. (1950) *One Hundred Years of Archaeology*, Duckworth.

Davies, K.C. & Hull, J. (1976) *The Zoological Collections of the Oxford University Museum*, Oxford.

Davies, S. (1985) *By the Gains of Industry: Birmingham Museum and Art Gallery 1885-1985*, Birmingham Museum and Art Gallery.

De Beer, Sir G. (1953) *Sir Hans Sloane and the British Museum.*

Desmond, R. (1982) *The India Museum, 1801-1879*, HMSO, London.

Durbin, G. (1983) A museum in the Great War - Norwich Castle Museum 1914-1919, *Museums Journal*, 83(2/3), 168-70.

Edwards, W. (1905) Hastings Museum, Victoria institute, Worcester, *Museums Journal*, 5(6), 179-90.

Edwards, W. (1976) *The Early Histoy of Palaeontology*, British Museum (Natural History), London.

Esdaile, A. (1948) *The British Museum Library*, London.

Evans, J. (1943) *Time and Chance: The Story of Arthur Evans and His Forebears*, Longman, Green & Co.

Follett, D. (1978) *The Rise of the Science Museum Under Henry Lyons*, Science Museum, London.

Gibson, M. & Wright, S. (eds.) (1988) *Joseph Meyer of Liverpool 1803-1886*, London and Liverpool.

Gould, C. (1974) *Failure and Success: 150 Years of the National Gallery 1824-1974*, National Gallery, London.

Greenhalgh, P. (1988) *Ephemeral Vistas*, Manchester University Press.

Gunther, A.E. (1975) *A Century of Zoology At the British Museum Through the Lives of Two Keepers 1815-1914*, Dawson.

Gunther, A.E. (1980) *The Founders of Science At the British Museum 1753-1900*, Halesworth Press, Suffolk.

Gutfleisch, B. & Menzhausen, J. (1989) How a Kunstkammer should be formed, *Journal of History of Collections*, 1, 3-32.

Hancock, E.G. (1980) One of those dreadful combats - a surviving display from William Bullocks London museum 1807-1818, *Museums Journal*, 79(4), 172-75.

Hardy, C.E. (1970) *John Bowes and the Bowes Museum*, Gateshead.

Harrison, M. (1950) *Museum Adventure: The Story of the Geffrye Museum*, University of London Press.

Harrison, S. (ed.) (1986) *100 Years of Heritage: The Work of the Manx Museum and National Trust*, Manx Museum and National Trust.

Haynes, P. (1975) *The Arundel Marbles*, Oxford.

Herrmann, F. (1972) *The English as Collectors*, Chatto & Windus, London.

Holmes, M. (1957) *Personalia*, Museums Association, London.

Hooley, R.W. (1920) The Winchester City and Westgate Museums, *Museums Journal*, 20(5), 103-10.

Howden, D. (1983) *Sir Arthur Evans: A Memoir*, Ashmolean Museum, Oxford.

Hunt, C. (1974) Ethnography in Liverpool Museum 1800-1900, *Museums*

Journal, 74(1), 15-16.

Hunter, M. (1983) *Elias Ashmole and His World*, Ashmolean Museum, Oxford.

Hunter, M. (ed.) (1983) *Elias Ashmole 1617-1692*, Ashmolean Museum, Oxford.

Hutchinson, S.C. (1968) *The History of the Royal Academy 1768-1968*, Chapman & Hall, London.

Jenkins, I. (1992) *Archaeologists and Aesthetes in the Sculpture Galleries of the British Museum 1800-1939*, British Museum, London.

Kaeppler, A. (1979) Tracing the History of Hawaiian Cook Voyage Artefacts in the Museum of Mankind, *British Museum Yearbook*, 3, 67-186.

Kidd, D. (1977) Charles Roach Smith and his Museum of London Antiquities, *The British Museum Yearbook*, 2, 105-35.

Leicestershire Museums (1949) *City of Leicester Museum 1849-1949*, Leicester.

Lloyd, D. (1983) *The History of Ludlow Museum 1833-1983*, Shropshire County Museum Service.

Lowe, E.E. (1910) The Plymouth Museum and Art Gallery, *Museums Journal*, 10(5), 133-38.

MacDonald, S. (1986) For "Swine of discretion": design for living: 1884, *Museums Journal*, 86 (3), 123-129.

MacGregor, A. (1983) Three centuries (and more) of the Ashmolean collections, *Museums Journal*, 83(2/3), 135-37.

MacGregor, A. (ed.) (1983) *Tradescants Rarities*, Oxford University Press.

Mallett, D. (1979) *The Greatest Collector: Lord Hertford and the Founding of the Wallace Collection*, Macmillan.

Marks, R. (1983) *Burrell: A Portrait of a Collector*, R. Drew.

Markus, T.A. (1985) Domes of enlightenment: two Scottish museums, *International J. of Museum Management and Curatorship*, 4(3), 215-42.

Martin, G. (1974) The founding of the National Gallery in London, *The Connoisseur*, 185.

McDowall, S.A. (1920) Winchester College Museum, *Museums Journal*, 20(4), 77-83.

Miller, E. (1973) *That Noble Cabinet*, Andre Deutsch, London.

Newberry, E. (1987) *Appaldurcombe House*, English Heritage.

Nicholson, S. & Warhurst, M. (1983) *Joseph Mayer 1803-1886*, Merseyside County Museums, Liverpool.

Nisbitt, N. (1979) *A Museum in Belfast*, Ulster Museum, Belfast.

Orange, A.D. (1973) *Philosophers and Provincials*, Yorkshire Philosophical Society, York.

Ovenell, R.F. (1986) *The Ashmolean Museum 1683-1894*, Oxford.

Penniman, T.K. (1953) The Pitt Rivers Museum, *Museums Journal*, 52(10), 243-6.

Physick, K.J. (1982) *The Victoria and Albert Museum: A History of Its Building*, Plaidon Christies, Oxford.

Price, D. (1989) John Woodward and a surviving British Geological Collection for the early eighteenth century, *Journal of History Collections*, 1, 79-95.

Pyrah, B. (1988) *The History of the Yorkshire Museum and Its Geological Collections*, The Yorkshire Museum, York.

Rosse, Earl of (1963) *Survey of Provincial Museums and Galleries*, Standing Commission on Museums and Galleries, HMSO, London.

Royal Academy of Arts (1980) *Lord Leverhulme: Founder of the Lady Lever Art Gallery and Port Sunlight on Merseyside*, Royal Academy of Arts.

Schadla-Hall, R.T. (1989) *Tom Sheppard*, Beverley.

Shelley, H.C. (1911) *The British Museum, Its History and Treasures*, L.C. Page, London.

Sheppard, F. (1991) *The Treasury of London's Past*, HMSO, London.

Simcock, A.V. (1984) *The Ashmolean Museum and Oxford Science 1683-1983*, Oxford.

Simcock, A.V. (ed.) (1985) *Robert T. Gunther and the Old Ashmolean Museum of History of Science*, Oxford.

Speakman, C. (1982) *Adam Sedgwick*, London and Cambridge.

Stearn, W.T. (1981) *The Natural History Museum At South Kensington: A History of the British Museum (Natural History) 1753-1980*, Heinemann, London.

Stevens, F. (nd) *The Salisbury Museums 1861-1947: A Record of Eighty-Six Years Progress*, Bennett Brothers, Salisbury.

Swann, J. (1969) Shoes concealed in buildings, *Journal of Northampton Museums*, 6, 8-21.

Swanton, E.W. (1947) *A Country Museum: The Rise and Progress of Sir Jonathan Hutchinsons Educational Museum At Haslemere Museum*, Haslemere Educational Museum, Surrey.

Tattersall, W.M. (1921) The Manchester Museum, *Museums Journal*, 21(5), 98-102.

Thomson, J. A. et al. (eds) (1930) *The North-East: The Land and Its People*, Aberdeen University Press.

Torrens, H.S. & Taylor, M.A. (1990) Geological collectors and museums in Cheltenham 1810-1988: a case history and its lessons, *The Geological Curator*, 5(5), 175-213.

Turner, H. (1980) *Henry Wellcome: The Man, His Collections and His Legacy*, Wellcome Trust and Heinemann.

Usherwood, P. & Bowden, K. (1984) *Art of Newcastle: Thomas Miles Richardson and the Newcastle Exhibitions 1822-1843*, Tyne and Wear Museums and Art Galleries.

Wainwright, C. (1989) *The Romantic Interior: The British Collector At*

Home 1750-1850, Yale University Press.

Walton, K.-M. (1980) *75 Years of Bristol Art Gallery*, Bristol Museum and Art Gallery.

Welch, M. (1978) The New Tradescant Room at the Ashmolean Museum, *Museums Journal*, 78(2), 65-66.

Welch, M. (1983) The Foundation of the Ashmolean Museum in MacGregor, A. (ed.), *Tradescants Rarities*, 40-58.

Whitehead P. & Keates, C. (1981) *The British Museum (Natural History)*, Scala & Philip Wilson, London.

Wilson, D.M. (1985) *The Forgotton Collector: Augustus Wollaston Franks of the British Museum*, Thames & Hudson, London.

Woolnough, F. (1908) History of Ipswich Museum, *Museums Journal*, 8(6), 191-200.

2.3 Europe

Bazin, G. (1979) *The Louvre,*, Thames & Hudson, London.

Beck, H. *et al.* **(eds.)** (1981) *Anti Kensammlungen Im 18. Jahrhundert*, Gebr. Manu Verlag, Berlin.

Boesen, G. (1966) *Danish Museums*, Committee for Danish Cultural Activities Abroad, Copenhagen.

Descargues, P. (1961) *The Hermitage*, Thames & Hudson, London.

Dube, W.D. (1970) *The Munich Gallery - Alte Pinakotek*, Thames & Hudson, London.

Fijalkowski, W. (1986) The Residence-Museum at Wilanow,, *International J. of Museum Management and Curatorship*, 5(2), 109-126.

Gaya-Nuno, J.A. (1968) *Historia Y Guia De Los Museos De Espana,*, Espasa-Calpa S.A., Madrid.

Klessmann, R. (1971) *The Berlin Gallery*, Thames & Hudson, London.

Lapaire, C. (1980) Evolution des collections Suisse, *Guide Des Musées Suisse*, Paul Haupt, Berne, 23-8.

Levere, T.H. (1973) Tayler's Museum, in Turner, G.L.E. & Levere, T.H. (eds.), *Martinus Van Marum: Life and Work*, Noordhof, Leyden, 39-102.

Lorentz, S. (1956) *Museums and Collections in Poland*, Polonia, Warsaw.

Luttervelt, R. Van (1967) *The Rijkmuseum and Other Dutch Museums*, Thames & Hudson, London.

Menz, H. (1962) *The Dresden Gallery*, Thames & Hudson, London.

Ministry of Culture, USSR (1980) *Museums in the USSR*, Moscow, USSR.

Rossi, F. (1967) *The Uffizi and Pitti Florence*, H.N. Abrams, inc. New York.

Sanchez Canton, F.J. (1973) *The Prado*, Thames & Hudson, London.

Selmeczi, L. (1983) Museums and national identity, (Hungary), *Museum*, 35(4), 204-08.

Serner, G. (ed.) (1960) *A Key to the Museums of Sweden*, The Swedish Institute, Stockholm.

Turner, G. Le. (1973) A very scientific century, in Lefebvre, E. & de Bruijn, J.G. (eds.), *Martinus Van Marum: Life and Work*, Noordhof, Leyden, 102-50.

2.4 America

Alderson, W.T. (ed.) (1992) *Mermaids, Mummies and Mastodons: the Emergence of the American Museum*, American Association of Museums, Washington DC.

Alexander, E.P. (1987) Early American museums: from collection of curiosities to popular education, *International J. of Museum Management and Curatorship*, 6(4), 337-351.

Alexander, E.P. (1988) The American Museum chooses education, *Curator*, 31(1), 61-77.

Dickson, L. (1993) *The Museum Makers: The Story of the Royal Ontario Museum*, Royal Ontario Museum, Toronto.

Goler, R (1986) Here the book of nature is unfolded: the American Museum and the diffusion of scientific knowledge in the early republic, *Museum Studies Journal*, 2(2), 10-21.

Gonzalez, A. L. (1980) *El Museo De Ciencias Naturales De Buenos Aires*, Ministerio de Cultura y Educacion, Argentina.

Hellman, G. (1968) *Bankers, Bones and Beetles: The First Century of the American Museum of Natural History*, Natural History Press, New York.

Howe, W.E. (1913) *A History of the Metropolitan Museum of Art*, 2 vols., New York.

Karp, W. (1965) *The Smithsonian Institution*, Smithsonian Institution Press, Washington DC.

Kogan, H. (1973) *The Continuing Marvel*, (Chicago Museum of Science & industry), New York.

Kohlstedt, S.G. (1985) Collectors, cabinets and summer camp: natural history in the public life of nineteenth century Worcester, *Museum Studies Journal*, 2(1), 10-23.

Lawrence, D.E. (1987) From library to art museum: the evolution of the Brooklyn Museum, *International J. of Museum Management and*

Curatorship, 6(4), 381-386.

Lerman, L. (1969) *100 Years and the Metropolitan Museum of Art*, Viking, New York.

Miers, Sir H.A. & Markham, S.F. (1932) *The Museums of Canada*, Museums Association, London.

Oehser, P.H. (1970) *The Smithsonian Institution*, Praeger, New York.

Orosz, J.J. (1985) Pierre Eugene du Simitiere: museum pioneer in America, *Museum Studies Journal*, 1(5), 8-18.

Orosz, J.J. (1986) Disloyalty, dismissal and a deal: the development of the National Museum at the Smithsonian institution, 1846-1855, *Museum Studies Journal*, 2(2), 22-23.

Orosz, J.J. (1987) In defense of the deal: a rebuttal to S. Dillon Ripley's and Wilcomb Washburn's "response", *Museum Studies Journal*, 3(1), 7-12.

Pickman, D. (1969) Museum of Fine Arts, Boston - the first 100 years, *Curator*, 12(4), 237-56.

Ripley, S.D. & Washburn, W.E. (1987) The development of the National Museum at the Smithsonian institution, 1846-1855: a response to Joel J. Orosz's article, *Museum Studies Journal*, 2(4), 6-11.

Sellers, C.C. (1980) *Mr. Peales Museum*, Norton, New York.

Stewart, S. (1984) *On Longing: Narratives of the Miniature, the Gigantic, the Souvenir, the Collection*, John Hopkins, Baltimore.

Tomkins, C. (1970) *Merchants and Masterpieces: The Story of the Metropolitan Museum of Art*, Dutton, New York.

Zeller. T. (1987) Arthur C. Parker: a pioneer in American Museums, *Curator*, 30(1), 41-62.

2.5 Asia & Australasia

Baglin, D. & Austin, Y. (1980) *Australia's Museums*, Child & Henry, Sydney.

Lloyd, C. & Sekuless, P. (1980) *Australia's National Collections*, Cassell Australia, Ltd., Ryde NSW.

Markham, S.F. & Oliver, W.R.B. (1933) *A Report on the Museums and Art Galleries of New Zealand*, Museums Association, London.

Markham, S.F. & Richards, H.C. (1933) *A Report on the Museums and Art Galleries of Australia*, Museums Association, London.

Specht, J. (1980) Lasting memorials: the early years of the Australian Museum, *Kalori*, 58, 7-11.

Strahan, R. et al. (1979) *Rare and Curious Specimens - An Illustrated History of the Australian Museum*, The Australian Museum, Sydney.

Thompson, K.W. (1981) *Art Galleries and Museums in New Zealand*, A.H. & A.W. Reed, Ltd., Wellington, New Zealand.

UNESCO-Japan (1960) *Museums in Japan*, Japanese National Commission for UNESCO, Tokyo.

Webber, K. (1987) Constructing Australia's past: the development of historical collections 1888-1938, *Museums Australia 1987*, 155-173.

3 Material Culture

3.1 Theory

Alpers, S. (1977) Is art history?, *Daedalus*, 107, 1-13.

Ames, K.L. (1978) Meaning in artifacts: hall furnishings in Victorian America, *Journal of Interdisciplinary History*, 9(1), 19-46.

Ames, K.L. (1980) Material culture as non-verbal communication: an historical case study, *Journal of American Culture*, 3(4), 619-641.

Ames, K.L. (1984) Material culture as non-verbal communication: a historical case study, in Mayo, E. (ed.), *American Material Culture: The Shape of Things Around Us*, Bowling Green University Popular Press, Ohio, 25-47.

Ames, K.L. & Martinez, K. (eds.) (1992) *Material culture of gender/gender of material culture*, University of Michigan Research Press, Ann Arbor.

Appadurai, A. (ed.) (1986) *The Social Life of Things*, Cambridge University Press.

Armstrong, R.P. (1971) *The Affecting Presence*, University of Illinois Press, Urbana.

Atkin, R. (1981) *Multidimensional Man: Can Man Live in 3-Dimensional Space?*, Penguin, Harmondsworth.

Badcock, C.R. (1975) *Levis-Strauss, Structuralism and Social Theory*, Hutchinson, London.

Bailey, S. (1979) *In Good Shape - Style in Industrial Products 1900-1960*, Design Council.

Barley, N. (1983) *Symbolic Structures: An Explanation of the Culture of the Dowagos*, Cambridge University Press.

Bartel, B. (1982) A historical review of ethnological and archaeological analyses of mortuary practice, *Journal of Anthropological Archaeology*, 1, 32-58.

Barthes, R. (1968) *Elements in Semiology*, Hills and Wang, New York.

Batchelor, R. (1986) Not Looking at Kettles, *Museum Professionals Group (MPG) News*, 23, 1-3.

Baudrillard, J. (1968) *Le Systeme des Objets*, Gallimard, Paris.

Beckow, S.M. (1975) Culture, history and artifact, *Canadian Museums Association (CMA) Gazette*, 8(4), 13-15.

Beckow, S.M. (1976) On the nature of an artifact, *Canadian Museums Association (CMA) Gazette*, 9(1), 24-7.

Birren, F. (1969) *Principles of Colour*, Van Nostrand Reinhold Company,

New York.

Boas, F. (1907) Some Principles of Museum Administration, *Science*, 25, 921-33.

Bourdieu, P. (1977) *Outline of a Theory of Practice*, Cambridge University Press.

Bourdieu, P. (1984) *Distinction: A social critique of the judgement of taste*, Harvard University Press, Cambridge, Mass..

Braudel, F. (1974) *Capitalism and Material Life, 1400-1800*, Fontana, London.

Briggs, A. (1990) *Victorian Things*, Penguin.

Bronner, S. (1979) Concepts in the study of material aspects of American folk culture, *Folklore Forum*, 12, 133-172.

Bronner, S. (1983) Toward a philosophy of folk objects: a praxic perspective, *Journal of American Culture*, 6, 712-743.

Bronner, S. (ed.) (1985) *American material culture and folklore: A prologue and dialogue*, UMI Press, Ann Arbor.

Bronner, S. (ed.) (1985) Material Culture: a Symposium, *Material Culture*, 17, 2-3.

Browne, R.B. (1980) Introduction, *Objects of Special Devotion: Fetishes and Fetishism in Popular Culture*, Bowling Green University Popular Press, Bowling Green, Ohio.

Bryant, C. & Jary, D. (eds.) (1990) *Gidden's Theory of Structurization*, Routledge, London.

Buck, L. & Dodd, P. (1991) *Relative Values, or What is Art Work?*, BBC, London.

Carrington, N. (1976) *Industrial Design in Britain*, George Allen & Unwin, London.

Carson, C. (1978) Doing history with material culture, in Quimby, I.M.G. (ed.), *Material Culture and the Study of American Life*, Norton, New York.

Chavis, J. (1964) The artefact and the study of history, *Curator*, 7, 156-62, New York.

Chenhall, R.G. (1978) *Nomenclature for Museum Cataloguing - A System for Classifying Man-Made Objects*, American Association for State and Local History (AASLH), Nashville, Tennessee, 3-20.

Collier, J. (1972) *Visual Anthropology - Photography as a Research Method*, New York.

Coulson, A.J. (1979) *A Bibliography of Design in Britain, 1851-1970*, Design Council, London.

Craig, T.L. (1982) Aesthetics aside: how to find historical information in works of art, *History News*, 37(6), 17-19.

Csikszentmihalyi, M. (1975) Play and intrinsic rewards, *Journal of Humanistic Psychology*, 15(3), 41-63.

Csikszentmihalyi, M. & Csikszentmihalyi, I. (1988) *Optimal Experience*,

Cambridge University Press, New York.

Csikszentmihalyi, M. & Rochberg-Halton, E. (1981) *The Meaning of Things: Domestic Symbols and the Self*, Cambridge University Press.

Deetz, J. (1967) *An Invitation to Archaeology*, Doubleday, Natural History Press, Garden City, New York.

Deetz, J. (1977) *In Small Things Forgotten*, Doubleday, Natural History Press, Garden City, New York.

Design Council (1979) *Design History: Past Process, Product*, London.

Douglas, M. & Isherwood, B. (1979) *The World of Goods: Towards an Anthropology of Consumption*, Allen Lane, London.

Duncan, C. & Wallach, A. (1980) The universal survey museum, *Art History*, 3(4), 448-469.

Eagleton, T. (1989) *Literary Theory: An Introduction*, Blackwell, Oxford.

Ellen, R. (1988) Fetishism, *Man*, 23, 213-235.

Elliott, R. et al. (1985) Towards a material history methodology, *Material History Bulletin*, 22(Fall), 31-40.

Fakete, J. (ed.) (1984) *The Structural Allegory: Reconstructive Encounters with the New French Thought*, Manchester University Press.

Ferebee, A. (1970) *A History of Design from the Victorian Era to the Present*, Van Nostrand Renhold Company, New York.

Ferguson, L. (ed.) (1977) *Historical Archaeology and the Importance of Material Things*, Society for Historical Archaeology, Columbia (South Carolina).

Findlen, P. (1989) The museum: its classical etymology and its renaissance genealogy, *Journal of History of Collections*, 1, 59-78.

Firth, R. (1973) *Symbols: Public and Private*, Cornell University Press, Ithaca.

Fisher, J.L. (1961) Art styles as cultural cognitive maps, *American Anthropologist*, 63, 71-93.

Fishwick, M. & Browne, R.B. (1970) *Icons and Popular Culture*, Bowling Green University Press, Bowling Green, Ohio.

Fleming, E. McC. (1974) Artefact study: a proposed model, *Winterthur Portfolio*, 9, 153-161.

Foucault, M. (1973) *The Order of Things*, Vintage Books, New York.

Friedman, J. & Rowlands, M. (1982) *The Evolution of Social Systems*, Duckworth.

Frye, M.Y. (1977) Costume as history, *Museum News*, 56(2), 37-42.

Fyfe, G. & Law, J. (eds.) (1988) *Picturing Power: Visual Depiction and Social Relations*, Sociological Review Monograph 35, Routledge, London.

Gathercole, P. (1989) The fetishism of artefacts, in Pearce, S. (ed.), *Museum Studies in Material Culture*, Leicester University Press, Leicester, London and New York, 73-81.

Geary, P. (1986) Sacred commodities: the circulation of mediaeval relics, in

Appadurai, A. (ed.), *The Social Life of Things*, Cambridge University Press, 169-191.

Giedien, S. (1948) *Mechanization Takes Command*, Oxford University Press.

Gilborn, C. (1968) Pop iconology: looking at the coke bottle, *Museum News*, 47(4), 12-18.

Glassie, H. (1968) *Pattern in the Material Folk Culture of the Eastern United States*, University of Pennsylvania Press, Philadelphia.

Glassie, H. (1973) Structure and function, folklore and the artifact, *Semiotica*, 7, 313-51.

Glassie, H. (1975) *Folk Housing in Middle Virginia: A Structural Analysis of Historic Artifacts*, University of Tennessee Press, Knoxville.

Goffman, E. (1969) *The Presentation of Self in Everyday Life*, Allen Lane (The Penguin Press), London.

Gombrich, E. (1962) *Art & Illusion: A Study in the Psychology of Pictorial Representation*, Phaidon Press, London.

Gombrich, E. (1984) *The Sense of Order: A Study in the Psychology of Decorative Art*, Phaidon Press, London.

Gombrich, E. (1991) *Topics of Our Time*, Phaidon Press, London.

Gombrich, E.H. (nd) *The Sense of Order*, Cornell University Press, Ithaca, N.Y.

Goody, J. (1983) *The Development of the Family and Marriage in Europe*, Cambridge University Press.

Gossman, E. (1975) *Frame Analysis*, Penguin Books, London.

Gould, R.A. & Schiffer, M.B. (eds.) (1981) *Modern Material Culture: The Archaeology of Us*, Academic Press, New York.

Gowans, A. (1972) *On Parallels in Universal History - Discoverable in Arts and Artefacts*, University of Victoria Monograph Series: History in the Arts, 6, Victoria. B.C.

Greenhalgh, M. & Megaw, V. (1978) *Art in Society: Studies in Style, Culture and (eds.) Aesthetics*, St. Martins Press, New York.

Grillo, P. (1960) *Form, Function and Design*, Dover Publications, New York.

Hamilton, N. (ed.) (1980) *Design and Industry: The Effects of Industrialisation and Technical Change on Design*, Design Council, London.

Hamp, S.K. (1980) Meaning in material culture: bibliographical references towards an analytical approach to artefacts, *Living Historical Farms Bulletin*, V, 9-13.

Harris, M. (1979) *Cultural Materialism: A Struggle for a Science of Culture*, Random House, New York.

Hill, C. (1979) Pictures as evidence: history of technology or history of art, *Museums Journal*, 78(4), 169-70.

Hindle, B. (1978) How much is a piece of the true cross worth?, in Quimby, I.M.G. (ed.), *Material Culture and the Study of American Life*, Norton,

New York, 5-20.

Hodder, I. (1982) *Symbols in Action*, Cambridge University Press.

Hodder, I. (1982) *The Present Past*, Cambridge University Press.

Hodder, I. (ed.) (1989) *The Meaning of Things*, One World Archaeology, vol. 6, Unwin Hyman.

Hoffmann, H. (1977) *Sexual and Asexual Pursuit: A Structuralist Approach to Greek Vase Painting*, Royal Anthropological Institute, Occasional Paper no. 34.

Horn, M.J. (1975) *Second Skin - An Interdisciplinary Study of Clothing*, Houghton Mifflin, Boston.

Jenkins, J.G. (1972) The use of artifacts and folk art in the folk museum, in Dorson, R.M. (ed.), *Folklore and Folklife: Aan Introduction*, University of Chicago, Chicago, 497-516.

Jones, M. (1990) *Fake? The Art of Deception*, British Museum, London.

Jones, M.O. (1975) *The Handmade Object and Its Maker*, University of California Press, Los Angeles.

Jung, C.G. (ed.) (1964) *Man and His Symbols*, Aldus Books.

Knight, D. (1981) *Ordering the World: A History of Classifying Man*, Burnett Books & Andre Deutsch, London.

Kubler, G. (1968) *The Shape of Time - Notes on the History of Things*, Yale University Press, New Haven.

La Fontaine, J.S. (ed.) (1972) *The Interpretation of Ritual*, Tavistock Publications, London.

Leach, E. (1976) *Culture and Communication*, Cambridge University Press, Cambridge.

Leach, J. & Leach, E. (eds.) (1983) *The Kula*, Cambridge University Press.

Lechtman, H. (1977) *Material Culture: Styles, Organization and Technology*, West Publishing Co., St. Paul, Minnesota.

Levi-Strauss, C. (1968) *Structural Anthropology*, Volumes 1 & 2, Allen Lane, Penguin Press, London.

Lewis, P. (1975) Common houses, cultural spoor, *Landscape*, 19, 1-22.

Lubar, S. & Kingery, W.D. (eds.) (1993) *History from Things:Essays on Material Culture*, Smithsonian Institution Press, Washington DC.

Lurie, N. O. (1981) Museumland Revisited, *Human Organization,*, 40, 180-7.

Lustig-Arrecco, V. (1975) *Technology: Strategies for Survival*, Holt, Rinehart & Winston Inc., London/New York.

MacCarthy, F. (1972) *A History of British Design 1830-1970*, Allen & Unwin, London.

Mayo, E. (ed.) (1984) *American Material Culture: The Shape of Things Around Us*, Bowling Green University Popular Press, Ohio.

McClung Fleming, E. (1959) Early American decorative arts as social documents, *Mississippi Valley Historical Review*, 45, 276-84.

McGhee, R. (1977) Ivory for the sea woman: symbolic attributes of a prehistoric technology, *Canadian Journal of Archaeology*, 1, 141-149.

Meltzer, D.J. (1981) Ideology and material culture, in Gould, R.A. & Schiffer, M.B. (eds.), *Modern Material Culture: The Archaeology of Us*, Academic Press, New York, 113-25.

Mergen, B. (1980) Toys and American culture: objects as hypotheses, *Journal of American Culture*, 3(4), 743-51.

Miller, D. (1985) *Artefacts as Categories*, Cambridge University Press.

Miller, D. (1987) *Material Culture and Mass Consumption*, Blackwell, Oxford.

Naylor, G. (1971) *The Arts and Crafts Movement*, Studio Vista, London.

Panofsky, E. (1962) *Studies in Iconography*, Harper & Row, New York.

Papanek, V. (1974) *Design for the Real World*, Paladin, London.

Papanek, V. (1975) Edugraphology - the myths of design and the design of myths, *Icongraphic*, 9.

Pearce, S.M. (1986) Objects as signs and symbols, *Museums Journal*, 86(3), 131-135.

Pearce, S.M. (1986) Objects, High and Low, *Museums Journal*, 86(2), 79-82.

Pearce, S.M. (1986) Thinking about things: approaches to the study of artefacts, *Museums Journal*, 85(4), 198-201.

Pearce, S.M. (1986) Thinking about things: approaches to the study of artefacts, *Museums Journal*, 82(2), 198-201.

Pearce, S.M. (1987) Ivory, antler, feather and wood: material culture and cosmology of the Cumberland Sound Inuit, Baffin Island, Canada, *Canadian Journal of Native Study*, 7(2), 307-321.

Pearce, S.M. (1987) Objects in structures, *Museums Journal*, 86(4), 178-181.

Pearce, S.M. (1989) *Museum Studies in Material Culture*, Leicester University Press, Leicester, London and New York.

Pearce, S.M. (1989) Objects in structures, in Pearce, S. (ed.), *Museum Studies in Material Culture*, Leicester University Press, Leicester, London and New York, 47-60.

Pearce, S.M. (1992) *Museums, Objects and Collections: A Cultural Study*, Leicester University Press, Leicester, London and New York.

Pearce, S.M. (1993) Artefacts as the social anthropologist sees them, in Fleming, D., Paine C. & Rhodes, J.G. (eds.), *Social History in Museums: A Handbook for Professionals*, HMSO, London, 65-72.

Pearce, S.M. (ed.) (1989) *Museum Studies in Material Culture*, Leicester University Press, Leicester, London and New York.

Pearce, S.M. (ed.) (1990) *Objects of Knowledge*, New Research in Museum Studies, Vol. 1, Athlone, London.

Pointon, M. (1980) *History of Art: A Students Handbook*, Allen & Unwin, London.

Prown, J. (1982) Mind in matter: an introduction to material culture theory and method, *Winterthur Portfolio*, 17(1), 1-19.

Pye, D. (1982) The six requirements for design, in Schlereth, T.J. (ed.), *Material Culture Studies in America*, American Association for State and Local History (AASLH), Nashville, Tennessee, 153-61.

Quimby, I.M.G. (1978) *Material Culture and the Study of Early American Life*, Norton, New York.

Rabinowitz, R. & Warner, S.B. (1982) From old to ordinary: a new approach to the artifact, *History News*, 37(11), 34-5.

Rapoport, A. (1969) *House Form and Culture*, Prentice Hall, Englewood Cliffs, New Jersey.

Renfrew, C. (1982) Space, time and polity, in Friedman, J, & Rowlands, M. (eds.), *The Evolution of Social Systems*, Duckworth, 89-112.

Reynolds, B. (1983) The Relevance of Material Culture to Anthropology, *Journal of Anthropological Society of Oxford*, 2, 63-75.

Richardson, M. (ed.) (1974) *The Human Mirror - Material and Spatial Images of Man*, Louisiana State University Press, Baton Rouge.

Royal Academy (1968) *50 Years Bauhaus*, Royal Academy Exhibition.

Schlebecker, J.T. (1977) The use of objects in historical research,, *Agricultural History*, 51, 200-08.

Schlereth, T.J. (1980) *Artifacts and the American Past*, American Association for State and Local History (AASLH), Nashville, Tennessee.

Schlereth, T.J. (1982) Material culture studies in America 1876-1976, in Schlereth, T.J. (ed.), *Material Culture Studies in America*, American Association for State and Local History (AASLH), Nashville, Tennessee, 1-75.

Schlereth, T.J. (1982) Pioneers of material culture, *History News*, 37(9), 28-32.

Schlereth, T.J. (1985) *Material Culture: A Research Guide*, University Press, Kansas.

Schlereth, T.J. (1993) *Cultural History & Material Culture: Everyday Life, Landscapes and Museums*, University Press of Viginia.

Schlereth, T.J. (ed.) (1982) *Material Culture Studies in America*, American Association for State and Local History (AASLH), Nashville, Tennessee.

Service, E.R. (1971) *Cultural Evolutionism*, New York.

Shanks, M. & Tilley, C. (1987) *Re-Constructing Archaeology*, Cambridge University Press, Cambridge.

Simmel, G. (1978) *The Philosophy of Money*, Routledge and Kegan Paul, London.

Spiers, R.F.G. (1970) *From the Hand of Man: Primitive and Pre-Industrial Technologies*, Houghton Mifflin Co., Boston.

Stewart, S. (1984) *On Longing: Narratives of the Miniature, the Gigantic, the Souvenir, the Collection*, John Hopkins, Baltimore.

Stocking, G.W. (ed) (1986) *Objects and Others: Essays on Museums and*

Material Culture, History of Anthropology, Vol. 3, University of Wisconsin Press.

Sturtevant, W.C. (1977) *Guide to Field Collecting of Ethnographic Specimens*, Smithsonian Information Leaflet 503, Washington, DC.

Tippett, A.R. (1968) *Fijian Material Culture: A Study of Cultural Context, Function and Change*, Bishop Museum Press, Honolulu.

Tuan, Y.F. (1980) The significance of the artifact, *Geographical Review*, 70(4), 462-74.

White, H. (1974) Structuralism and popular culture, *Journal of Popular Culture*, 759-775.

Williamson, J. (1978) *Decoding Advertisements*, Marion Boyars.

Winner, L. (1980) Do artifacts have politics?, *Daedalus*, 109, 121-36.

3.2 General

Clifton-Taylor, A. (1972) *The Pattern of English Building*, Faber, London.

Cotterill, R. (1985) *The Cambridge Guide to the Material World*, Cambridge University Press.

Fall, F.K. (1973) *Art Objects: Their Care and Preservation*, McGilvery, London.

Fleming, J. & Honour, H. (1979) *Penguin Dictionary of the Decorative Arts*, Penguin, London.

Harris, N. (1978) Museums, merchandising and popular taste: the struggle for influence, in Quimby, I.M.G. (ed.), *Material Culture and the Study of American Life*, Norton, New York, 140-74.

Hartley, D. (1977) *Made in England*, Eyre Methuen, London.

Hodges, H. (1964) *Artefacts: An Introduction to Early Metals and Technology*, John Baker, London.

Jenkins, J.G. (1978) *Traditional Country Craftsmen*, Routledge & Kegan Paul, London.

Knudsen, S.J. (1978) *Culture in Retrospect*, Rand McNally College Publishing Co., Chicago.

Plenderleith, H.J. & Werner, A.E.A. (1979) *The Conservation of Antiquities and Works of Art, Treatment, Repair and Restoration*, Oxford University Press.

Singer, C. *et al.* (1954) *A History of Technology*, volumes I-V, Oxford University Press, Oxford.

Spiers, R.F.G. (1970) *From the Hand of Man: Primitive and Pre-Industrial Technologies*, Houghton Mifflin Co., Boston.

Van Amerogen, C. (1972/4) *How Things Work*, volumes 1-2, Paladin, St.

Albans.
Van Oss, J.F. & Van Thor, T.J.W. (eds.) (1968) *Materials and Technology,* Vols I-VIII, Longman, London.

3.3 Animal Derivative

Attwater, W.A. (1961) *Leathercraft, Batsford,* London.
Clarke, D.J. & Kurashina, H. (1981) A study of the work of a modern tanner in Ethiopia and its relevance for archaeological interpretation, in Gould, R. & Schiffer, M. (eds.), *Modern Material Culture: The Archaeology of Us,* Academic Press, New York, 303-21.
Haines, B.M. (1981) *The Fibre Structure of Leather,* Leather Conservation Centre, London.
Hardwick, P. (1981) *Discovering Horn,* Lutterworth Press, Guildford, Surrey.
Humphreys, G.H.W. (1967) *Manufacture of Sole and Other Heavy Leathers,* Pergamon, London.
MacGregor, A. (1984) *Bone, Antler, Ivory and Horn,* Croom Helm, London.
Monfit, C. (1852) *The Arts of Tanning, Curing and Leather-Dressing,* Henry Carey Baird, Philadelphia.
Penniman, T.K. (1952) *Pictures of Ivory and Other Animal Teeth, Bone and Antler,* Oxford University Press.
Pyne, W.H. (1806) *Microcosm,* London, republished (1971) by Benjamin Blom Inc., New York.
Salaman, R.A. (1986) *Dictionary of Leather-Working Tools C.1700-1950,* Allen and Unwin, London.
Tomlinson, C. (1852) *Cyclopedia of Useful Arts,* George Virtue & Co., London.
Waterer, J.W. (1963) *Leathercraftsmanship,* Bell, London.
Waterer, J.W. (1973) *Spanish Leather,* Bell, London.
Welsh, P.C. (1964) *Tanning in the United States to 1850,* Smithsonian Institution, Washington, DC.
Williamsburg Craft Series (1973) *The Leatherworker in Eighteenth Century Williamsburg,* Colonial Williamsburg.
Williamson, G.C. (1938) *The Book of Ivory,* London.

3.4 Ceramic

Adams, P.J. (1961) *Geology and Ceramics*, Geological Survey and Museum, HMSO, London.

Anderson, A. (1984) *Interpreting Pottery*, Batsford, London.

Arnold, D.E. (1985) *Ceramic Theory and Cultural Process*, Cambridge University Press.

Brears, P.C.D. (1971) *English Country Potteries*, David & Charles, Newton Abbott.

Chaffers, W. (1972) *Marks and Monograms on Pottery and Porcelain*, 15th edition, Faber & Faber, London.

Clifton-Taylor, A. (1972) *The Pattern of English Building*, Faber & Faber, London.

Cushion, J.B. (1980) *Handbook of Pottery and Porcelain Marks*, 4th edition, (with W.B. Honey) Faber & Faber, London.

Dodd, E. (1964) *Dictionary of Ceramics*, Philosophical Library, New York.

Fontana, B.L. (1973) The cultural dimensions of pottery: ceramics as social documents, in I.M.G. Quimby (ed.), *Ceramics in America*, Winterthur Museum, Delaware, 1-12.

Green, D. (1972) *Pottery, Materials and Techniques*, McGraw Hill, New York.

Hartley, D. (1977) *Made in England*, Eyre Methuen, London, 164-79.

Hillier, B. (1968) *Pottery and Porcelain 1700-1914: English, European and American*, Weidenfeld & Nicholson, London.

Hodges, H.W.M. (1963) The examination of ceramic materials in thin section, in E. Pyddoke (ed.), *The Scientist and the Archaeologist*, Phoenix House, London, 114-23.

Honey, W.B. (1952) *European Ceramic Art from the End of the Middle Ages to About 1815: A Dictionary of Factories, Artists, Technical Terms etc.*, A. & C. Black, London.

Kempton, W. (1981) *Folk Classification of Ceramics: A Study of Cognitive Prototypes*, Academic Press, London.

Kenny, J.B. (1976) *Complete Book of Pottery Making*, 2nd edition, Pitman, London.

Lloyd, N. (1925) *A History of English Brickwork from Medieval Times to the End of the Georgian Period*, H.G. Montgomery, London.

Quimby, I.M.G. (ed.) (1973) *Ceramics in America*, Winterthur Museum, Delaware.

Rhodes, A. (1973) *Clays and Glazes for the Potter*, Pitman, London.

Shaw, K. (1969) *Ceramic Colours and Pottery Decoration*, Praeger, New York.

Shepard, A.O. (1974) *Ceramics for the Archaeologist*, Carnegie Institute of Washington, Washington, DC.

Wylde, J. (1866) *The Book of Trades*, C. Griffin & Co., London.

3.5 Glass

Burgoyne, I. (1980) The evolution of glass-making techniques, *Museums Journal*, 80(1), 28-30.

Caley, E.R. (1962) *Analysis of Ancient Glasses 1790-1957*, Corning Museum of Glass, Corning, New York.

Charleston, R.J. *et al.* (1977) *Glass and Stained Glass and Limoges and Other Painted Enamels*, Office du Livre (for the National Trust), Fribourg.

Clifton-Taylor, A. (1972) *The Pattern of English Building*, Faber & Faber, London.

Garner, H. (1970) *Chinese and Japanese Cloisonne Enamels*, Faber & Faber, London.

Harden, D. (1972) *Ancient Glass*, Royal Archaeological Institute, London.

Honey, W.B. (1948) *Glass: A Handbook for the Study of Glass Vessels of All Periods and Countries, and a Guide to the Collections*, Victoria & Albert Museum, London.

Lang, B. (1978) Glass: handle with care!, *Canadian Museums Association (CMA) Gazette*, 11(4), 37-40.

Morey, G.W. (1961) *The Properties of Glass*, Reinhold, London.

Tooley, F.V. (1961) *Handbook of Glass Manufacture*, 2 volumes, Ogden, New York.

Vavra, J.R. (c1957) *5000 Years of Glass Making*, Artia, Prague.

Vose, R.H. (1975) *Glass*, The Connoisseur, London.

Weiss, G. (1971) *The Book of Glass*, Barrie & Jenkins, London.

Wilkinson, O.N. (1968) *Old Glass - Manufacture, Styles and Uses*, Ernest Benn Ltd., London.

3.6 Man-made

Blow, C.M. (1971) *Rubber Technology and Manufacture*, Butterworth, London.

Briston, J.H. & Gosselin, C.C. (1968) *Introduction to Plastics*, Newnes, London.

Brydson, J.A. (1966) *Plastics Materials*, Illife, London.

Carrol-Parczynski, C.Z. (1961) *Natural-Polymer Man-Made Fibres*, National Trade Press, London.

Cook, J.G. (1968) *Your Guide to Plastics*, Merrow, Watford.

Couzens, E.G. & Yarsley, V.E. (1968) *Plastics in the Modern World*, Penguin.

Fraser, W.H. (1981) *The Coming of the Mass Market, 1850-1914*, Macmillan.

Hall, J. (1985) *Powers and Liberties: An Account of the Causes and Consequences of the Rise of the West*, Blackwell, Oxford.

Katz, S. (1978) *Plastics, Designs and Materials*, Studio Vista, London.

Lever, A.E. (ed.) (1966) *The Plastics Manual*, Scientific Press, London.

Moncrieff, R.W. (1963) *Man-Made Fibres*, Heywood, London.

Newport, R. (1976) *Plastic Antiques*, British Industrial Plastics Ltd./Wolverhampton Polytechnic, (3 booklets), Wolverhampton.

Simmonds, H.R. & Church, J.M. (1963) *A Concise Guide to Plastics*, Reinhold, New York.

3.7 Metalwork

Aitchison, L. (1960) *A History of Metals*, 2 volumes, MacDonald & Evans, London.

Brooke, C.N.L. (1983) *Studies in Numismatic Method*, Cambridge University Press.

Bullock, T.K. (1956) *The Silversmith in Eighteenth Century Williamsburg*, Colonial Williamsburg Craft Series, Williamsburg.

Caley, E.R. (1964) *Analysis of Ancient Metals*, Pergamon Press, Oxford.

Haedeke, H.-U. (1970) *Metalwork*, Weidenfeld & Nicholson, London.

Kauffmann, H.J. (1960) *Decorative Wrought Ironwork in Great Britain*, Bell, London.

Kauffmann, H.J. (1960) *Early American Ironware, Cast & Wrought*, C.E. Tuttle & Co., Rutland, Vermont.

Kauffmann, H.J. (1968) *American Copper & Brass*, T. Nelson & Co., Cambridge, New Jersey.

Lister, R. (1957) *Decorative Cast Ironwork in Great Britain*, Bell, London.

Montgomery, C.F. (1973) *A History of American Pewter*, Praeger, New York.

Rickard, T. (1932) *Metals and Man: A History of Mining in Relation to the Development of Civilization*, McGraw Hill, New York.

Street, A. & Alexander, W. (1954) *Metals in the Service of Man*, 3rd edition, Pelican, London.

3.8 Painters' Materials

Alberti, L.B. (1956) *On Painting*, Yale University Press.

Ayres, J. (1985) *The Artists Craft: A History of Tools Techniques and Materials*, Phaidon Press, London.

Becker, H.S. (1974) Art as collective action, *American Sociological Review*, 39(6).

Burcaw, G.E. (1983) *Introduction to Museum Work*, American Association for State and Local History (AASLH), Nashville, Tennessee.

Canaday, J. (1980) *What Is Art: an Introduction to Painting, Sculpture and Architecture*, Hutchinson, London.

Cole, B. (1983) *The Renaissance Artist at Work*, John Murray, London.

Collins, J. et al. (1983) *Techniques of Modern Artists*, MacDonald & Co., London and Sydney.

Constable, W.G. (1954) *The Painters Workshop*, Oxford University Press, Oxford.

Cox, T. (1955) *Handbook for Museum Curators*, Part D, Sections 1 & 2, Museums Association, London.

Dubery, F. & Willats, J. (1972) *Perspective and Other Drawing Systems*, The Hubert Press, London.

Evans, H. & Nelki, A. (1975) *Picture Researchers Handbook: An International Guide to Picture Sources and How to Use Them*, David & Charles (Holdings) Ltd..

Fall, F.K. (1973) *Art Objects: Their Care and Preservation*, McGilvery, London.

Fletcher, J. (1974) Tree-ring dates for some panel paintings in England, *Burlington Magazine*, 116, 250-58.

Fletcher, J. (1976) A group of English royal portraits painted soon after 1513, *Studies in Conservation*, 21, 171-78.

Fuller, P. (1972) The Tate, the state and the English tradition, *Studio International*, 194(988).

Gilmour, P. (1978) *The Mechanized Image: An Historical Perspective on 20th Century Prints*, Arts Council of Great Britain, London.

Goldman, P. (1979) *Looking at Drawings - A Guide to Technical Terms*, British Museum, London.

Gorine, I. (1967) The restoration of works of art in the USSR, *Museum*, 20(2), 121-23.

Hayes, C. (1978) *The Complete Guide to Painting and Drawing Techniques* *and Materials*, Phaidon.

Hendon, W.S. (1972) Problems of the museum of contemporary art in the west, *Museum*, 24(1), 4-32.

Hendon, W.S. (1979) *Analyzing an Art Museum*, Praeger Publisher, New York.

Plenderleith, H.J. & Werner, A.E.A. (1979) *The Conservation of Antiquities and Works of Arts, Treatment, Repair and Restoration*, Oxford University Press.

Simpson, I. (ed.) (1983) *Painters Progress*, Allen Lane, London.

Stout, G.L. (1978) *The Care of Pictures*, Dover Publications, New York.

Vasani, G. (1960) *Vasani on Technique*, Dover Publications, New York.

3.9 Photography

Coe, B. & Haworth Booth, M. (1983) *A Guide to the Early Photographic Processes*, Victoria and Albert Museum, London.

Holt, G.E. (1982) Chicago through the lens: an essay on photography as history, in Schlereth, T.J. (ed.), *Material Culture Studies in America*, American Association for State and Local History (AASLH), Nashville, Tennessee, 278-88.

Rempel, S. (1980) *The Care of Black and White Photographic Collections: Cleaning and Stabilization*, Canadian Conservation Institute Technical Bulletin 9.

Schlereth, T.J. (1980) Mirrors of the past: historical photography and American history, in Schlereth, T.J. (ed.), *Artefacts and the American Past*, American Association for State and Local History (AASLH), Nashville, Tennessee, 11-47.

Time Life Books (1973) *Caring for Photographs*, Time-Life International, Netherlands.

Ward, S. (1978) *Museum Procedure: Photographs*, Museum of English Rural Life, Reading.

Weinstein, R.A. & Booth, L. (1977) *Collections, Use and Care of Historical Photographs*, American Association for State and Local History (AASLH), Nashville, Tennessee.

3.10 Printing

Brunner, F. (1968) *A Handbook of Graphic Reproduction Processes*, Arthur Niggli Tenfen, Switzerland.

Calloway, S. (1980) *English Prints for the Collector*, Lutterworth Press, London & Guildford.

Chamberlain, W. (1978) *Thames & Hudson Manual of Wood Engraving*, Thames & Hudson, London.

Dawson, J. (ed.) (1981) *The Complete Guide to Prints and Printmaking: Techniques and Materials*, Phaidon Press, Oxford.

Goldman, P. (1981) *Looking at Prints - A Guide to Technical Terms*, British Museum, London.

Griffiths, A. (1980) *Prints and Printmaking: An Introduction to the History and Techniques*, British Museum, London.

Hayter, S.W. (1962) *About Prints*, Oxford University Press, London.

Hind, A.M. (1963) *A History of Engraving and Etching*, Dover Publications, New York.

Ivins, W.M. (1953) *Prints and Visual Communication*, Routledge & Kegan Paul, London.

Ivins, W.M. (1964) *How Prints Look*, Beacon, Boston.

Lister, R. (1984) *Prints and Printmaking*, Methuen, London.

Mara, T. (1979) *Thames & Hudson Manual of Silk Screen Printing*, Thames & Hudson, London.

Marzio, P.C. (1980) *The Democratic Art, Chromolithography 1840-1900, Pictures for a 19th Century America*, Scolar Press, London.

Mayor, A. H. (1971) *Prints and People: A Social History of Printed Pictures*, Metropolitan Museum of Art, New York.

Russell, R. (1979) *Guide to British Topographical Prints*, David & Charles, Newton Abbott.

Sotriffer, K. (1968) *Printmaking - History & Techniques*, McGraw Hill, New York.

Turk, F.A. (1967) *The Prints of Japan*, Marlborough Books, New York.

Twyman, N. (1970) *Printing 1770-1970: An Illustrated History of Its Development and Uses in England*, Eyre & Spottiswood, London.

Vicary, R. (1977) *Thames & Hudson Manual of Advanced Lithography*, (post 1950 methods), Thames & Hudson, London.

Zigrosser, C. & Gaehde, C.M. (1965) *A Guide to the Collecting and Care of Original Prints*, Crown Publications, New York.

3.11 Stone

Arkell, W.J. (1947) *Oxford Stone*, Faber & Faber, London.
Arkell, W.J. & Tomkeieff, S (1953) *English Rock Terms*, Oxford University Press.
Boardman, J. (1970) *Greek Gems and Finger Rings*, Thames & Hudson, London.
Clifton-Taylor, A. (1972) *The Pattern of English Building*, Faber & Faber, London.
Clough, T.H. McK. & Cummins, W.A. (eds.) (1979) *Stone Axe Studies - Archaeological, Petrological, Experimental, Ethnographic*, Council for British Archaeology Research Report, 23, London.
Davey, N. (1961) *A History of Building Materials*, Phoenix House, London.
Gould, R.A. (1981) Brandon revisited: a new look at an old technology, in Gould, R.A. & Schiffer, M.B. (eds.), *Modern Material Culture: The Archaeology of Us*, Academic Press, New York, 269-82.
Harley, R. (1982) *Artists Pigments C1600-1835*, Butterworth, London.
Hester, T.R. & Heizer, R.F. (1981) Making stone vases: contemporary manufacture of material culture items Upper Egypt, in Gould, R. & Schiffer, M. (eds.), *Modern Material Culture: Ahe Archaeology of Us*, Academic Press, New York, 283-302.
International Institute for Conservation (1972) *Conservation of Stone Objects*, International Institute for Conservation, New York.
Miller, K. (1948) *Stone and Marble Carving*, Studio Press, London.
Shackley, M. (1977) *Rocks and Man*, George Allen & Unwin, London.
Simpson, B. (1966) *Rocks and Minerals*, Pergamon Press, Oxford.
Sinkankas, J. (1968) *Van Nostrands Standard Catalogue of Gems*, Van Nostrand, Reinhold, New York.
Webster, R. (1970) *Gems: Their Sources, Descriptions and Identification*, Butterworth, London.

3.12 Textile

Burkett, M.E. (1979) *The Art of the Felt Maker*, Abbott Hall Art Gallery, Kendal.
Burnham, D.K. (1966) *Warp and Weft: ATextile Terminology*, Royal Ontario Museum, Toronto.
Catling, D. & Grayson, J. (1982) *Identification of Vegetable Fibres*, Chapman & Hall, London.

Clabburn, P. (1976) *The Needleworkers Dictionary*, MacMillan, London.

Collier, A.M. (1980) *A Handbook of Textiles*, Wheaton, Oxford.

Diehl, J.M. (1972) Natural dyestuffs, in Leeve, J. (ed.), *Textile Conservation*, 23-31.

Earnshaw, P. (1980) *The Identification of Lace*, Shire Publications, Aylesbury.

Emery, I. (1966) *The Primary Structures of Fabrics*, Textile Museum, Washington, DC.

Fleming, E.R. (1958) *Encyclopaedia of Textiles*, Praeger, New York.

Geifer, A. (1979) *A History of Textile Art*, Sotheby, Parke Bernet Publications, London.

Gostelow, M. (1979) *The Art of Embroidery*, Weidenfeld & Nicholson, London.

Hartley, D. (1977) *Made in England*, Eyre Methuen, London.

Hudson, K. (1978) *Food, Clothing and Shelter*, John Baker, London.

Jenkins, G. (1978) *Traditional Country Craftsmen*, Routledge & Kegan Paul, London.

Miller, E. (1968) *Textiles - Properties and Behaviour*, Batsford, London.

Montgomery, F.M. (1970) *Printed Textiles - English and American Cottons and Linens, 1700-1850*, Thames & Hudson, London.

Palliser, B. (1875) *A History of Lace*, 1971 facsimile edition, Tower Books, Detroit.

Picton, J. & Mack, J. (1979) *African Textiles*, British Museum, London.

Putnam, G. & Finch, K. (1975) *Caring for Textiles*, Barrie & Jenkins, London.

Storey, J. (1974) *The Thames and Hudson Manual of Textile Printing*, Thames & Hudson, London.

Tattersall, C.E.C. (1969) *Notes on Carpet Knotting and Weaving*, HMSO for Victoria and Albert Museum, London.

Textile Institute (1975) *Identification of Textile Materials*, Textile Institute, Manchester.

Werbel, A.C. (1952) *2000 Years of Textiles*, Pantheon, New York.

Wigginton, E. (1973) *Foxfire 2*, Anchor Press/Doubleday, Garden City, New York.

3.13 Vegetable

Blow, C.M. (ed.) (1971) *Rubber Technology & Manufacture*, Butterworth, London.

Cooke, G.B. (1961) *Cork and the Cork Tree*, Pergamon Press, London.

Hartley, D. (1977) *Made in England,* (originally published 1939), Eyre Methuen, London.

Haylock, E.W. (1974) *Paper: Its Making, Merchanting and Usage,* 3rd edition, National Association of Papermakers & Longman, London.

Hubner, M. (1981) What you need to know about paper, *History News,* 36(3), 46.

Hunter, D. (1980) *The History and Techniques of an Ancient Craft,* (paper-making), Dover, London.

Jenkins, J.G. (1978) *Traditional Country Craftsman,* Routledge & Kegan Paul, London.

Lasansky, J. (1979) *Willow, Oak and Rye: Basket Traditions in Pennsylvania,* Keystone Books, Pennsylvania State University Press, Philadelphia.

Long, P. (ed.) (1981) *Paper - Art and Technology,* World Print Council, San Francisco.

Moir, G. (1980) The care of papier mache, *History News,* 35(6), 57-8.

Usher, G. (1974) *A Dictionary of Plants Used by Man,* Constable, London.

Whitlock, N. (1837) *Complete Book of Trades,* J. Bennett, London.

3.14 Woodwork

Barclay, R., Eames, R. & Todd, A. (1980) *The Care of Wooden Objects,* Canadian Conservation Institute Technical Bulletin, 8.

Blandford, P. (1974) *Country Craft Tools,* David & Charles, London.

Edlin, H.L. (1969) *What Wood Is That? - A Manual of Wood Identification,* Thames & Hudson, London.

Edlin, H.L. (1973) *Woodland Crafts in Britain,* Batsford, London.

Everett, T.H. (1969) *Living Trees of the World,* Thames & Hudson, London.

Fitzrandelph, H.E. & Hay, M.D. (1977) *The Rural Industries of England & Wales,* Part I, E.P. Publishing, Wakefield.

Friedman, J. (1978) *Wood Identification,* Heritage Record No.5, British Columbia Provincial Museum.

Goodman, W.L. (1964) *The History of Woodworking Tools,* Bell, London.

Hora, B. (ed.) (1981) *The Oxford Encyclopaedia of Trees of the World,* Oxford University Press.

International Institute for Conservation (1972) *Conservation of Wooden Objects,* International Institute for Conservation, New York.

McGiffen, R.W. (1992) *Furniture - Care and Conservation,* 3rd edition, American Association of State and Local History (AASLH), Nashville, Tennessee.

Mercer, H.C. (1960) *Ancient Carpenters Tools*, Bucks County Historical Society, Doylestown, Pennsylvania.
Phillips, E.W.J. (1948) *Identification of Hard Woods*, HMSO, London.
Phillips, E.W.J. (1979) *Identification of Soft Woods*, HMSO, London.
Pinto, E.H. (1969) *Treen and Other Wooden Bygones*, Bell, London.
Rackham, O. (1980) *Ancient Woodland*, Edward Arnold, London.
Rood, J. (1968) *Sculpture in Wood*, University of Minnesota Press, Minneapolis.
Salaman, R.A. (1975) *Dictionary of Tools Used in the Wood-Working and Allied Trades C1700-1970*, George Allen & Unwin, London.

3.15 Fakes

Anon. (1979) Where is it now?, *Geological Curators Group Newsletter*, 2(7), 436-38.
Anscombe, I. (1981) Daylight robbery? Exposing the shady side of the collotype, *Connoisseur*, 207(831), 49-51.
Boyd, M. (1980) Fossil forgeries: the smallest improved ammonite?, *Geological Curators Group Newsletter*, 2(9/10), 609-10.
Boylan, P.J. (1979) The controversy of the Moulin-Quinon Jaw: the role of Hugh Falconer, *British Society for the History of Environmental Sciences Monograph*, No 1, 171-99.
Carr, J.R. (1978) Fakes and forgeries in maritime art, *International Congress of Maritime Museums Proceedings*, Mystic Seaport, Connecticut, USA.
Cole, S. (1955) *Counterfeit*, John Murray, London.
Coremans, P.B. (1949) *Van Meegerens Faked Vermeers and De Hooghs: A Scientific Examination*, J.M. Meulenhoff, Amsterdam.
Crawley, W. (1971) *Is It Genuine? A Guide to the Identification of Eighteenth Century English Furniture*, Eyre & Spottiswoode, London.
Dance, P. (1976) *Animal Fakes and Frauds*, Sampsen Low, London.
Dunn, P.J., Bentley, R.E. & Wilson, W.E. (1981) Mineral fakes, *Mineralogical Record*, 12(4), 197-220.
Dutton, D. (1979) Artistic crimes: the problems of forgery in the arts, *British Journal of Aesthetics*, 19(4), 302-14.
Fleming, S.J. (1975) *Authenticity in Art: The Scientific Detection of Forgeries*, The Institute of Physics, London and Bristol.
Gray, R. (1980) The Hilditch affair, *Museums Journal*, 80(2), 93-4.
Haywood, I. (1987) *Faking It: Art and the Politics of Forgery*, Harvester Press, London.

Irving, C. (1969) *Fake!*, Heinemann, New York.

Jaffe, H.L.C., Storm Van Leeuwen, J. & Van Tweel, L.H (1979) *Authentication in the Visual Arts*, B.M. Israel.BV, Amsterdam.

Jones, M. (ed.) (1992) *Why Fakes Matter: Essays on Problems of Authenticity*, British Museum, London.

Keating, T. & Norman, G. & Norman, F. (1977) *The Fakes Progress*, Hutchinson, London.

Keck, S. (1948) The laboratory detection of fraud, *Magazine of Art*, 41, 172-77.

Kurz, O. (1967) *Fakes*, (Originally published by Faber & Faber, 1948), revised edition, Dover, New York.

McCrone, W. (1975) The Vineland map, *Physics in Technology*, 6, 18-21.

Meyer, K.E. (ed.) (1977) *The Plundered Past, the Traffic in Art Treasures*, Pelican.

Millar, R. (1974) *The Piltdown Men*, Paladin, St. Albans.

Mills, J. (1973) *Treasure Keepers*, Aldus Books Ltd., London, 75-95.

Mills, J. & Mansfield, J.M. (1979) *The Genuine Article*, BBC, London.

Munro, R. (1903) *Archaeology and False Antiquities*, Methuen & Co., London.

Nobli, R. (1922) *The Gentle Art of Faking*, Seeley, Service & Co., London.

Peterson, H.L. (1975) *How Do You Know Its Old?*, Charles Scribner and Sons, New York.

Philips, D. (1980) Fossil forgeries: constructed cephalopods at the British Museum, *Geological Curators Group Newsletter*, 2(9/10), 599-603.

Plenderleith, H.J. (1952) Fakes and forgeries in museums, *Museums Journal*, 52, 143-48.

Rieth, A. (1970) *Archaeological Fakes*, Barrie & Jenkins, London.

Savage, G. (1963) *Forgeries, Fakes and Reproductions*, Barrie & Rockliff, London.

Tietze, H.S. (1934-6) The psychology and aesthetics of forgery in art, *Metropolitan Museum of Art Studies*, 5.

Tietze, H.S. (1948) *Genuine and False*, Max Parish & Co. Ltd., London.

Weiner, H.S. (1955) *The Piltdown Forgery*, Oxford.

Weisenauer, E. (1980) "Complete" belemnite animals from the Posidonia shales of Holzmaden, *Geological Curators Group Newsletter*, 2(9/10), 605-08.

Whitworth, H.F. (1953) A faked fossil, *Museums Journal*, 53, 319.

Williams, R.S. (1980) Northwest coast masks salmon egg paint unmasks fakes, *CCI Journal*, 4, 2-11.

Wright, C. & De Marley, D. (1980) Fake?, *Connoisseur*, 205(283), 22-5.

4 Collection Management

4.1 General

American Association of Museums (1984) *Caring for Collections: Strategies for Conservation, Maintenance and Documentation*, American Association of Museums, Washington DC.

Anon. (1985) The cost of managing collections, *Museums Journal*, 85(3), 147.

Anon. (1988) Museum Automation: defining the need, *Museum News*, 66(6), 42-48.

Appelbaum, B. (1991) *Guide to Environmental Protection of Collections*, Sound View Press, Connecticut.

Area Museums Service for South Eastern England (1992) *Collection Management Plan Guidelines*, AMSSEE, London.

Bachmann, K. (1992) *Conservation Concerns: A Guide for Collectors and Conservators*, Smithsonian Institution & Cooper Hewitt.

Bandes, S.J. (1984) Caring for collections, *Museum News*, 63(1), 68-71.

Beelitz, P.F. (1990) The relative linearity of ethnographic collections, *Curator*, 33(1), 40-8.

Bott, V. (1990) Beyond the museum, *Museums Journal*, 90(2), 28-30.

Boylan, P.J. (1977) *Towards a Policy for the Leicestershire Museums, Art Galleries and Records Service*, Leicestershire County Council.

Bradley, S.M. (1990) Do objects have a finite lifetime, in Keene, S. (ed.), *Managing Conservation*, United Kingdom Institute for Conservation, London.

Bradley, S.M., Uprichard, K. & Munday, V. (1990) *A Guide to the Storage, Exhibition and Handling of Antiquities, Ethnographia and Pictorial Art*, Occasional Paper 66, British Museum, London.

Brunton, C.H.C., Besterman, T.P. & Cooper, J.A. (eds.) (1985) *Guidelines for the Curation of Geological Materials*, Miscellaneous Paper No. 17, Geological Society, London/Geological Curators Group.

Case, M. (ed.) (1988) *Registrars on Record: Essays on Museum Collections Management*, Registrars Committee of the American Association of Museums.

Caton, J. (1991) Setting Standards, *Museums Journal*, 91(1), 34-35.

Croucher, R. & Woolley, A.R. (1982) *Fossils, Minerals and Rocks: Collection and Preservation*, British Museum (Natural History), London.

Dickerson, A. (1991) Redressing the Balance, *Museums Journal*, 91(2), 21-23.

Doughty, P.S. (1981) *The State & Status of Geology in Museums*, Geological Society, Miscellaneous Paper 13, London.

Fall, F.K. (1973) *Art Objects: Their Care and Preservation*, McGilvery, California.

Fewster, C. (1990) Beyond the Showcase, *Museums Journal*, 90(6), 24-27.

Forman, L. & Bridson, D. (1990) *The Herbarium Handbook*, Royal Botanic Gardens, Kew.

Fussell, A. (1991) Adding to the Collection, *Museums Journal*, 91(2), 28-29.

Gallagher, D.T. (1982) Role specialisation and collection management, *Canadian Museums Association (CMA) Gazette*, Winter, 24-9.

Gallagher, D.T. (1983) Planning for collections in Lord, B & Lord, G.D. (eds.), *Planning Our Museums*, National Museums of Canada, Ottawa,, 75-83.

Garfield, D. *et al.* (1990) *Conservation in Storage*, Getty Conservation Institute, California.

Genoways, H.H., Jones, C. & Rossolimo, O.L. (eds.) (1987) *Mammal Collection Management*, Texas Technical University Press.

Herholdt, E.M. (1990) *Natural History Collections: Their Management and Value*, Special Publication No. 1, Transvaal Museum, Pretoria.

Image (1991) *Image Databases Proceedings*, IMAGE:International Meeting on Museums & Art Galleries, London.

Johnstone, C. (1991) Documenting Diversity, *Museums Journal*, 91(2), 29-30.

Jones, D.L. (1982) *The Care of Ethnographic Material*, Occasional Paper No. 1, Museum Ethnographers Group.

Keefe, L.E. & Inch, D. (1990) *Life of a Photograph: Archival Processing, Matting, Framing and Storage*, 2nd edition, Butterworth.

Keene, S. (ed.) (1990) *Managing Conservation*, United Kingdom Institute for Conservation.

King, E. (1990) Collecting for Cultural Identity, *Museums Journal*, 90(12), 26-28.

Knell, S.J. (1991) The most important fossil in the world, *Geology Today*, 7(6), 221-224.

Knell, S.J. & Taylor, M.A. (1989) *Geology and the Local Museum*, HMSO, London.

Knell, S.J. & Taylor, M.A. (1991) Museums on the Rocks, *Museums Journal*, 91(1), 23-25.

Lincoln, M. (1990) Fingertip Control, *Museums Journal*, 90(8), 29.

Lord, B., Lord, G.D. & Nicks, J. (1989) *The Cost of Collecting: Collection Management in UK Museums*, HMSO, London.

Malaro, M.C. (1979) Collection management policies, *Museum News*, 58(2), 57-61.

Malaro, M.C. (1985) *A Legal Primer on Managing Museum Collections*, Smithsonian Institution Press, Washington DC.

Malaro, M.C. (1990) Moving People Towards Change, *MDA Information*, 14(2/3/4), 18-23.

Manning, A. (1987) Self-study: how one museum got a handle on collection management, *Museum News*, 65(6), 61-67.

Martin, E. (1988) *Collecting and Preserving Old Photographs*, Collins, London.

Morrison, A. (1990) Words and Images, *Museums Journal*, 90(8), 30-31.

Museums Association (1991) Code of Conduct for Museum Curators, *Museums Yearbook*, Museums Association, London, 13-20.

Museums Association (1991) Code of Practice for Museum Authorities, *Museums Yearbook*, Museums Association, London, 9-12.

Museums & Galleries Commission (1988) *Guidelines for a Registration Scheme for Museums in the United Kingdom*, Museums and Galleries Commission, London.

Museums & Galleries Commission (1990) *Report 1989-90*, Museums and Galleries Commission, London..

Museums & Galleries Commission (1992) *Standards in the Museum Care of Archaeological Collections*, Museums & Galleries Commission, London.

Museums & Galleries Commission (1993) *Museums of Music: A Review of Musical Collections in the UK*, HMSO, London.

Museums & Galleries Commission (1993) *Standards in the Museum Care of Biologicial Collections*, Museums & Galleries Commission, London.

Museums & Galleries Commission (1993) *Standards in the Museum Care of Geologicial Collections*, Museums & Galleries Commission, London.

Museums & Galleries Commission (1994) *Registration Scheme for Museums & Galleries in the UK, Second Phase*, Museum & Galleries Commission, London.

Museums & Galleries Commission (1994) *Standards in the Museum Care of Industrial Collections*, Museums & Galleries Commission, London.

Museums & Galleries Commission (1994) *Standards in the Museum Care of Photographic Collections*, Museums & Galleries Commission, London.

National Audit Office (1988) *Management of the Collections of the English National Museums and Galleries*, HMSO, London.

National Committee to Save America's Cultural Collections (1992) *Caring for your Collections: Preserving and Protecting your Art and other Collectibles*, Harry N. Abrams, Inc..

National Park Service (1990) *Museum Handbook Part 1: Museum Collections*, Department of the Interior, USA.

Neal, A., Haguland, K. & Webb, E. (1978) Evolving a policy manual, *Museum News*, 56(3), 26-30.

North West Museums Service (1992) *Collection Management Plan Guidelines,* NWMS, Blackburn.

Orna, E. (1987) *Information Policies for Museums,* Museum Documentation Association, Cambridge.

Peake, L. (1990) Blowing the dust off scholarship, *Museums Journal,* 90(12).

Pinkerton, L. F. (1987) Preventive legal audits for museums, *Museum News,* 66(1), 36-9.

Pittman, N. (1990) Influence of funding agencies, *MDA Information,* 14(2/3/4), 23-29.

Porter, D.R. (1985) *Current Thoughts on Collections Policy,* Technical Report No.1, American Association for State & Local History, Nashville, Tennessee.

Porter, D.R. (1986) *Developing a Collection Management Manual,* Technical Report No. 7, American Association for State and Local History, Nashville, Tennessee.

Putnam, G. & Finch, K. (1985) *The Care and Preservation of Textiles,* Batsford, London.

Rempel, S. (1987) *The Care of Photographs,* Lyons & Burford, New York.

Roberts, D.A. (ed.) (1988) *Collection Management for Museums,* Museum Documentation Association, Cambridge.

Roberts, D.A. (ed.) (1990) *Terminology for Museums,* The Museum Documentation Association, Cambridge.

Sandwith, H. & Stanton, S. (1993) *The National Trust Manual of Housekeeping,* Penguin.

Schumann, Y. (1986) *Survey of Ethnographic Collections in the UK, Eire and the Channel Islands,* Occasional Paper No. 2, Museum Ethnographers Group.

Shelley, M. *et al.* (1987) *The Care and Handling of Art Objects: Practices in the Metropolitan Museum of Art,* Harry N. Abrams, Inc..

Simmons, M. (1993) *Discovering Green Treasure: The Findings and Work of the NEMS Peripatetic Biology Curator,* North of England Museums Service, Newcastle Upon Tyne.

Stansfield, G. (1985) Collection management plans, *Museum Professionals Group (MPG) News,* 20.

Suggitt, M. (1990) Emissaries from the Toy Cupboard, *Museums Journal,* 90(12), 30-33.

Vance, D. (1980) Planning ahead: the registrar's role in a building program, *Museum News,* 58(4), 60-86.

Vulpe, M. (1986) Collection management action support systems, *International J. of Museum Management and Curatorship,* 5(4), 349-356.

Walker, A.K. & Crosby, T.K. (1979) *The Preparation and Curation of Insects,* Dept of Scientific & Industrial Research, Auckland.

Walley, G. & Edgar, J. (1989) The Experience of Nottingham City Museums, *MDA Information*, 13(3/4), 44-51.

Williams, S.L., Laubach R. & Genoways, H.H. (1977) *A Guide to the Management of Recent Mammal Collections*, Special Publication No. 4, Carnegie Museum of Natural History, Pittsburgh.

Yamamoto, T. (1985) The Royal Ontario Museum system of collections management, *International J. of Museum Management and Curatorship*, 4(3), 273-8.

4.2 Collecting & Acquisition

Anderson, R.M. (1965) *Methods of Collecting and Preserving Vertebrate Animals*, National Museums of Canada, Ottawa.

Anon. (1971) Harvard University approves policy governing acquisition of art objects from foreign countries, *Curator*, 14, 83-7.

Anon. (1971) Policy statement concerning acquisition of antiquities, *Curator*, 14, 232-35.

Anon. (1971) Science policy report, *Curator*, 14(4), 235-40.

Anon. (1973) Ethics of acquisition, *ICOM (International Council of Museums) News*, 26(1), 77.

Atkinson, F. (1985) The unselective collector, *Museums Journal*, 85(1), 9-11.

Babbidge, A. (1983) Collecting policies and ethics of ownership - industrial museums, *Museum Professionals Group (MPG) Transactions*, 17, 44-46.

Boodle, C. (1991) National Art Collectors Fund, *Scottish Museums News*, 7(3), 19.

Boston, D. (1985) Successful business sponsorship - two cases, *Museums Journal*, 85(3), 131-2.

Boston, D. & Harrison, R. (1969) Why collect what?, *Museums Journal*, 69(3), 110-15.

Bott, V. (1983) Collecting policies and ethics of ownership - publicly funded museums, *Museum Professionals Group (MPG) Transactions*, 17, 40-3.

Boylan, P.J. (1976) An East Midlands regional agreement on industrial and technological material, *Museums Journal*, 76(2), 67-8.

Boylan, P.J. (1992) The UK and the cultural clause, *Museums Journal*, 92(3).

Boylan, P.J. (ed.) (1977) *Towards a Policy for the Leicestershire Museums, Art Galleries, and Records Service*, Leicestershire County Council.

British Museum (Natural History) (1953) *Instructions for Collectors No. 3:*

Reptiles, Amphibia and Fish, British Museum (Natural History), London.

British Museum (Natural History) (1968) *Instructions for Collectors No. 1: Mammals*, British Museum (Natural History), London.

British Museum (Natural History) (1974) *Instructions for Collectors No. 4a: Insects*, BM(NH), London.

Burcaw, G.E. (1967) Active collecting in history museums, *Museum News*, 45(7), 21-2.

Byrne-Sutton, Q. (1992) The Goldberg case: a confirmation of the difficulty of acquiring good title to valuable stolen cultural objects, *International Journal of Cultural Property*, 1(1), 151-168.

Cheape, H. (1990) Collecting on a national scale, *Museums Journal*, 90(12), 34-37.

Cole, R. (1988) The Bencroft Bequest, *Museums Journal*, 88(1), 41-2.

Cook, B.F. (1993) Conference report. International conference on the theme "Eredita Contestata?", *International Journal of Cultural Property*, 1(2), 189-195.

Davies, S. (1992) Yesterday's collecting: tomorrow's collections, *Museums Journal*, 92(7), 19-20.

Deecke, T. (1991) Old traditions and new ways in the acquisition policies of German public art galleries, *Museum Management & Curatorship*, 10, 168-171.

Elder, B.D. (1981) Collecting the 20th century, *History News*, 36(11), 9-12.

Elsner, J. & Cardinal, R. (eds.) (1993) *The Cultures of Collecting*, Reaktion Books, London.

Evans, G. (1987) The National Museums of Scotland Grants Fund, *Museums Journal*, 86(4), 214-218.

Farnell, G. & Heath, M. (1993) *Handbook of Grants: The Guide to sources of public funding for museums, galleries, heritage and visual arts organisations*, Museum Development Company.

Faul, R. (1973) Forum, *Museum News*, 51(9), 21-4.

Feest, C.F. (1993) European collecting of American Indian artefacts and art, *Journal of the History of Collections*, 5(1), 1-11.

Field Museum of Natural History (1977) *Policy Statements on Accessions and Deaccessions and Loans from the Reference Collections*, Field Museum of Natural History, Chicago.

Forder, C. (1993) The Breduis Museum case: public interest and private law, *International Journal of Cultural Property*, 2(1), 117-125.

Frigo, M. (1993) The proposed EEC Council Directive on the return of unlawfully exported cultural objects, *International Journal of Cultural Property*, 1(2), 73-80.

Gathercole, P. & Lowenthal, D. (eds.) (1989) *The Politics of the Past*, Routledge, London.

Gilbert, C. (1991) New perspectives in collecting decorative art, *Museum*

Management & Curatorship, 10, 172-176.

Goyder, J. (1992) European Community free movement of cultural goods and European Community law, *International Journal of Cultural Property*, 1(1), 219-225.

Goyder, J. (1992) European Community free movement of cultural goods and European Community law: Part II, *International Journal of Cultural Property*, 1(2), 403-411.

Goyder, J. (1993) European Community free movement of cultural goods and European Community law: Part III, *International Journal of Cultural Property*, 2(1), 403-411.

Green, O. (1977) Collecting for the future, *Museum Assistants Group News*, 1, 9-11.

Hall, D. (1969) Some thoughts on policy in the acquisition of modern art from Scottish public collections, *Museums Journal*, 69(1), 3-6.

Harrison, C.J.O., Cowles, G.S. & Dahl, A.L. (1970) *Instructions for Collectors No. 2: Birds*, British Museum (Natural History), London.

Hitchcock, A. (1980) Collections policy, *Canadian Museums Association (CMA) Gazette*, 13(2), 40-68.

Hoving, T.P. (1973) A policy statement from the Met, *Museum News*, 51(9), 43-5.

Inland Revenue (1986) *Capital Taxation and the National Heritage*, Board of Inland Revenue, London.

Inland Revenue (1986) *Gift Aid: A Guide for Donors and Charities*, Board of Inland Revenue, London.

International Council of Museums (1971) *Ethics of Acquisition*, ICOM (International Council of Museums), Paris.

International Council of Museums (1987) *Code of Professional Ethics*, ICOM (International Council of Museums), Paris.

Irvin, A.D., Cooper, J.E. & Hedges, S.R. (1972) Possible health hazards associated with the collection and handling of post-mortem zoological material, *Mammal Review*, 2, 43-54.

Karageorghis, V. (1992) The trade in Cypriot antiquities in London, *International Journal of Cultural Property*, 1(2), 331-332.

Kenyon, J. (1992) *Collecting for the 21st Century*, Yorkshire and Humberside Museums Council.

King-Farlow, C. (1986) Capital taxation and heritage reliefs, *International J. of Museum Management and Curatorship*, 5(1), 81-3.

Lacey, G.W.B., Scholes, J. & Thomson, A.G. (1966) Collecting large objects (technological material), *Museums Journal*, 66(4), 248-53.

Lalive, P. (ed.) (1987) *International Sales of Works of Art*, International Chamber of Commerce, Geneva.

Lee, W.L., Bell, B. & Sutton, J.F. (1982) *Guidelines for the Aquisition and Management of Biological Specimens*, Association of Systematics Collections, Lawrence, Kansas.

Lewis, S. (1982) Beyond traditional boundaries - collecting for black art museums, *Museum News*, 60(3), 41.

Lewison, J. (1991) New directions for a national collection, *Museum Management & Curatorship*, 10, 198-203.

Lincoln, R.J. & Sheals, J.G. (1979) *Invertebrate Animals: Collection and Preservation*, British Museum (Natural History), London.

Lyster, S. (1985) *International Wildlife Law*, Grotius Publications.

Malaro, M.C. (1979) Collections management policies, *Museum News*, 58(2), 57-61.

Malaro, M.C. (1993) The anatomy of a loan, *Museum International*, 178(2), 51-54.

Manitoba Museum of Man and Nature (1980) Collections policy, *Canadian Museums Association (CMA) Gazette*, 13, 45-8.

Maurice, C. and Turnor, R. (1992) The export licensing rules in the United Kingdom and the Waverley Criteria, *International Journal of Cultural Property*, 1(2), 273-295.

Meltzer, R. (1987) The long and winding tax road, *Museum News*, 66(1), 32-35.

Merrin, L. (1990) Tax effective giving to the arts and museums: a guide for fundraisers, *Museum Development*, November, 14-17.

Merryman, J. H. (1992) Limits on state recovery of stolen artifacts: Peru v Johnson, *International Journal of Cultural Property*, 1(1), 169-173.

Messenger, P. (ed.) (1989) *The Ethics of Collecting Cultural Propery: Whose Ethics? Whose Property?*, University of New Mexico, Albuquerque.

Montias, J.M. (1973) Are museums betraying the publics interest?, *Museum News*, 51(9), 25-31.

Mossman, S. (1986) Collecting policies - conflict or co-operation, *Museum Professionals Group (MPG) News*, 24, 1-2.

National Art Collections Fund (1984) *National Art Collections Fund Review*.

National Heritage Memorial Fund (1984) *National Heritage Memorial Fund Annual Report for 1982/83*, National Heritage Memorial Fund, London.

National Museums of Canada (1981) *Collections Policy and Procedure*, National Museums of Canada, Ottawa.

National Museums of Canada (1983) *Collection Policy Procedures, 2*, National Museums of Canada, Ottawa.

Naumer, H.J. & Kendall, A. (1973) Acquisitions and old lace, *Museum News*, 51(9), 40-2.

Naylor, G. (1991) Public funding in Great Britain, *Museum Management & Curatorship*, 10, 143-148.

Neal, A., Haglund, K. & Webb, E. (1978) Evolving a policy manual, *Museum News*, 56(3), 26-30.

Nicholson, T.D. (1974) Policy on the acquisition and disposition of collection material, *Curator*, 17(1), 5-9.

Norton, M. (1990) *Tax Effective Giving*, Directory of Social Change, London.

O'Keefe, P.J. & Prott, L.V. (1993) The European Convention on the protection of the archaeological heritage, *Antiquity*, 67(255), 406-413.

Office of Arts & Libraries (1978) *Purchase Grant Fund*, Victoria & Albert Museum.

Polzer, A.D. (1993) A clock in court: East German export of cultural property considered by West German courts, *International Journal of Cultural Property*, 2(1), 111-115.

Prott, L. (1993) War, heritage and normative action, *Museum International*, 178(2), 45-48.

Robinson, J.C. (1988) The Science Museum Grant in Aid Fund, *Museums Journal*, 88(1), 43-46.

Robinson, J.C. (1989) The Science Museum Fund, *Science Museum Review*, Science Museum, London.

Rushing, B. (1982) Afro-Americana - defining it, finding it and collecting it, *Museum News*, 60(3), 33.

Schlereth, T.J. (1984) Contemporary collecting for future recollecting, *Museum Studies Journal*, 1(3), 23-30.

Science Museum (1973) *Grant in Aid - Fund for the Preservation of Technological and Scientific Material*, Science Museum, London.

Science Museum (1991) *Museum Collecting Policies in Modern Science and Technology*, Science Museum, London.

Siehr, K. (1993) The UNIDROIT draft convention on the international protection of cultural property, *International Journal of Cultural Property*, 1(2), 321-330.

Silber, E. (1991) Acquisitions policy in local authorities, *Museum Management & Curatorship*, 10, 177-181.

Sizer, C. (1979) The purchase of the Silchester Collection, *Museums Journal*, 79(2), 58-60.

Smith, A. (1991) A university collection in a northern climate, *Museum Management & Curatorship*, 10, 182-185.

Southworth, E. (ed.) (1991) *What's Mine is Yours - Museum Collecting Policies*, The Museum Archaeologist 16, Society of Museum Archaeologists.

Summerfield, P. (1988) *Historical Collections Scheme for Small Museums*, Museums Association of Australia, Western Australian Branch, Perth.

Trevelyn, V.M. (1987) The V & A Grant Fund, *Museums Journal*, 86(4), 205-213.

Tweedy, C. (1991) Sponsorship of the Arts - an outdated fashion or the model of the future?, *Museum Management & Curatorship*, 10, 161-166.

Wakefield, P. (1991) The role of trusts in the acquisitions policy of British art galleries, *Museum Management & Curatorship*, 10, 149-152.

Ware, M. (1988) *Museum Collecting Policies and Loan Agreements*, AIM Guideline 14, Association of Independent Museums.

Weil, S.E. (1985) *Beauty and the Beasts: On Museums, Art, the Law and the Market*, Smithsonian Institution Press, Washington DC.

Werner, K. (1991) Inheritance and acquisitions: East German collections and their future, *Museum Management & Curatorship*, 10, 186-191.

Wilson, D.M. (1989) *The British Museum: Purpose and Politics*, British Museum, London.

Wilson, H. & Longman, P. (1985) Tax incentives - can museums benefit?, *Museums Journal*, 85(3), 134-142.

Wyrwoll, R. (1991) Collecting activities and perspectives in the 1990's: Germany, *Museum Management & Curatorship*, 10, 136-131.

Zelle, A. (1972) ICOM ethics of acquisition, *Museum News*, 50(8), 31-3.

4.3 Disposal & Restitution

Anon. (1986) Return and restitution of cultural property - a brief resume, *Museum*, 38(1), 61-63.

Archibald, R.R. (1993) The ethics of collections, *History News*, 48(3), 22-26.

Babbidge, A. (1991) Disposals from museum collections: a note on legal considerations in England and Wales, *Museum Management & Curatorship*, 10, 255-261.

Barr, D.W. (1990) Legacies and Heresies: Some Alternatives in Disposing of Museum Collections, *Muse*, Summer, 14-16.

Besterman, T. (1992) Disposal from museum collections: ethics and practicalities, *Museum Management & Curatorship*, 11, 29-45.

Bromilow, G. (1993) Finders keepers?, *Museums Journal*, 93(3), 31-34.

Browning, R. (1984) The case for the return of the Parthenon Marbles, *Museum*, 36(1), 38-41.

Capstick, B. (ed.) (1979) The return and restitution of cultural property, *Museums Journal*, 79(2), 67-71.

Clarke, B. (1991) Scottish sense, *Museums Journal*, 91(9), 34-35.

Clement, E. (1992) Return and restitution of cultural property: towards co-ordination of efforts to combat illicit traffic, *Museum*, 44(1), 32.

Davies, S. (1987) Social history collections, *Museums Journal*, 87(3), 124-126.

Field Museum of Natural History (1977) *Policy Statements on Accessions* *and Deaccessions and Loans from the Reference Collections*, Field Museum of Natural History, Chicago.

Fleming, D. (1987) Sense or suicide, (disposal), *Museums Journal*, 87(3), 119-20.

Fleming, D. (1991) Immaculate collections, speculative conceptions, *Museum Management & Curatorship*, 10, 263-272.

Gathercole, P. (1986) Recording ethnographic collections: the debate on the return of cultural property, *Museum*, 38(3), 187-92.

Gazi, A. (1990) Museums and National Cultural Property - 1: the Question of Restitution, *International J. of Museum Management and Curatorship*, 9(2), 121-35.

Gazi, A. (1990) Museums and National Cultural Property - 2: the Parthenon Marbles, *International J. of Museum Management and Curatorship*, 9(3), 241-55.

Gonyea, R.W. (1993) Give me that old time religion, *History News*, 48(2), 4-7.

Greenfield, J. (1989) *The Return of Cultural Treasures*, Cambridge University Press.

Hill, R. (1993) Beyond repatriation, *History News*, 48(2), 9-10.

Jacob, J. (1971) The sale and disposal of museum objects, *Museums Journal*, 71(3), 112-16.

Konecny, T.A. (1991) Deaccessioning from the Historic Houses Trust of New South Wales, *Museum Management & Curatorship*, 10, 281-292.

Lewis, G.D. (1992) Attitudes to disposal from museum collections, *Museum Management & Curatorship*, 11, 19-29.

Lloynd, M. (1987) The law, *Museums Journal*, 87(3), 122-123.

Malaro, M.C. (1991) Deaccessioning: the American perspective, *Museum Management & Curatorship*, 10, 273-279.

Miller, S. (1985) Selling items from museum collections, *International J. of Museum Management and Curatorship*, 4(3), 289-94.

Miller, S. (1991) Deaccessioning: sales or transfers, *Museum Management & Curatorship*, 10, 245-253.

Mitchell, W. (1973) When you run out of money.... sell, *Museum News*, 51(11), 36-9.

Monroe, D.L. (1993) Repatriation: a new dawn, *Museums Journal*, 93(3), 29-31.

Murdin, L. (1991) Derbyshire's Sale is the final step, *Museums Journal*, 91(2), 8.

Museums Association (1991) Code of conduct for museum curators, *Museums Yearbook*, Museums Association, London, 13-20.

Museums Association (1991) Code of practice for museum authorities, *Museums Yearbook*, Museums Association, London, 9-12.

Nicholson, T.D. (1974) Policy on the acquisition and disposition of collection material, *Curator*, 17(1), 5-9.

Norgate, M. (1987) Disposal is a dirty word, *South West Museum News.*, 6, 5-6.

Robertson, I. (1987) Archaeological collections, (disposal), *Museums Journal*, 87(3), 127-9.

Robertson, I. (1990) Infamous deaccessions, *Museums Journal*, 90(3), 32-4.

Spalding, J. (1987) Art collections, *Museums Journal*, 87(3), 130-1.

Sullivan, A.McC. (1991) Law and diplomacy in cultural property, *Museum Management & Curatorship*, 10, 219-243.

Terrell, J. (1993) We want our treasures back, *Museums Journal*, 93(3), 34-36.

Tivy, M. (1993) Passing the point of no return, *Museums Journal*, 93(3), 25-28.

Tolmatch, E. (1990) A Case Study: the Deaccession and Disposal Controversy at the New Brunswick Museum (1985-1990), *Muse*, Summer, 20-27.

Weil, S.E. (1987) Deaccession practices in American museums, *Museum News*, 66(1), 44-50.

Wheatcroft, P. (1987) Natural history collections, *Museums Journal*, 87(3), 133-134.

Woroncow, B. (1987) Ethnographical collections, *Museums Journal*, 98(3), 137-139.

4.4 Legal Aspects of Acquisition & Disposal

Bator, P.M. (1988) *The International Trade in Art*, University of Chicago Press.

Burnham, B. (1974) *The Protection of Cultural Property: Handbook on National Legislations*, ICOM (International Council of Museums), Paris.

Cameron, D.F. (1977) *An Introduction to the Cultural Property Export and Import Act*, Arts and Culture Branch, Department of the Secretary of State, Canada, Ottawa.

Chamberlain, R. (1983) *Loot! The Heritage of Plunder*, Thames & Hudson, London.

Clark, I. C. (1986) Illicit traffic in cultural property: Canada seeks a bilateral agreement with the U.S, *Museum*, 38(3), 182-7.

Cleere, H. (1990) Heritage Protection, *Museums Journal*, 90(5), 37-38.

Cottesloe, Lord (1964) *Report of the Committee of Enquiry Into the Sale of Works of Art by Public Bodies*, HMSO, London.

Council of Europe (1973) *European Convention on the Protection of the Archaeological Heritage 1969*, HMSO, London.

Council of Europe (1988) *The Art Trade: Report of the Committee on*

Culture and Education and Related Documents, Strasbourg.

Export of Works of Art Reviewing Committee (1987) *Thirty-Third Report*, HMSO, London.

Hanley, R. (1992) The Museum Firearms Licence: a case study, *Scottish Museum News*, 8(1), 5.

HM Government (1939) *Import, Export and Customs Powers (Defence) Act*, HMSO, London.

HM Government (1968) *Firearms Act*, HMSO, London.

HM Government (1973) *The Protection of Wrecks Act*, HMSO, London.

HM Government (1976) *Endangered Species (Import & Export) Act*, HMSO, London.

HM Government (1979) *Ancient Monuments and Archaeological Areas Act*, HMSO, London.

HM Government (1980) *National Heritage Act*, HMSO, London.

HM Government (1981) *Wildlife and Countryside Act*, HMSO, London.

HM Government (1988) *Firearms (Amendment) Act*, HMSO, London.

HM Government (1989) *The Firearms Rules*, HMSO, London.

International Council of Museums (1971) *Ethics of Acquistion*, ICOM (International Council of Museums), Paris.

King-Farlow, C. (1983) Capital taxation relief and the heritage route, *International J. of Museum Management and Curatorship*, 2(2), 135-46.

King-Farlow, C. (1986) Capital taxation and heritage reliefs, *International J. of Museum Management and Curatorship*, 5(1), 81-83.

Kouroupas, M.P. & Guthrie, A.J. (1985) The cultural property act: what it means for museums, *Museum News*, 63(5), 47-52.

Lalive, P. & Brat, M. (eds.) (1990) *International Art Trade and Law*, ICC Publishing, Deventer.

Lewis, G.D. (1981) The return of cultural property, *Journal of the Royal Society of Arts*, 129, 435-43.

Lewis, G.D. (1983) Attitudes towards cultural property, *Museum Ethnographers Group Newsletter*, 14, 16-33.

Lewis, G.D. (1988) Museums: international and national self-regulation, in Lalive, P. (ed.), *International Sales of Works of Art*, ICC and Faculty of Law, University of Geneva.

Lewis, G.D. (1990) Heritage giving through taxation in the United Kingdom, in Lalive, P. & Briat, M. (eds.), *International Art Trade and Law*, Vol. 2, ICC Publishing and Kluwer Publishers, Deventer.

Lochnan, K.A. (1986) The ethics of attribution or the name of the game, *Muse*, 4(3), 20-24.

Malaro, M.C. (1985) *A Legal Primer on Managing Museum Collections*, Smithsonian Institution Press, Washington DC.

Malaro, M.C. (1988) Deaccessioning: the importance of procedure, *Museum News*, 66(4), 74-5.

Marsam, A.G. (1991) 1993: A protectionist Europe, *The Art Newspaper*, 2,

4.

Marsam, A.G. (1991) Art exports: DGIII still has the upper hand to the relief of the British, *The Art Newspaper*, 2, 5.

Merriman, J.H. & Elsen, A.E. (1987) *Law, Ethics and the Usual Arts*, 2 volumes, University of Pennsylvania Press.

National Heritage Memorial Fund (1980) *Guidelines Issued to the Trustees*, 11 August.

O'Keefe, P.J. & Prott, L.V. (1984) *Law and the Cultural Heritage: Volume 1 Discovery and Excavation*, Professional Books, Butterworths, Abingdon.

O'Keefe, P.J. & Prott, L.V. (1990) *Law and the Cultural Heritage, Vol. 3: Movement*, Professional Books, Butterworths, Abingdon.

Office of Arts & Libraries (1986) *New Tax Benefits for the Arts (Leaflet)*.

Palmer, N. (1989) Museums and cultural property, in Virgo, P. (ed.), *The New Museology*, Reaktion Books, London.

Phelan, M. (1982) *Museums and the Law*, American Association for State and Local History (AASLH), Nashville, Tennessee.

Scottish Federation of Museums and Art Galleries (1966) Memorandum of Treasure Trove and Bona Vacantia in Scotland, *Museums Journal*, 66(3), 175-86.

Simpson, S. (1989) *Museums and Galleries: A Practical Legal Guide*, Redfern, New South Wales.

Stansfield, G. (ed.) (1983) *The Wildlife and Countryside Act 1981 and Its Implications for Museums*, Biology Curators Group Report No 2.

Staunton, I. & McCartney, M. (1981) *Lost Heritage*, Commonwealth Arts Association and the Africa Centre, London.

Taylor, M.A. & Harte, J.D. (1991) Fossils, minerals and the law, *Geology Today*, 7, 189-193.

UNESCO (1954) *Final Act of the Intergovernmental Conference on the Protection of Cultural Property in the Event of Armed Conflict*, The Hague.

UNESCO (1956) *Recommendation on International Principles Applicable to Archaeological Excavations*, New Delhi.

UNESCO (1960) *Recommendation Concerning the Most Effective Means of Rendering Museums Accessible to Everyone*, Paris.

UNESCO (1964) *Recommendation on the Means of Prohibiting and Preventing the Illicit Export, Import and Transfer of Ownership of Cultural Property*, Paris.

UNESCO (1968) *Recommendation Concerning the Preservation of Cultural Property Endangered by Public or Private Works*, Paris.

UNESCO (1970) *Convention on the Means of Prohibiting and Preventing the Illicit Import, Export and Transfer of Ownership of Cultural Property*, Paris.

UNESCO (1972) *Convention Concerning the Protection of the World*

Cultural and Natural Heritage, Paris.

UNESCO (1972) *Recommendation Concerning the Protection, at National Level, of the Cultural and Natural Heritage*, Paris.

UNESCO (1976) *Recommendation Concerning the International Exchange of Cultural Property*, Nairobi.

UNESCO (1976) *Recommendation Concerning the Safeguarding and Contemporary Role of Historic Areas*, Nairobi.

UNESCO (1978) *Recommendation for the Protection of Movable Cultural Property*, Paris.

UNESCO (1980) *Recommendation for the Safeguarding and Preservation of Moving Images*, Belgrade.

UNESCO (1980; 1981; 1983; 1985; 1987) *Report of the Intergovernmental Committee for Promoting the Return of Cultural Property to Its Countries of Origin or Its Restitution in the Case of Illicit Appropriation*, Belgrade, Paris, Istanbul, Athens and Paris.

UNESCO (1982) *The Cultural Heritage of Mankind: a Shared Responsibility*, Division of Cultural Heritage, Unesco, Paris.

UNESCO (1982) *World Conference on Cultural Policies, Final Report*, Unesco, Paris.

UNESCO (1984) *The Protection of Movable Cultural Property, I & II.*, Paris.

UNIDROIT (1991) Preliminary draft UNIDROIT Convention on Stolen or Illegally Exported Cultural Objects, *Museum*, 43(4), 223-224.

Weil, S.E. (1987) A checklist of legal considerations for museums, *Museum News*, 66(1), 40-42.

Weil, S.E. (1987) Deaccession practices in American museums, *Museum News*, 65(3), 44-50.

West, R.M. (1989) State regulation of geological, palaeontological and archaeological collecting, *Curator*, 32(4), 281-319.

Williams, S.A. (1979) *The International and National Protection of Movable Cultural Property: A Comparative Study*, Dobbs Ferry, New York.

Williams, S.A. (1984) Recent developments in restitution and return of cultural property, *International J. of Museum Management and Curatorship*, 3(2), 117-29.

Wilson, H. & Longman, P. (1985) Tax incentives - can museums benefit?, *Museums Journal*, 85(3), 139-142.

4.5 Documentation

Allan, D.A., Owen, D.E. & Wallis, F.S. (1960) *Administration*, Handbooks for Curators Series, Museums Association, London.

Bergengren, G. (1978) Towards a total information system, *Museum*, 36(3/4), 213-7.

Blackaby, J.R., Greeno, P. & the Nomenclature Committee (1988) *The Revised Nomenclature for Museum Cataloging: A Revised and Expanded Version of Robert G. Chenhall's System for Classifying Man-Made Objects*, American Association for State and Local History, Nashville, Tennessee.

Bruckner, G. (1979) A standard terminology for describing objects in a museum of anthropology, in Dudley, D.H. & Wilkinson, I.B. (eds.), *Museum Registration Methods*, 3rd edition, American Association of Museums, Washington, DC, 267-80.

Brundin, J.A. (1984) Inventorying a historic property, *Museum News*, 63(1), 17-25.

Buchanan, S. & Burnett, J. (1990) Where do you come from?, *Museums Journal*, 90(8), 28.

Buck, A. (1976) Cataloguing Costume, *Museums Journal*, 76(3), 109-10.

Buck, R.D. (1979) Inspecting and describing the condition of art objects, in Dudley, D.H. & Wilkinson, I.B. (eds.), *Museum Registration Methods*, American Association of Museums, Washington, DC, 237-44.

Burcaw, G.E. (1978) Registration and cataloguing, *Introduction to Museum Work*, American Association for State and Local History, Nashville, Tennessee, 84-92.

Burnett, J. & Morrison, I. (1989) *Wimps, Worms and Winchesters, a Guide to Documentation in Museums*, National Museums of Scotland, Edinburgh.

Burnett, J. & Wright, D. (1982) Practical problems in cataloguing the Wellcome collection, *Museums Journal*, 82(2), 86-8.

Burns, W.A. & Rozen, J.G. (1979) Accessioning, marking and storing scientific collections, in Dudley, D.H. & Wilkinson, I.B. (eds.), *Museum Registration Methods*, American Association of Museums, Washington, DC, 301-06.

Butler, S. & Webb, P. (1987) A cataloguing system for a medium-sized museum, *Museums Journal*, 86(4), 199-201.

Case, M. (ed.) (1988) *Registrars on Record*, American Association of Museums Registrars Committee, Washington, DC.

Chenhall, R.G. (1978) *Nomenclature for Museum Cataloguing: A System for Classifying Man-Made Objects*, American Association for State and Local History, Nashville, Tennessee.

Choudhury, A.R. (1964) *Art Museum Documentation and Practical Handling*, Choudhury & Choudhury, Hyderabad, India.

Coleman, L.V. (1927) Museum records, *Manual for Museums*, Putnam, New York.

De Borhegyi, S.F. & Marriott, A. (1958) Proposals for a standardized museum accessioning and classification system, *Curator*, 1(2), 77-86.

Diess, W.A. (1984) *Museum Archives: An Introduction*, Society of American Archivists.

Dixon, R. (1987) CMASS: a response to the Smithsonian institutions Statement of Problem document, *International J. of Museum Management and Curatorship*, 6(2), 201-6.

Dudley, D.H. & Wilkinson, I.B. (eds.) (1979) *Museum Registration Methods*, 3rd edition, American Association of Museums, Washington, DC.

Graham, J.M. (1964) A method of museum registration, *Museum News*, 42(8), Technical Supplement.

Hanna, M.G. & Conaty, G.T. (1987) Expanding the mandate of museum collections: Saskatchewan's collection registration program, *International J. of Museum Management and Curatorship*, 6(3), 252-8.

Harty, M.C., Vilcek, M. & Rhyne, B. (1979) Cataloguing in the Metropolitan Museum of Art, with a note on adaptation for small museums, in Dudley, D.H. & Wilkinson, I.B. (eds.), *Museum Registration Methods*, American Association of Museums, Washington, DC, 219-27.

Herrin, T.E. & Steele, J.L. (1987) A custom designed free-form computer data management system, *Curator*, 30(3), 216-226.

Hoachlander, M.E. (1979) *Profile of a Museum Registrar*, Academy of Education Development, Washington, DC.

Holm, S.A. (1991) *Facts & Artefacts: How to Document a Museum Collection*, Museum Documentation Association, Cambridge.

Hurst, R.M. (1970) Putting a collection on film, *Curator*, 13, 199-203.

Institute of Agricultural History/ Museum of English Rural Life (1978) *Museum Procedure: Classification*, Universityof Reading.

International Committee for Museums and Collections of Costume (1982) *Vocabulary of Basic Terms for Cataloguing Costume*, International Council of Museums.

Jeffrey, C. (1989) *Biological Nomenclature*, 3rd edition, Cambridge University Press.

Jewett, D.F. (1983) *A Glossary for Recording the Condition of an Artefact*, Canadian Heritage Information Network, Ottawa.

Kennedy, W. (1979) A classification system for art objects, in Dudley, D.H. & Wilkinson, I.B. (eds.), *Museum Registration Methods*, American Association of Museums, Washington, DC, 205-07.

Kley, R. T. (1987) Whatchamacalit: problems and potentials in nomenclature & classification, *Curator*, 30(2), 107-112.

Leicestershire County Council (1986) *Written Statement of Registration Policy for the Leicestershire Museums, Art Galleries and Records Service 1986 - 1990.*

Lewis, G.D. (1979) Documentation as an aid in the protection of the international heritage, *Museums and Cultural Exchange*, Papers from the Eleventh General Conference, ICOM (International Council of Museums), Paris, 128-36.

Light, R.B., Roberts, D.A., & Stewart, J.D. (eds.) (1986) *Museum Documentation Systems: Developments and Applications*, Butterworth, London.

Lytle, D.L. & Castleman, R. (1979) Cataloguing prints in the Museum of Modern Art, in Dudley, D.H. & Wilkinson, I.B. (eds.), *Museum Registration Methods*, American Association of Museums, Washington, DC, 228-36.

Majewski, L.J. (1979) Classifying paintings, drawings and prints by media with a note on classifying instructions, in Dudley, D.H. & Wilkinson, I.B. (eds.), *Museum Registration Methods*, American Association of Museums, Washington, DC, 208-18.

Mann, V. (1988) From clay tablet to hard disk, in M. Case (Ed.), *Registrars on Record*, American Association of Museums, Washington DC, 3-12.

Manning, A. (1979) A registrars role in a natural history museum, in Dudley, D.H. & Wilkinson, I.B. (eds.), *Museum Registration Methods*, American Association of Museums, Washington, DC, 281-300.

McBeath, G. & Gooding, S.J. (1969) Registration methods, *Basic Museum Management*, Canadian Museums Association, Ottawa, 49-58.

Miles, G. (1988) Conservation and collection management: integration or isolation, *International J. of Museum Management and Curatorship*, 7, 159-163.

Museum Documentation Association (1981) *Practical Museum Documentation*, 2nd edition, Museum Documentation Association, Duxford.

Museum Documentation Association (1989) *An Introduction to MDA Catalogue Cards*, MDA, Cambridge.

Museum Documentation Association (1991) *The MDA Data Standard*, Museum Documentation Association, Cambridge.

Museum Documentation Association (1992) Sharing the Information Resources of Museums, *Proceedings from the 3rd International Conference, 1989*, Museum Documentation Association, Cambridge.

Museum Documentation Association Development Committee (1982) The future development of the Museum Documentation Association, *Museums Journal*, 82(2), 71-76.

Museum Documentation Association Terminology Working Group (1992) *Thesauri for Museum Documentation*, Museum Documentation Association, Cambridge.

Museums Association (1976) The value of museums as record centres, *Museums Association Conference Proceedings*, 19-24.

Norgate, M. (1982) Museum record, *Museums Journal*, 82(2), 83-6.

Nystrom, B. & Cedrenius, G. (nd) *Spread the Responsibility for Museum*

Documentation - A Programme for Contemporary Documentation At Swedish Museums of Cultural History, Nordiska Museet, SAMDOK, National Council for Cultural Affairs.

Orna, E. (1982) Information management in museums: there's more to it than documentation and computers, *Museums Journal*, 82(2), 79-82.

Orna, E. (1987) *Information Policies for Museums*, The Museum Documentation Association, Cambridge.

Orna, E. & Pettitt, C. (1980) *Information Handling in Museums*, Bingley, London.

Pearsall, M.P. & Ulseth, H.B. (1979) Registration records in a history museum, Dudley, D.H. & Wilkinson, I.B. (eds.), *Museum Registration Methods*, American Association of Museums, Washington, DC, 245-52.

Prince, D.R. (1987) *Museums UK: The Findings of the Museums Database Project*, Museums Association, London.

Prince, D.R. & Higgins-McLoughlin, B. (1987) *Museums UK: The Findings of the Museums Database Project, Update 1*, Museums Association, London.

Pullen, D.L. (1985) Inventorying historical collections in the small museum, *Curator*, 28(4), 271-286.

Reibel, D.B. (1978) *Registration Methods for the Small Museum: A Guide for Historical Collections*, American Association for State and Local History, Nashville, Tennessee.

Reilly, P. & Rahtz, S. (1992) *Archaeology and the Information Age*, Routledge, London.

Rivard, P.E. & Miller, S. (1991) Cataloguing collections - erratic starts and eventual success: a case study, *Curator*, 34(2), 119-124.

Roberts, D.A. (1985) *Planning the Documentation of Museum Collections*, Museum Documentation Association, Duxford, England.

Roberts, D.A. (ed.) (1988) *Collection Management for Museums*, Museum Documentation Association, Cambridge.

Roberts, D.A. (ed.) (1990) *Terminology for Museums*, Museum Documentation Association, Cambridge.

Roberts, D.A. (ed.) (1993) *Staff Development and Training: Meeting the Needs of Museum Documentation*, Museum Documentation Association, Cambridge.

Roberts, D.A., Light, R.B. & Stewart, J.D. (1980) The Museum Documentation Association, *Museums Journal*, 80(2), 81-5.

Rosander, G. (ed.) (1980) *Today for Tomorrow: Museum Documentation of Contemporary Society in Sweden by Acquisition of Objects*, SAMDOK Council, Stockholm.

Rose, C. (1985) A code of ethics for registrars, *Museum News*, 63 (3), 42-6.

Rubenstein, H.R. (1985) Collecting for tomorrow - Sweden's contemporary documentation programme, *Museum News*, 63(6), 55-60.

Ruston, S.H. (1979) Registration methods in a museum of science and industry, in Dudley, D.H. & Wilkinson, I.B. (eds.), *Museum Registration Methods*, American Association of Museums, Washington, DC, 307-10.

Seaborne, M.J. & Neufeld, S. (1982) Historic photograph collection management at the Museum of London, *Museums Journal*, 82(2), 99-104.

Social History and Industrial Classification Working Party (1983) *Social History and Industrial Classification*, Centre for English Cultural Tradition and Language, University of Sheffield.

Stam, D.C. (1989) Public access to museum information, pressures and policies, *Curator*, 32(3), 190-7.

Stone, S. (1992) Documenting collections, in Thompson, J.M.A. *et al. (eds.)*, *Manual of Curatorship*, Butterworth, London, 213-228.

Taylor, D.G. (1979) Registration in historic house museums, in Dudley, D.H. & Wilkinson, I.B. (eds.), *Museum Registration Methods*, American Association of Museums, Washington, DC, 253-66.

Thornton, J.H. & Swann, J.M. (1986) *A Glossary of Shoe Terms*, Northampton Museum.

Townsend, J. (1990) Labelling and Marker Pens, *Conservation News*, 42, 8-10.

Washburn, W.E. (1984) Collecting information, not objects, *Museum News*, 62(3), 5-15.

Webb, V. (1987) Collected images: a research file of photographs of art, *Curator*, 30(1), 77-84.

4.6 Computers & Computer Documentation

Alsford, S. & Granger, E. (1987) Image automation in museums: the Canadian Museum of Civilizations optical disc project, *International J. of Museum Management and Curatorship*, 6(2), 187-200.

Art Museum Association of America (1984) *A Reference List of in-House Computer Use in Art Museums*, San Francisco.

Avendon, E.M. (1985) A community museum computer network, *Muse*, 3(2), 18-24.

Bacharach, J. (1987) Automation of the NPS Museum collections, *Curator*, 30(2), 146-158.

Bailey, L., Steigman, K. & Peterman, B. (1990) Application of dBase III plus to database needs of small museum, *Curator*, 33(3).

Bearman, D. (1987) Automated systems for archives and museums: acquisition and implementation issues, *Archival Informatics Technical*

Report, 1(4).

Bearman, D. (1987) Functional requirements for collections management systems, *Archival Informatics Technical Report*, 1(3).

Bearman, D. (1988) Directory of software for archives and museums, *Archival Informatics Technical Report*, 2(1).

Binder, R.H. (1988) *Videodiscs in Museums: A Project and Resource Directory.*, American Association of Museums, Washington DC.

Blackaby, J.R. (1991) Museum computerisation: making a glass slipper fit, *Muse*, Spring, 14-17.

Blackwood, B. (1970) *Classification of Artefacts in the Pitt Rivers Museum, Oxford*, Occasional Paper on Technology 1, Pitt Rivers Museum, Oxford.

Cash, J. (1986) Spinning towards the future, *Museum News*, 63(6), 19-36.

Cato, D.S. & Folse, L.J. (1985) A microcomputer/mainframe hybrid system for computerizing specimen data, *Curator*, 28(2), 105-116.

Chadburn, A. (1988) A review of approaches to controlling archaeological vocabulary for data retrieval, in Ratz, S.P.Q. (ed.), *Proceedings of the 1988 Computer Applications in Archaeology Conference*, B.A.R. International Series, 315-322.

Chenhall, R.G. (1975) *Museum Cataloguing in the Computer Age*, American Association for State and Local History, Nashville, Tennessee.

Chenhall, R.G. (1978) Computer use in museums today, *Museum*, 30(3/4), 139-45.

Chenhall, R.G. (1978) Museums and computers: a progress report, *Museum*, 30(1), 52-4.

Chenhall, R.G. (1987) Museums and computers: a world view, *Curator*, 30(2), 1-2-106.

Chenhall, R.G. & Vance, D. (1988), *Museum Collections and Today's Computers*, Greenwood Press, London.

Cutbill, J.L. (1973) *Computer Filing Systems for Museums and Research*, Sedgwick Museum, Cambridge.

Cutbill, J.L., Hallan, A.J. & Lewis, G.D. (1971) A format for the machine exchange of museum data, in Cutbill, J.L. (ed.), *Data Processing in Biology and Geology*, Academic Press, London, 311-20.

Dixon, R. (1983) A modern computer cataloguing and administration system for museums, *International J. of Museum Management and Curatorship*, 2(4), 335-46.

Dixon, R. (1986) Using computers for art history & collection management, *International J. of Museum Management and Curatorship*, 4(1), 56-63.

Dobbs, G. (1982) *A National Survey of Current Technology in Museum Environments and Anticipated Use in Art Museums*, The Art Museums Association, San Francisco.

Dudley, D.H. & Wilkinson, I.B. (eds.) (1979) *Museum Registration*

Methods, American Association of Museums, Washington, DC.

Eades, C. (1987) A systems framework for museums, *Curator*, 30(2), 118-123.

Ellin, E. (1970) Scientific documentation, *ICOM (International Council of Museums), 8th General Conference Report*, Deutsches Museum, Munich, 67-86.

Englander, N. (1983) Museum computer systems and the J. Paul Getty Trust, *International J. of Museum Management and Curatorship*, 2(3), 229-34.

Eri, I. & Vegh, B. (1986) *Dictonarium Museologicum*, CIDOC Working Group on Terminology, Hungarian Esperanto Association, Budapest.

Femenias, B. (1985) ARTSearch: an interactive loans videodisc computer system for museum collections, *Museum Studies Journal*, 2(1), 50-58.

Folse, L.J. & Cato, P.S. (1985) Software made for collection management, *Curator*, 28(2), 97-104.

Forbes, C.L., Harland, W.B. & Cutbill, J.L. (1971) A uniform cataloguing system in the Department of Geology, Cambridge, in Cutbill, J.L. (ed.), *Data Processing in Biology and Geology*, Academic Press, London, 320-331.

Foster, R. & Phillips, P. (1987) New applications for computers in the National Museums and Galleries on Merseyside, in Roberts, D.A. (ed.), *Collection Management for Museums*, Museums Documentation Association, Cambridge.

Gartenberg, J. (1987) Cataloguing films on a PC, *Curator*, 30(2), 131-145.

Gautier, T.G. (1978) Automated collection documentation at the National Museum of Natural History, Smithsonian institution, Washington, DC, *Museum*, 30, 160-68.

Goodwin, L. & Conaway, M.E. (1984) The micro and the muse, *Museum News*, 62(4), 55-63.

Granger, F. & Alsford, S. (1988) *The Canadian Museum of Civilisation Optical Disc Project: A Report*, Canadian Museum of Civilisation, Ottawa.

Hackmann, W.D. (1973) *The Evaluation of a Museum Communication Format*, Organisation of Scientific and Technological institutions Report 5154, Museum of History of Science, Oxford.

Hart, C.W., Clark, J. & Manning, R. (1983) Mythology and microcomputers, *Curator*, 26(3), 199-202.

Hicks, E.C. & Walker, C.B. (1986) Streamlined systems- computers make museums manageable, *Museum News*, 63(6), 36-47.

Holland, K.C. (1985) Creating a permanent collection catalogue, *Museum Studies Journal*, 85(5), 26-34.

IRGMA Standards Sub-Committee (1977) Ten years of IRGMA, 1967-1977, *Museums Journal*, 77(1), 11-14.

Kirk, J.J. (1979) Using a computer in Brighton's museums, *Museums*

Journal, 79(1), 17-20.

Kley, R.J. (1987) Museum computer network: an introduction, *Curator*, 30(2), 100-101.

Lewis, G.D. (1979) Documentation as an aid in the protection of the international heritage, *ICOM (International Council of Museums), 11th General Conference Report*, 128-36.

Lewis, G.D. (ed.) (1967) Information retrieval for museums: report of a colloquium, *Museums Journal*, 67(2), 88-120.

Lewis, G.W. & Paull, T. (1984) Towards computer literacy, *Muse News*, Winter, 30-39.

Light, R. (1982) Today's microcomputers for museum documentation, *Museums Journal*, 82(2), 77-8.

Mackie, E.W. (1980) Using the MDA cards in the Hunterian Museum, *Museums Journal*, 80(2), 66-89.

McVey, M.E., Fairchild, L. & Gaunt, S.L.L. (1989) A Microcomputer DBMS for a sound-recording collection, *Curator*, 32(2), 91.

Morrison, I.O. (1992) Towards a national database, *Scottish Museums News*, 8(2), 6-7.

Museum Documentation Association (1980) *Introduction to the Museum Documentation Association*, MDA, Duxford.

Museum Documentation Association (1981) *Guide to the Museum Documentation System*, 2nd edition, MDA, Duxford.

Museum Documentation Association (1981) *International Museum Data Standards*, MDA, Duxford.

Museum Documentation Association (1981) *Practical Museum Documentation*, MDA, Duxford.

Museum Documentation Association (1981) *The MDA Systems and Services: A User's View*, MDA, Duxford.

Museum Documentation Association (1984) *Microcomputers in Museums*, MDA, Duxford.

Museum Documentation Association (1989) *Computer Support for Fieldwork and Site Recording*, MDA Occasional Paper 15, MDA Cambridge.

Museum Documentation Association (1989) *Computerization of Museum Management Practices and Gallery Displays*, MDA Occasional Paper 12, MDA Cambridge.

Museum Documentation Association (1989) *Computers in Conservation and Environmental Control*, MDA Occasional Paper 14, MDA Cambridge.

Museum Documentation Association (1989) *Management of the Use of Automated Systems*, MDA Occasional Paper 11, MDA Cambridge.

Museum Documentation Association (1989) *Modes: The Museum Cataloguing System*, MDA, Cambridge.

Museum Documentation Association (1989) *The Use of Computers for*

Collections Documentation, MDA Occasional Paper 13, MDA Cambridge.

Museum Documentation Association (1990) *The UK Museum Databases Project - Report on Progress*, Museums Documentation Association and Chadwick Healey Ltd.

Neri, J. (1988) Museum application software survey responses, *MDA Information*, 12(1), 2-8.

Orna, E. (1993) Interaction: liberation or exploitation?, *Museums Journal*, 93(2), 27-28.

Orna, E. & Pettit, C. (1980) *Information Handling in Museums*, Clare Bingley, London.

Parker, S. (1987) Relational database technology, *Curator*, 30(2), 124-130.

Perkins, J. (1992) CIMI's data movement, *Museum News*, 71(4), 24-26.

Pettit, C.W. (1981) The Manchester Museum Computer Cataloguing Unit, *Museums Journal*, 80(2), 187-91.

Porter, M.F., Light, R.B. & Roberts, D.A. (1977) *A Unified Approach to the Computerization of Museum Catalogues*, British Library Research and Development Report 5338 HC, London.

Pring, I. (ed.) (1990) *Image '89: The Internation Meeting on Museums and Art Galleries Image Database*, IMAGE, London.

Prochnak, M. (1990) Computers in Museums, *Museums Journal*, 90(5), 9.

Prochnak, M. (1990) Multimedia is the Message, *Museums Journal*, 90(8), 25-27.

Roberts, D.A. (1980) The Museum Documentation Association, *Museums Association Conference Proceedings*, 16-17.

Roberts, D.A. (ed.) (1987) *Collection Management for Museums*, Museum Documentation Association, Cambridge.

Roberts, D.A., Light, R.B. & Stewart, J.D. (1980) The Museum Documentation Association, *Museums Journal*, 80(2), 81-5.

Rowlison, E.B. (1984) Towards discovering our cultural heritage: a progress report on cataloguing gallery collections, *Museum Australia*, 26-30.

Rush, C.E. & Chenhall, R.G. (1979) Computers and registration: principles of information management, in Dudley, D.H & Wilkinson, I.B. (eds.), *Museum Registration Methods*, American Association of Museums, Washington, DC.

Sarasan, L. (1979) An economical approach to computerization, *Museum News*, 57(4), 61-4.

Sarasan, L. (1981) Why museum computer projects fail, *Museum News*, 59(4), 40-9.

Sarasan, L. (1987) What to look for in an automated collections management system, *Museum Studies Journal*, 3(1), 82-93.

Sarasan, L. (1988) Standards: how do we get from here to there, *Museum News*, 66(6), 36.

Sarasan, L. & Neuner, A.M. (eds.) (1983) *Museum Collections and*

Computers: Report on an ASC Survey., Association of Systematics Collections, Lawrence, Kansas.

Sargent, G.F. (1990) Trends in mass storage products for computers, *Museum Documentation Association Information*, 14(1), 9-14.

Squires, D.F. (1970) An information storage and retrieval system for biological and geological data, *Curator*, 13(1), 43-62.

Squires, D.F. (1971) Implications of data processing for museums, in Cutbill, J.J. (ed.), *Data Processing in Biology and Geology*, Academic Press, London, 235-53.

Stewart, J.D. (1983) Museum documentation in Britain - a review of some recent developments, *Museums Journal*, 82(1), 61-4.

Urice, J.K. (1984) Information systems and the arts, *Journal of Arts Management & Law*, 14(1).

Vance, D. (1970) Museum computer network: the second phase, *Museum News*, 48(9), 15-20.

Varveris, T. (1979) Computers and registration: practical applications, in Dudley, D.H. & Wilkinson, I.B. (eds.), *Museum Registration Methods*, American Association of Museums, Washington, DC, 340-54.

Veiner, S.B. (1985) Designing a collections information system for the Smithsonian institution, *Curator*, 28(4), 237-248.

Vulpe, M. (1986) Collection Management Action Support Systems - CMASS, *International J. of Museum Management and Curatorship*, 5(4), 349-356.

Wentz, P. (1989) Museum information systems: the case for computerization, *International J. of Museum Management and Curatorship*, 8, 313-25.

Wheeler, S. (1987) Information management in a small collection, *Curator*, 30(2), 159-167.

Wilcox, V. (1980) Collections management with the computer, *Curator*, 23(1), 43-54.

Will, L., Robinson, D., Rhodes, K., Quickfall, J. & Kirk, J. (1989) Planning to automate: 1.The National Museum of Science and Industry, *Museum Documentation Association Information*, 13(3/4), 33-44.

Williams, D.W. (1987) *A Guide to Museum Computing*, American Association for State and Local History, Nashville, Tennessee.

4.7 Conservation Issues

American Institute of Conservation (1980) Code of Ethics and standards of practice, *American Institute of Conservation Directory*, AIC,

Washington DC, 9-22.

Anon. (1980) A code of ethics for conservators, *Museum News*, 58(4), 27-34.

Anon. (1987) The conservation-restorer: a definition of the profession, *Museum*, 39(4), 231-3.

Ashley-Smith, J. (1978) Why conserve collections?, *Museum Professionals Group (MPG) Transactions*, 15.

Ashley-Smith, J. (1982) The ethics of conservation, *The Conservator*, 6, 1-5.

Ballestrem, A., Von Immhof., McMillan, E., & Perrot, P.M. (1984) The conservator-restorer: a draft definition of the profession, *International J. of Museum Management and Curatorship*, 3, 75-78.

Brown, C.E. (1992) Selecting a conservator or restorer, *Scottish Museum News*, 8(4), 2-3.

Cadorin, P. (1982) Inadequate precautions for temporary exhibitions, *Museum*, 34(1), 48-50.

Cannon-Brookes, P. (1988) The role of the scholar-curator in conservation, *International J. of Museum Management and Curatorship*, 7, 323-325.

Carlyle, L. (ed.) (1990) *Appearance, Opinion, Change: Evaluating the Look of Paintings*, United Kingdom Institute for Conservation, London.

Daley, M. (1993) Solvent abuse, *The Spectator*, 30 January, 55-58.

Drish, D. & Summers, C. (1989) Know what you want, *Museum News*, 68(4).

Edwards, Y. (1987) Museums must decide:hands-on or hands-off?, *Muse*, 5(1).

Fielden, J.F. (1982) Museums:the right places for conservation, *Museum*, 34(1), 10-20.

Getty Conservation Institute (1992) Preventative conservation, *Conservation*, 7(1), 4-7.

Hedley, G. (1986) Cleaning and meaning: the 'Ravished Image' reviewed, *The Conservator*, 10, 2-6.

International Institute for Conservation (1974) *Conservation in Museums and Galleries, - A Survey of Facilities in the United Kingdom* International Institute for Conservation, UK Group.

King, M.E. (1980) Curators:Ethics and Obligations, *Curator*, 23(1), 10-18.

Kopec, D.R. (1991) Conservation cure, *Museum News*, 70(3), 60-63.

Krahn, A.H. (1984) Access and public trust: a conservation perspective, *Muse*, 1(4).

Krasnow, C.C. (1981) Legal aspects of conservation - basic consideration of contracts and negligence, *Technology & Conservation*, 7(1), 38-40.

Lewis, G.M. (1986) The conservation service at the National Maritime Museum, Greenwich *International J. of Museum Management and Curatorship*, 5(4), 383-390.

Mann, P.R. (1989) Working exhibits and the destruction of evidence in the Science Museum, *International J. of Museum Management and Curatorship*, 8, 369-387.

Marijnissen, R.H. (1986) May we keep the Breughel?, *Museum*, 38(4), 249-252.

Miles, G. (1988) Conservation and collection management: integration or isolation, *International J. of Museum Management and Curatorship*, 7, 159-163.

Monger, G. (1984) Conservation or restoration, *International J. of Museum Management and Curatorship*, 7, 375-380.

Museums & Galleries Commission (1989) *Conservation Research in the UK*, London.

Museums & Galleries Commission (1989) *Education and Training for Conservation*, London.

National Conservation Advisory Council (1976) *Conservation of Cultural Property in the U.S.*, Smithsonian Institution Press, Washington DC.

National Conservation Advisory Council (1979) *Report of the Study on Scientific Support*, Washington, DC.

National Fire Protection Association (1987) *Protection of Museums and Museum Collections*, NFPA, 911.6-911.7.

National Museums of Canada (1983) *National Museums of Canada Conservation Policy*, Ottawa.

Oakley, V. (1990) Vessel Glass Deterioration at the Victoria and Albert Museum:Surveying the Collections, *The Conservator*, 14.

Oddy, W.A. (1992) *The Art of the Conservator*, British Museum, London.

Organ, R.M. (1982) Errors of preservation, *Museum*, 34(1), 51-2.

Percival-Prescott, W. (1982) The complexities of conservation of paintings, *International J. of Museum Management and Curatorship*, 1, 243-247.

Ramer, B.L. (1989) *A Conservation Survey of Museum Collections in Scotland*, Edinburgh, HMSO.

Sidey, T. (1989) Making the case for conservation, *Museums Journal*, 89(2), 28-31.

Standing Commission on Museumsand Galleries (1980) *Conservation*, HMSO, London.

Staniland, K. (1973) Modern display versus conservation, *Museum Assistants Group (MAG) Newsletter*, 10 June.

Storer, J.D. (1989) *Conservation of industrial Collections: A Survey*, Science Museum and Museums and Galleries Commission, London.

Sykas, P. (1987) Caring or wearing? The case against the showing of costume on live models, *Museums Journal*, 87(3), 155-157.

Todd, V. (ed.) (1988) *Conservation Today*, Preprints of the 30th Anniversary Conference, United Kingdom Institute for Conservation.

Ullberg, A.D. & Lind, R.C. (1989) Consider the potential liability of failing to conserve collections, *Museum News*, 68(1), 32-3.

UNESCO (1968) *The Conservation of Cultural Property*, Museums and Monuments Series No XI.

UNESCO (1981) *Appropriate Technologies in the Conservation of Cultural*

Property, Technical Handbooks for Museums and Monuments No.7.

UNESCO (1981) *Protection of the Underwater Heritage*, Technical Handbooks for Museums and Monuments No.4.

United Kingdom Institute for Conservation (1984) Guidance for Conservation Practice, *Museums Journal*, 84(2), 92.

United Kingdom Institute for Conservation (1989) *The Survey: Conservation Facilities in Museums and Galleries*, UKIC, London.

Various (1982) Conservation - a challenge to the profession, Special issue, *Museum*, 34(1).

Walters, J. (1989) Tracking advances, *Museum News*, 68(1), 44-9.

Ward, P. (1989) *The Nature of Conservation: A Race Against Time*, Getty Conservation Institute, California.

Ward, P.R. (1982) Poor support: the forgotten factor, *Museum*, 34(1), 55-6.

Watkins, C.S. (1989) Conservation:a cultural challenge, *Museum News*, 68(1), 36-43.

Webster, L. (1990) Altered states:documenting changes in anthropology museum objects, *Curator*, 33(2), 130-60.

4.8 Conservation Practice

Baer, N. (1988) Maintenance of outdoor bronze sculpture, *International J. of Museum Management and Curatorship*, 7, 71-75.

Baynes-Cope, A.D. (1981) *Caring for Books and Documents*, British Library.

Berner, A., Van Der Meer, J.H. & Thibault, G. (1967) *Preservation and Restoration of Musical Instruments*, International Council of Museums, London.

Black, J. (ed.) (1987) *Recent Advances in the Conservation and Analysis of Artefacts*, University of London, Institute of Archaeology.

Clapp, A.F. (1987) *Curatorial Care of Works of Art on Paper*, Lyons, New York.

Clydesdale, A. (1990) *Chemicals in Conservation: A Guide to Possible Hazards and Safe Use*, Scottish Society for Conservation and Restoration, Edinburgh.

Conservation Unit, Museums & Galleries Commission (1991) *Conservation Sourcebook*, HMSO, London.

Conservation Unit, Museums & Galleries Commission (1992) *Science for Conservators 1: An Introduction to Materials*, MGC/Routlege.

Conservation Unit, Museums & Galleries Commission (1992) *Science for Conservators 2: Cleaning*, MGC/Routledge.

Conservation Unit, Museums & Galleries Commission (1992) *Science for Conservators 3: Adhesives and Coatings*, MGC/Routlege.

Cronyn, J.M. (1990) *Elements of Archaeological Conservation*, Routledge, London.

Cross, C.F. & Hauser, R.A. (1979) Reducing the perils of textile display, *Museum News*, 58(1), 60-4.

Crowther, P.R. & Collins, C.J. (eds.) (1987) The Conservation of Geological Material, *Geological Curator*, 4.

Dollof, F.W. & Perkinson, R.L. (1985) *How to Care for Works of Art on Paper*, Boston Museum of Fine Art, Boston.

Dowmann, E.A. (1970) *Conservation in Field Archaeology*, Methuen, London.

Ellis, M.H. (1988) *The Care of Prints and Drawings*, American Association for State and Local History (AASLH), Nashville, Tennessee.

Fall, F.K. (1973) *Art Objects: Their Care and Preservation*, McGilvery, California.

Finch, K. & Putman, G. (1977) *Caring for Textiles*, Barrie & Jenkins, London.

Florian, M.-L.E., Norton, R., & Kronkright, D. (1990) *Conservation of Artifacts Made from Plant Materials*, Getty Conservation Trust, California.

Flury-Lemberg, M. (1988) *Textile Conservation and Research*, Abegg-Stifung, Bern.

Fogle, S. (ed.) (1985) *Recent Advances in Leather Conservation*, American Institute for Conservation, Washington DC.

Garfield, D. (1989) Filling the gaps (work of Getty Conservation Institute), *Museum News*, 68(1), 50-3.

Gerhard, C. (1990) *Preventative Conservation in the Tropics: A Bibliography*, Institute of Fine Arts, New York.

Glover, J.M. (1973) *Textiles: Their Care and Protection in Museums*, Museums Association Information Sheet No 18, London.

Griset, S. (1986) Preventative conservation measures for an ethnographic collection, *International J. of Museum Management and Curatorship*, 5, 371-382.

Guldbeck, P. (1972) *The Care of Historical Collections*, American Association for State and Local History, Nashville, Tennessee.

Hackney, S. (1990) Framing for conservation at the Tate Gallery, *The Conservator*, 14.

Horie, C.V. (1987) *Materials for Conservation*, Butterworth, London.

Horie, C.V. (1987) *Materials for Conservation*, Butterworths, London.

Horie, C.V. (ed.) (1989) *Conservation of Natural History Specimens: Spirit Collections*, Department of Environmental Biology/Manchester Museum, University of Manchester.

Horie, C.V. (ed.) (1989) *Conservation of Natural History Specimens:*

Vertebrates, Department of Environmental Biology/Manchester Museum, University of Manchester.

Howie, F.M.P. (1978) Storage environment and the conservation of geological material, *Conservator*, 2, 13-19.

Howie, F.M.P. (1986) Conserving and mounting fossils: a historical review, *Curator*, 29(1), 5-24.

Howie, F.M.P. (ed.) (1992) *The Care and Conservation of Geological Material: Minerals, Rocks, Meteriorites and Lunar Finds*, Butterworth-Heinemann, London.

International Centre for the Study of the Preservation and Restoration of Cultural Property (ICCROM) & Washington Conservation Analytical Laboratory (1988) *International Conservation Research*, ICCROM, Rome.

International Council of Museums (1985) Developments in Protection Methods, *ICOM (International Council of Museums) News*, 43, 2.

International Institute for Conservation (1961) *Conservation of Paintings and the Graphic Arts*, Lisbon Conference, IIC.

International Institute for Conservation (1961) *Recent Advances in Conservation*, Rome Conference, IIC.

International Institute for Conservation (1964) *Textile Conservation*, Delft Conference, IIC.

International Institute for Conservation (1970) *Conservation of Stone and Wooden Objects*, New York Conference, International Institute for Conservation.

International Institute for Conservation (1975) *Conservation in Archaeology and the Applied Arts*, International Institute for Conservation.

International Institute for Conservation (1978) *Conservation of Wood in Paintings and the Decorative Arts*, International Institute for Conservation.

International Institute for Conservation (1983) *Science and Technology in the Service of Museums*, International Institute for Conservation.

Keck, C.K. (1965) *A Handbook on the Care of Paintings*, American Association for State and Local History, Nashville, Tennessee.

Keene, S. (1991) Audits of care: a framework for collections condition surveys, in Norman, M. & Todd, V. (eds.), *Storage*, United Kingdom Institute for Conservation, London, 6-14.

Kenjo, T. (1986) Certain deterioration factors for works of art and simple devices to monitor them, *International J. of Museum Management and Curatorship*, 5(3), 295-300.

Knell, S.J. & Collins, C.J. (1992) Extinct again!, *Geology Today*, 8(2), 62-65.

Koe, F.T. (1990) Fabrics on file, *Museum News*, 69(1).

Kuhn, H. (1986) *Conservation and Restoration of Works of Art and*

Antiquites, Butterworth-Heinemann, London.

Kuhn, H. (1989) The restoration of historic technological artefacts, scientific instruments and tools, *International J. of Museum Management and Curatorship*, 8(4), 389-405.

Landi, S. (1992) *The Textile Conservator's Manual*, 2nd edition, Butterworth-Heinemann, London.

Leene, J.E. (ed.) (1972) *Textile Conservation*, Butterworth, London.

London, M. (1988) *Masonry: How to Care for Old and Historic Brick and Stone*, Preservation Press, Washington.

MacLeish, B. (1985) *The Care of Antiquities and Historical Collections*, American Association for State and Local History (AASLH), Nashville, Tennessee.

Mills, J. (1987) *The Organic Chemistry of Museum Objects*, Butterworth, London.

Mora, P., Mora, L. & Philippot (1984) *Conservation of Wall Paintings*, Butterworth-Heinemann, London.

Morgan, J. (1991) *Conservation of Plastics: An Introduction*, The Conservation Unit, Museums & Galleries Commission, London.

Newton, R.G. & Davidson, S. (1989) *Conservation of Glass*, Butterworth-Heinemann, London.

Oakley, V. (1990) Vessel glass deterioration at the Victoria and Albert Museum: surveying the collections, *Conservator*, 14.

Organ, R.M. (1968) *Design for Scientific Conservation of Antiquities*, Butterworths, London.

Park, D. & Cather, S. (eds.) (1991) *The Conservation of Wall Paintings*, Getty Conservation Institute, California.

Pearson, C. (1987) *The Conservation of Marine Archaeological Objects*, Butterworths, London.

Plenderleith, H.J. & Werner, A.E.A. (1971) *The Conservation of Antiquities and Works of Art*, 2nd edition, Oxford University Press.

Rempel, S. (1980) *The Care of Black and White Photographic Collections: Cleaning and Stabilization*, Canadian Conservation Institute Technical Bulletin 9.

Rempel, S. (1987) *The Care of Photographs*, Lyons & Burford, New York.

RILEM (1993) *Conservation of Stone & Other Materials*, Chapman & Hall, London.

Rixon, A.E. (1976) *Fossil Animal Remains - Their Preparation and Conservation*, Athlone Press, London.

Serjeant, D. (1986) The protection of paintings in loan exhibitions, *Museum*, 38(4), 246-8.

Waterer, J.W. (1971) *A Guide to the Conservation and Restoration of Leather*, G. Bell & Sons, London.

Watkinson, D. (ed.) (1987) *First Aid for Finds*, UKIC Archaeology Section/Rescue.

Weinstein, R.A. & Booth, L. (1977) *Collection, Use and Care of Historical Photographs*, American Association for State and Local History (AASLH), Nashville, Tennessee.

Wilks, H. (ed.) (1982) *Science for Conservation, Book 1, Introduction to Materials*, Crafts Council.

Williams, M.A. (1988) *Keeping it all Together: The Preservation and Care of Historic Furniture*, Ohio Antique Review.

4.9 Conservation Laboratories

Al-Naqshbandi, A. (1973) The Iraq Museum Laboratory, Baghdad, *Studies in Conservation*, 18(1), 36-42.

Augusti, S. (1959) The Conservation Laboratory of the Museo e Gallerie Nazionali di Capido-monte, *Studies in Conservation*, 4(3).

Baer, N.S. & Blair, C. (1989) Conservation 1. Scientific instrumentation for the conservation laboratory, *International J. of Museum Management and Curatorship*, 8, 241-5.

Boustead, W. (1960) The Conservation Department of the New South Wales Art Gallery, Australia, *Studies in Conservation*, 5(4), 121ff.

Brommelle, N.S. (1963) Conservation studios, *Museums Journal*, 63(1/2), 74-9.

Daifuku, H. (1968) Equipping the laboratory, *The Conservation of Cultural Property*, Museums and Monuments, 11, UNESCO, Paris.

Gettens, R.J. (1959) The Freer Gallery Laboratory for Technical Studies in Oriental Art and Archaeology, *Studies in Conservation*, 4, 140ff.

Hodges, H.W.M. (1968) Equipping the laboratory, *The Conservation of Cultural Property*, Museums and Monuments, 11, UNESCO, Paris.

Muhlethaler, B. (1962) The research laboratory of the Swiss National Museum, *Studies in Conservation*, 7, 35-.

National Museums & Galleries on Merseyside (1993) *The Conservation Centre*, National Museums & Galleries on Merseyside, Liverpool.

Organ, R.M. (1968) *Design for Scientific Conservation of Antiquities*, Butterworth, London.

Schur, S.E. & Weiss, N.R. (1979) Establishing laboratories for treatment of cultural properties, *Technology and Conservation*, 3, 26-30.

Slabczynski, S. (1964) Establishing a laboratory for the restoration of paintings, *Museums Journal*, 64(1), 36-49.

Straub, R.E. (1961) The laboratories of the Swiss institute for Art Research, *Studies in Conservation*, 6(2), 41ff.

Walden, T.A. (1963) Laboratories and workshops, *Museums Journal*,

63(1/2), 70-3.

Werner, A.E.A. (1962) The British Museum research laboratory, *Museums Journal*, 62(3), 153-59.

Werner, A.E.A. & Organ, R.M. (1962) The new laboratory of the British Museum, *Studies in Conservation*, 7, 70ff.

4.10 Relative Humidity

Amdur, H.J. (1964) Humidity control - isolated area plan, *Museum News*, 43(6) Technical Supplement.

Anderson, R.G.W. & Simpson, A.D.C. (1973) Control of the museum environment, *Royal Scottish Museum Triennial Report*, 38-40.

Anon. (1984) The Smithsonian's new museum support centre, *Museum News*, 62 (4), 32-5.

Anon. (1988) Insulating tactics...to win the collections survival battle, *Technology and Conservation*, March/April, 5-6, 8-9.

Appelbaum, B. (1991) *Guide to Environmental Protection of Collections*, Sound View Press, Connecticut.

Ashley-Smith, J. & Moncrieff, A. (1984) Experience with silica-gel for controlling humidity in showcases, *Preprints of the 7th Triennial Meeting of the ICOM (International Council of Museums) Committee for conservation*, Copenhagen, 17.1 - 17.5.

Ayres, J.M. *et al.* (1989) Energy conservation and climate control in museums: a cost simulation under various outdoor climates, *International J. of Museum Management and Curatorship*, 8(3), 299-312.

Baer, N.S. & Banks, P.N. (1987) Environmental standards, *International J. of Museum Management and Curatorship*, 6(2), 207-10.

Banks, P.N. & Baer, N.S. (1986) Ultrasonic humidifiers, *International J. of Museum Management and Curatorship*, 5(4), 395-8.

Barrette, B. (1984) Climate control: the Egyptian Galleries at the Metropolitan Museum of Art, *Preprints of the 7th Triennial Meeting of the ICOM (International Council of Museums) Committee for Conservation*, Copenhagen, 17.6-17.8.

Barrette, B. (1985) The Egyptian Galleries at the Metropolitan Museum of Art, *Museum*, 37(2), 81-4.

Bernardi, A. (1990) Microclimate in the British Museum, *International J. of Museum Management and Curatorship*, 9(2), 169-82.

Bosshard, E. (1992) Paintings: the (show)case for passive climate control, *Museum*, 44(1), 46-50.

Brimblecombe, P. & Ramer B. (1983) Museum display cases and the exchange of water vapour, *Studies in Conservation*, 24(4), 179-88.

Bryantseu, A.V. (1985) The Hermitage Museum; packing techniques for paintings, *Museum*, 37(2), 123-4.

Byrne, R.O. (1984) An Easter Island effigy figure display case, *Preprints of the 7th Triennial Meeting of the ICOM (International Council of Museums) Committee for Conservation*, Copenhagen, 17.9-17.10.

Calmes, A. (1985) Charters of freedom of the United States, *Museum*, 37(2), 99-101.

Cassar, M. (1984) Proposal for a typology of display case construction, design and museum climate control systems, *Preprints of the 7th Triennial Meeting of the ICOM (International Council of Museums) Committee for Conservation*, Copenhagen, 17.11-17.15.

Cassar, M. (1985) Case design and climate control: a typological analysis, *Museum*, 37(2), 104-7.

Cassar, M. (1986) A flexible climate-controlled storage system for a collection of ivory veneers from Nimrud, *International J. of Museum Management and Curatorship*, 5(2), 171-181.

Cassar, M. & Oreszczyn (1991) Environmental surveys in museums and galleries in the United Kingdom, *Museum Management & Curatorship*, 10, 385-402.

Child, R.E. (ed.) (1993) *Electronic Environmental Monitoring in Museums*, Archetype Books.

Deferne, J. (1992) Hygrometry and the happiness of a harpsichord, *Museum*, 1, 51-54.

Douglas, R.A. (1972) A commonsense approach to environmental control, *Curator*, 15(2), 139-44.

Guichen, G. De (1985) Controlling the atmosphere for 197 musical instruments, *Museum*, 37(2), 95-8.

Hall, R. (1987) Conservation in the computer age, *International J. of Museum Management and Curatorship*, 6, 291-294.

Harvey, J. (1973) Air conditioning for museums, *Museums Journal*, 73(1), 11-16.

Horton-James, D. (1984) A comparison of manual environmental systems with a computer based system, *Preprints of the 7th Triennial Meeting of the ICOM (International Council of Museums) Committee for Conservation*, Copenhagen, 17.26-17.28.

Keck, C.K. (1972) On conservation, *Museum News*, 50(8), 13-14.

Kenjo, T. (1982) A rapid-response humidity buffer composed of Nikka pellets and Japanese tissue, *Studies in Conservation*, 27, 19-24.

Lafontaine, R.H. & Michalski, S. (1984) The control of relative humidity - recent developments, *Preprints of the 7th Triennial Meeting of the ICOM (International Council of Museums) Committee for Conservation*, Copenhagen, 17.33-17.37.

Lewis, L.L. (1957) Air conditioning for museums, *Museum*, 10(2), 140.

Macleod, K.J. (1975) Relative humidity: its importance, measurement and control in museums, *Canadian Conservation Institute Technical Bulletin*, 1.

Marriner, P. (1980) Temperature and humidity control, *Canadian Museums Association (CMA) Gazette*, Winter, 12-17.

Martin, G. & Ford, D. (1992) Museums tune in to radio, *Museum Development*, November, 15-16.

Michalski, S. (1985) A relative humidity control module, *Museum*, 37(2), 85-8.

Motylewski, K. (1990) A matter of control, *Museum News*, 69(2), 64-7.

Nelson, E.R. (1968) Do we understand air-conditioning?, *Curator*, 11(2), 127-36.

Padfield, T. (1966) Control of relative humidity and air pollution in show cases and picture frames, *Studies in Conservation*, 11, 8-30.

Padfield, T. (1985) A cooled display case, *Museum*, 37(2), 102-103.

Padfield, T. et al. (1984) A cooled display case for George Washington: commission, *Preprints of the 7th Triennial Meeting of the ICOM (International Council of Museums) Committee for Conservation*, Copenhagen, 17.38-17.42.

Plenderleith, H.J. & Philpot, P. (1960) Climatology and conservation in museums, *Museum*, 13(4), 242-89.

Plenderleith, H.J. & Werner, A.E.A. (1971) *The Conservation of Antiquities and Works of Art*, Oxford University Press.

Ramer, B.L. (1984) The design and construction of two humidity controlled display cases, *Preprints of the 7th Triennial Meeting of the ICOM (International Council of Museums) Committee for Conservation*, Copenhagen, 17.46-17.49.

Ramer, B.L. (1984) The development of a local humidity control system, *International Journal of Museum Management and Curatorship*, 3, 183-191.

Ramer, B.L. (1985) Showcases modified for climate control, *Museum*, 37(2), 91-4.

Richard, M., Mecklenburg, M.F. & Merrill, R.M. (eds.) (1991) *Art in Transit: Handbook for Packing and Transporting Paintings*, National Gallery of Art, Washington.

Rothe, A. & Metro, B. (1985) Climate controlled showcases for paintings, *Museum*, 37(2), 89-91.

Saunders, D. (1991) Temperature and relative humidity conditions encountered in transportation, in Mecklenburg, M.F. (ed.), *Art in Transit: Studies in the Transport of Paintings*, National Gallery of Art, Washington, 299-309.

Schweizer, F. (1984) Stabilization of R.H. in exhibition cases - an experimental approach, *Preprints of the 7th Triennial Meeting of the ICOM (International Council of Museums) Committee for Conservation*,

Copenhagen, 17.50-17.53.

Scottish Society for Conservation & Restoration (1989) *Environmental Monitoring and Control*, SSCR and Museums Association.

Sekino, M. & Toishi, K. (1972) The fine arts museum at Expo, *Museum*, 24(2), 67-8.

Staniforth, S. (1987) Light and environmental measurement and control in National Trust houses, in Black, J. (ed.), *Recent Advances in the Conservation and Analysis of Artefacts*, University of London, institute of Archaeology.

Staniforth, S. (1987) Temperature and relative humidity measurement and control in National Trust houses, *Preprints of the 8th Triennial Meeting of the ICOM (International Council of Museums) Committee for Conservation*, Sydney, 915-926.

Staniforth, S. (1992) Control and measurement of the environment, in Thompson, J.M.A. *et al.* *(eds.)*, *Manual of Curatorship*, Butterworth, London, 234-245.

Stolow, N. (1966) *Controlled Environment for Works of Art in Transit*, Butterworth, London.

Stolow, N. (1966) Fundamental case design for humidity sensitive museum collections, *Museum News*, 44(6), Technical Supplement, 45-52.

Stolow, N. (1966) The action of environment on museum objects. Part 1: humidity, temperature, atmospheric pollution, *Curator*, 9(3), 175-85.

Stolow, N. (1977) Conservation of exhibition in the museum of the future, *Conference Proceedings for 2001 - The Museum and the Canadian Public*, Canadian Museums Association, Ottawa, 24-31.

Stolow, N. (1977) The microclimate; a localized solution, *Museum News*, 56, 52-63.

Stolow, N. (1978) The effectiveness of preconditioned silica gel and related sorbents for controlling humidity environments for museum collections, *ICCROM Conference on Climatology*, November.

Stolow, N. (1987) *Conservation and Exhibitions*, Butterworth, London.

Thomson, G. (1977) Stabilisation of R.H. in exhibition cases, *Studies in Conservation*, 22(2), 85-102.

Thomson, G. (1984) Specification and logging of the museum environment, *International Journal of Museum Management and Curatorship*, 3, 317-326.

Thomson, G. (1986) *The Museum Environment*, 2nd edition, Butterworth-Heinemann.

Thomson, G. & Bullock, L. (1980) *Simple Control and Measurement of Relative Humidity in Museums*, Museums Association Information Sheet, Museums Association, London.

Thomson, G. (ed.) (1968) *Museum Climatology*, Contributions to the IIC conference, 1967, International Institute for Conservation, London.

Tymchuk, M.P. (1983) Environmental control of museum collections - the

Nicholson project, *Curator*, 26(4), 265-74.

Volent, P. & Baer, N.T. (1985) Volatile enemies as corrosion inhibitors in museum humidification systems, *International J. of Museum Management and Curatorship*, 4(4), 359-64.

Weintraub, S. (1982) A new silica gel and recommendations, *American Institute for Conservation Preprints of the Papers Presented at the Tenth Annual Meeting*, Milwaukee.

Wilks, H. (1990) *Conservation in Storage*, Getty Conservation Institute, California.

Williams, M. (1986) Fresh-air climate conditioning at the Arthur M. Sackler Museum, *International J. of Museum Management and Curatorship*, 5(4), 328-36.

4.11 Light & Lighting

Allen, W.A. (1971) The museum in Lisbon for the Gulbenkian Collection. a new approach to illumination, *Museums Journal*, 71(2), 54-8.

Appelbaum, B. (1991) *Guide to Environmental Protection of Collections*, Sound View Press, Connecticut.

Brill, T.D. (1980) *Light: Its Interaction with Art and Antiquities*, Plenum Press, New York.

Brommelle, N.S. (1961) Museum lighting part 1 - colour rendering, *Museums Journal*, 61(3), 169-76.

Brommelle, N.S. (1962) Museum lighting part 3 - aspects of the effect of light on deterioration (includes bibliography), *Museums Journal*, 62(1), 337-46.

Brommelle, N.S. (1964) The Russel & Abney Report on the action of light on watercolours, *Studies in Conservation*, 9, 140-53.

Chartered Institute of Building Services (1980) *Lighting Guide - Museums and Art Galleries*, CIBS, London.

Concord Lighting Ltd (1986) *Light in Museums and Galleries*.

Crawford, B.H. (1960) Colour rendition and museum lighting, *Studies in Conservation*, 5, 41-51.

Crawford, B.H. (1973) Just perceptible colour differences in relation to level of lumination, *Studies in Conservation*, 18, 159-66.

Crawford, B.H. & Palmer, D.A. (1961) A new look at colour rendering and the classification of light sources, *Studies in Conservation*, 6, 71-81.

Crews, P.C. (1989) A comparison of selected UV filtering materials for the reduction of fading, *Journal of the American Institute for Conservation*, 28(2), 117-26.

David, J. (1986) Light in museums, *Museums Journal*, 85(4), 203-215.

David, J. (1987) Lighting (report of conference), *Museums Journal*, 87(3), 141-154.

Doe, B. (1965) Notes on museum and art gallery lighting in the tropics, *Studies in Conservation*, 10, 64-71.

Eastough, M. (1984) The effect of illumination on the appearance of objects, *Preprints of the 7th Triennial Meeting of the ICOM (International Council of Museums) Committee for Conservation*, Copenhagen, 17.16 -17.19.

Feller, R.L. (1964) The control of deteriorating effects of light upon museum objects (very comprehensive bibliography), *Museum*, 7(2), 57-8.

Feller, R.L. (1964) The deteriorating effect of light on museum objects: Principles of photochemistry. the effect on varnishes and paint vehicles and on paper, *Museum News*, 42(10) Technical Supplement.

Giles, C.H. (1966) The fading of colouring matter, *Curator*, 9(2), 95-102.

Hanlan, J.F. (1970) The effect of electronic photographic lamps on the materials of works of art, *Museum News*, 48(10) Technical Supplement.

Hansen, P. (1987) The Clore Gallery - designing for natural & artificial light, *International J. of Museum Management and Curatorship*, 6(1), 43-47.

Illuminating Engineering Society (1970) *Lighting of Art Galleries and Museums*, Illuminating Engineering Society, Technical Report 14.

International Council of Museums (1971) *La Lumière Et La Protection Des Objets Et Specimens Exposés Dans Les Musées Et Galeries Dart*, Paris.

Knox, B.J. (1988) Electric vs. Natural Lighting, *Museum News*, 67(3).

Loe, D.L., Rowlands, E. & Watson, N.F. (1982) Preferred lighting conditions for the display of oil and watercolour paintings, *Lighting Research and Technology*, 14, 173-192.

Macleod, K.J. (nd) *Museum Lighting*, Canadian Conservation Institute, Technical Bulletin 2.

Museums Association (1987) *Lighting in Museums, Galleries and Historic Houses*, Museums Association, London.

Nassau, K. (1983) *The Physics and Chemistry of Color*, Wiley & Sons, New York.

Norman, M. & Staniforth, S. (eds.) (1987) *Lighting in Museums, Galleries and Historic Houses*, United Kingdom Institute for Conservation.

Ridgway, B. (1985) Lighting in museums and galleries: a review of recent developments, *The Architectural Review*, 178(1065), 92-111.

Roveri, A. M. D. (1991) A 'first' in Italy, *Museum*, 43(4), 206-207.

Saunders, D. (1989) Portable instrument for logging light levels, *The Conservator*, 13.

Sease, C. (1984) Problems of lighting and display: an example from the Metropolitan Museum, *Preprints of the 7th Triennial Meeting of the*

ICOM *(International Council of Museums) Committee for Conservation*, Copenhagen, 17.54 - 17.55.

Shalkop, R. & Goldberg, S.M. (1987) Northern light in a Museum, *Museum News*, 65(4), 40-43.

Thompson, C. (1971) Daylight in art galleries, *Museums Journal*, 71(2), 59-62.

Thomson, G. (1986) *The Museum Environment*, 2nd edition, Butterworths, London.

Thomson, G. & Bullock, L. (1978) *Conservation and Museum Lighting*, 3rd edition, Museums Association information Sheet, London.

Thomson, G. & Staniforth, S. (1985) *Conservation and Museum Lighting*, 4th revised edition, Museums Association information Sheet, London.

4.12 Atmospheric Pollutants

Arni, P.C., Cochrane, G.D. & Gray, J.D. (1965) The emission of corrosive vapors from wood, *Journal of Applied Chemistry*, 15, 305-315, 463-468.

Baer, N.S. & Banks, P.N. (1985) Indoor air pollution - effects on cultural and historic materials, *International J. of Museum Management and Curatorship*, 4, 9-20.

Blackshaw, S.M. & Daniels, V.D. (1978) Selecting safe materials for use in the display and storage of antiquities, *ICOM (International Council of Museums) Committee for Conservation 5th Triennial Meeting*, Preprints, Zagreb.

Blackshaw, S.M. & Daniels, V.D. (1979) The testing of materials for use in storage and display in museums, *The Conservator*, 3, 16-19.

Blackshaw, S.M. & Daniels, V.D. (1984) Safe fabrics for permanent exhibitions, *Conservation News*, 23, 16-18.

Cass, G.R. & Nazaroff, W.W. (1993) *Research in Conservation-Technical Protection of Works of Art from Airborne Particles*, Getty Conservation Institute, California.

Daniels, V.D. & Ward, S. (1982) A rapid test for the detection of substances which will tarnish silver, *Studies in Conservation*, 27, 58-60.

Getty Conservation Institute (1993) Environmental research at the GCI, *Conservation*, 8(1), 5-9.

Hackney, S. (1984) The distribution of gaseous air pollution within museums, *Studies in Conservation*, 29, 105-116.

Hatchfield, P. B.& Carpenter, J.M. (1986) A problem of formaldehyde in museum collections, *International J. of Museum Management and Curatorship*, 5(2), 183-8.

Hodges, H. (1982) Showcases made of chemically unstable material, *Museum*, 34(1), 56-8.

Oddy, W.A. (1973) An unsuspected danger in display, *Museums Journal*, 73(1), 27-8.

Oddy, W.A. (1975) Corrosion of metals on display, *International Institute for Conservation (IIC) Congress Proceedings*, Stockholm.

Thomson, G. (1986) *The Museum Environment*, 2nd edition, Butterworths, London.

4.13 Infestation

Allsopp, D. & Seal, K.J. (1986) *Introduction to Biodeterioration*, Edward Arnold, London.

Armes, N. (1984) Aspects of the biology of the Guernsey carpet beetle - Anthrenus servicus Mroczk, *Preprints of the 7th Triennial Meeting of the ICOM (International Council of Museums) Committee for Conservation*, Copenhagen, 13.1 - 13.3.

Askew, R.R. (1988) Pests, pesticides and specimens in Horie, C.V. (ed.), *Conservation of Natural History Specimens, Vertebrates*, University of Manchester, Department of Environmental Biology and the Manchester Museum, Manchester, 93-107.

Ballard, M.W. & Baer, N.S. (1987) Is fumigation possible?, *International J. of Museum Management and Curatorship*, 6(1), 82-6.

Boulton, A. (1986) The examination, treatment and analysis of a pair of boots from the Aleutian Islands including a note about possible pesticide contamination., *Journal of the American Institute for Conservation*, 25(1), 1-14.

Bravery, A.F., Berry, R.W., Carey, J.K. & Cooper, D.E. (1987) *Recognising Wood Rot and Insect Damage in Buildings*, Building Research Establishment Report, Watford.

Busvine, J.R. (1986) *Insects and Hygene*, Chapman & Hall, London.

Butcher-Youngmans, S. & Anderson, G.E. (1990) *A Holistic Approach to Museum Pest Management*, American Association for State and Local History, Technical Leaflet, Nashville, Tennessee.

Child, B. & Pinniger, D. (1987) Insect pest control in museum in Black, J., *Recent Advances in the Conservation and Analysis of Artefacts*, London.

Child, R.E. (1989) Fumigation in museums - a possible alternative, *Museums Journal*, 88(4), 191-2.

Cornwell, P.B. (1979) *Pest Control in Buildings*, Rentokil, East Grinstead.

Dawson, J.E. & Strang, T.J.K. (1992) *Solving Museum Insect Problems:*

Chemical Control, Canadian Conservation Institute Technical Bulletin 15.

Derrick, M.R., Burgess, H.D., Baker, M.T. & Binnie, N.E. (1990) Sulfuryl fluoride (Vikane): a review of its use as a fumigant, *Journal of the American Institute for Conservation,* 29(1), 77-90.

Edwards, R. & Mill, A.E. (1986) *Termites in Buildings,* Rentokil, East Grinstead.

Edwards, S. (1980) *Pest Control in Museums,* American Society of Conservation, Kansas.

Florian, M.-L.E. (1987) Methodology used in pest surveys in museum buildings - a case study, *Preprints of the 8th Triennial Meeting of the ICOM (International Council of Museums) Committee for Conservation,* Sydney, 1169-1181.

Florian, M.-L.E. (1987) The effect of artefact materials on the fumigant ethylene oxide and freezing used in pest control., *Preprints of the 8th Triennial Meeting of the ICOM (International Council of Museums) Committee for Conservation,* Sydney, 199-208.

Florian, M-L.E. (1986) The freezing process - effects on insects and artifact materials, *Leather Conservation News,* 3(1), 1-13.

Florian, M-L.E. (1990) The effects of freezing and freeze-drying on natural history specimens, *Collection Forum,* 6(2).

Gilberg, M. (1989) Inert atmosphere fumigation of museum objects, *Studies in Conservation,* 34(2), 80-4.

Gilberg, M. (1991) The effects of low oxygen atmospheres on museum pests, *Studies in Conservation,* 36, 93-98.

Glastrup. J. (1987) Insecticide analysis by gas chromatography in the stores of the Danish National Museums Ethnographic collection, *Studies in Conservation,* 32(2), 59-64.

Haines, J.H. & Kohler, S.A. (1986) An evaluation of ortho phenyl phenol as a fungicidal fumigant for archives and libraries, *Journal of the American Institute for Conservation,* 25(1), 49-55.

Hall, A.V. (1988) Pest control in herbaria, *Taxon,* 37, 885-907.

Hall, D.W. (1981) Microwave: a method of control of herbarium insects, *Taxon,* 30(4), 818-9.

Hamlyn, P.F. (1983) Microbiological deterioration of textiles, *Textiles,* 12(3), 73-76.

Health & Safety Commission (1988) *Control of Substances Hazardous to Health in Fumigation Operations, Approved Code of Practice,* HSC.

Hickin, N. (1985) *Bookworms: The Insect Pests of Books,* Sheppard Press, London.

Hillyer, L. & Blyth V. (1992) Carpet beetle - a pilot study in detection and control, *The Conservator,* 16.

Hueck, H.J. (1972) Textile pests and their control, in Leene, J.E. (ed.), *Textile Conservation,* Butterworth, London.

Kleitz, M.O. (1987) L'oxyde dethylene. Utilisation et limites. Actions secondaire avec un residue de traitment anterieur, *Preprints of the 8th Triennial Meeting of the ICOM (International Council of Museums) Committee for Conservation*, Sydney, 1175-1181.

Lewis, R.H. (1976) *Manual for Museums*, US Government Printing Office, Washington, DC, 34-7, 39, 68-76.

Mallis, A. (1990) *Handbook of Pest Control*, Frasak & Foster, Cleveland.

McGriffin, R.F. (1985) *A Current Status Report on Fumigation in Museums and Historical Agencies*, American Association for State and Local History (AASLH), Nashville, Tennessee, Technical Report No.4.

Meynell, G.G. & Newcombe, R.J. (1978) Foxing a fungal infection of paper, *Nature*, 274, 466-468.

Meynell, G.G. & Newcombe, R.J. (1979) Foxed paper and its problems, *New Scientist*, 17 May, 567.

Ministry of Agriculture, Fisheries and Foods (1993) *Pesticides 1993*, Reference Book 500, MAFF/Health & Safety Executive, London.

Mourier, H. & Winding, O. (1986) *Collins Guide to Wildlife in the House and Home*, Collins.

National Audit Office (1988) *Management of the Collections of the English National Museums and Galleries*, HMSO, London.

Pardue, D. (1987) Integrated pest management in the United States National Park Service, *Preprints of the 8th Triennial Meeting of the ICOM (International Council of Museums) Committee for Conservation*, Sydney, 1183-7.

Parker, T.A. (1988) *Studies on Integrated Pest Management for Libraries and Archives*, UNESCO, Paris.

Peltz, P. & Rossa, M. (1983) *Safe Pest Control Procedures for Museum Collectors*, Center for Occupational Hazards, New York.

Philbrick, C.T. (1984) Comments on the use of microwave as a method of herbarium insect control - possible drawbacks, *Taxon*, 33.

Pinniger, D. (1989) *Insect Pests in Museums*, Institute of Archaeology Publications, London.

Pinniger, D. (1991) New development in the detection and control of insects which damage museum collections, *Biodeterioration Abstracts*, 2, 5.

Postlethwaite, A.W. (1987) Fumigation, choice of fumigants and design of facility, *Preprints of the 8th Triennial Meeting of the ICOM (International Council of Museums) Committee for Conservation*, Sydney, 1189-1196.

Reagan, B.M. (1984) Eradication of insects from wood textiles, *Journal of the American Institute for Conservation*, 21(2), 1-34.

Simmons, M. (1993) Mothballs, curators and the law, *Biology Curators Group Newsletter*, 10(1), 11.

Stansfield, G. (1985) Pest control - a collection management problem, *Museums Journal*, 85(2), 97-99.

Stoate, C. (1987) Beetles in store, *Museums Journal*, 86(4), 196-8.

Story, K.O. (1985) *Approaches to Pest Management in Museums*, Conservation Analytical Laboratory, Smithsonian Institution Press, Washington DC.

Strang, T.J.K. (1992) A review of published temperatures for the control of insect pests in museums, *Collection Forum*, 8(2).

Urban, J. & Justa. P. (1986) Conservation by gamma radiation: the museum of Central Bohemia in Roztoky, *Museum*, 38(3), 165-71.

Ward, P.R. (1976) *Getting the Bugs Out*, British Columbia Provincial Museum, Victoria.

Williams, S. L., Hawks, C.A. & Weber, S.G. (1984) Considerations in the use of DDVP resin strips for insect & pest control in biological research collections, *Bioterioration*, V1, 344-350.

Williams, S.L. & Walsh, E.A. (1989) Behaviour of DDVP in storage cases, *Curator*, 32(1), 41-49.

Williams, S.L. & Walsh, E.A. (1989) The effect of DDVP on a museum pest, *Curator*, 32(1), 34-41.

Williams, S.L., Walsh, E.A. & Weber, S.G. (1989) Effect of DDVP on museum materials, *Curator*, 32(1), 49-69.

Yaldon, V.L. (1966) A portable fumigation chamber for the small museum, *Museum News*, 44(5), 38-9.

Zaitseva, G.A. (1987) Chemical measures of protecting USSR museum collections against keratin destroying insects, *Preprints of the 8th Triennial Meeting of the ICOM (International Council of Museums) Committee for Conservation*, Sydney, 1211-1214.

Zycherman, L.A. & Schrock, J.R. (1988) *A Guide to Museum Pest Control*, Foundation of the American institute for Conservation of Historic and Artistic Works and Association of Systematics Collections, Washington, DC.

4.14 Storage & Access to Collections

Ames, M.M. (1977) Visible storage and public documentation, *Curator*, 20, 65-79.

Ames, M.M. (1985) De-schooling the museum:a proposal to increase public access to museums and their resources, *Museum*, 37(1), 25-31.

Anon. (1983) De-schooling the museum:a report on accessible storage, *ICOM (International Council of Museums) 13th General Conference Papers*, London.

Anon. (1983) Support centre solves storage problems, *Aviso*, 7, 1-2.

Arch, N.J. (1978) Technical notes: sword storage at the Castle Museum, *Museums Journal*, 78(1), 26-7.

Barrette, B. (1985) The Egyptian Galleries at the Metropolitan Museum of Art, *Museum*, 37(2), 81-4.

British Standards Institution (1989) *BS 5454, Recommendations for the Storage and Exhibition of Documents*, British Standards Institution, Milton Keynes.

Buechner, T.S. (1962) The open study-storage gallery, *Museum News*, 40(9), 34-7.

Cameron, D.F. (1982) Museums and public access: the Glenbow approach, *International J. of Museum Management and Curatorship*, 1(3), 177-96.

Cassar, M. (1986) A flexible climate-controlled storage system for a collection of ivory veneers from Nimrud, *International J. of Museum Management and Curatorship*, 5(2), 171-82.

Cumberland, D. (1985) *Museum Collection Storage*, National Park Service, Department of the Interior, Washington, DC.

Denford, G.T. (1984) A new store for Winchester City Museum, *Museums Journal*, 83(4), 239-40.

Duckworth, W.D. (1984) The Smithsonian's new museum support centre, *Museum News*, 62(4), 32-5.

Dudley, D.H. & Wilkinson, I.B. (eds.) (1979) *Museum Registration Methods*, American Association of Museums, Washington DC.

Elkin, P. (1975) Treasures in store:the Bristol Museum storage project, *Museums Journal*, 75(2), 57-60.

Hilberry, J.D. & Weinberg, S.K. (1981) Museum collection storage, Part 1, *Museum News*, 59(5), 7-21.

Hilberry, J.D. & Weinberg, S.K. (1981) Museum collection storage, Part 2, *Museum News*, 59(6), 5-23.

Hilberry, J.D. & Weinberg, S.K. (1981) Museum collection storage, Part 3, *Museum News*, 59(7), 49-60.

Hume, I. (1992) Floor loadings and historic buildings, *English Heritage Conservation Bulletin*, 18, 1-2.

Idiens, D. (1973) New ethnographical storage in the Royal Scottish Museum, *Museums Journal*, 73(2), 61-2.

Johnson, E.V. & Horgan, J.C. (1979) *Museum Collection Storage*, UNESCO, Paris (Protection of the Cultural Heritage.Technical Handbooks for Museums and Monuments, 2).

Knell, S.J. (1988) Rescue curation: restoring old geology collections, *Bulletin of the Scottish Society for Conservation and Restoration*, 10, 8-10.

Lambert, S. (1983) *Storage of Textiles and Costumes: Guidelines for Decision Making*, University of British Columbia, Museum of Anthropology.

Lamley, P.W. & Frodin, D.G. (1987) The Natural Sciences Resource

Centre at the University of Papua New Guinea, *Curator*, 30(3), 250-258.

MacFadden, B.J., Shaak, G.D., Webb, S.D. & Brown, E. (1988) Compactors in small collection-based museum libraries, *Curator*, 31(2), 137-40.

Murray, C. (1986) An act of providence, *Museums Journal*, 86(1), 11.

Norman, M. & Todd, V. (eds.) (1991) *Storage*, United Kingdom Institute for Conservation, London.

Owen, H.G. (1981) Rationalised storage of fossils in the British Museum (Natural History), *Curator*, 24(2), 77-88.

Pettit, C.W. (1989) The new zoology storage at Manchester Museum:an opportunity for a new curatorial strategy, *Journal of Biological Curation*, 1(1), 27-40.

Rebora, C. (1991) Curators' closet, *Museum News*, 70(4), 50-54.

Richoux, J.A., Serota-Braden, J. & Demyttenaere, N. (1981) A Policy for collections access, *Museum News*, 59(4), 43-47.

Stansfield, G. (1974) *The Storage of Museum Collections*, Museums Association Information Sheet No 10, Museums Association, London.

Stolow, N. (1987) *Conservation and Exhibitions*, Butterworths, London.

Terrones, A. (1989) Hermes what to consider in selecting high-density storage, *Museum News*, 68(2), 80-1.

Thistle, P.C. (1990) Visible storage for the small museum, *Curator*, 33(1), 49-62.

Walker, K. (1992) Taking control of the stores: a conservator in charge, *3 Colloque International de l'ARAAFU - Paris 1992*, 53-58.

Washburn, D.K. (1990) Curatorial or "Native" categories:their use in visible storage, *Curator*, 33(1), 63-71.

Watson, T.C. (1976) Archive and costume storage, *Curator*, 19(1), 29-36.

Wilcox, U.V. (1990) Managing museum space, in Keene, S. (ed.), *Managing Conservation*, United Kingdom Institute for Conservation, London, 7-10.

Wilson, D. (1992) *Showing the Flag - Loans from the National to Museums in the Regions*, HMSO, London.

Wolf, A.H. (1980) Open storage for a research collection, *Curator*, 23(4), 249-54.

Wolf, A.H. & Bell, J.R. (1976) Rolling your own:a new system for textile storage, *Curator*, 19, 246-49.

4.15 Handling, Packing & Transport

Area Museums Service for South Eastern England (1984) *AMSSEE*

Seminar on Moving Pictures, AMSSEE, Milton Keynes.

Bambos, G. (1985) The hazards of vibration during transport, *UKIC Meeting on Packing Cases, Safer Transport for Museum Objects*, Preprints, London.

Bauhof, W.A. (1965) The package engineer in the museum, *Museum News*, 44(4), 27-8.

Bogdanow, G. & Gorine, I. (1983) The Russian insert frame method of packing, *International J. of Museum Management and Curatorship*, 2(4), 354-62.

Booth, P., Green,T. & Sitwell, C.L. (1985) Moving pictures, *International J. of Museum Management and Curatorship*, 4, 41-52.

BP Chemicals Ltd (1992) *Foams Business: Cushion Packing Guide*, BP Chemicals Ltd.

Cannon-Brookes, P. (1982) A draft code of practice for escorts and couriers, *International J. of Museum Management and Curatorship*, 1, 41-60.

Cannon-Brookes, P. (1986) The evolution and implementation of a transportation strategy for works of art, *International J. of Museum Management and Curatorship*, 5(2), 163-9.

Choudhury, A.R. (1964) *Art Museum Documentation and Practical Handling*, Choudhury & Choudhury, Hyderabad, India.

Dudley, D.H. & Wilkinson, I.B. (eds.) (1979) *Museum Registration Methods*, 3rd edition, American Association of Museums, Washington, DC.

Fall, F.K. (1965) New industrial packing materials: their possible uses in museums, *Museum News*, 44(4), 47-52.

Fall, F.K. (1973) *Art Objects: Their Care and Preservation*, McGilvery, La Jolla, California.

Georgiou, B. & Staniforth, S. (eds.) (1985) The hazards of vibration during transport, *UKIC Meeting on Packing Cases, Safer Transport for Museum Objects*, Preprints, London.

Glover, J.N. (1973) *Textiles: Their Care and Protection in Museums*, Museums Association Information Sheet No 18.

Green, R. & Hackney, S. (1984) The evaluation of a packing case for paintings, *Preprints of the 7th Triennial Meeting of the ICOM (International Council of Museums) Committee for Conservation*, Copenhagen, 12.1-12.6.

Green, T. & Staniforth, S. (eds.) (1985) Observations on the vibration of canvases, *UKIC Meeting on Packing Cases, Safer Transport for Museum Objects*, Preprints, London.

Health & Safety Executive (1992) *Manual Handling: Guidance on Regulations 1992*, HMSO, London.

Holden, C. (1979) Notes on the protection of modern works of art during handling, packing and storage, *The Conservator*, 3, 20-24.

Jessup, W.C. (1983/4) Packing without crates, *Museologist*, 45(166), 12-17.

Keck, C.K. (1970) *Safeguarding Your Collection in Travel,* American Association for State and Local History, Nashville, Tennessee.

Lange, H. (1979) Technical notes: the construction of a thermobox, *Museums Journal,* 79(1), 27-8.

Leback, K. F. (1986) The art of conserving, shipping and packing museum objects, *International J. of Museum Management and Curatorship,* 5(4), 341-4.

Lewis, R.H. (1976) *Manual for Museums,* United States Government, Printing Office.

Matteo, C. De (1982) The pitfalls of transport, *Museum,* 34(1), 46-7.

Mecklenburg, M.F. (ed.) (1991) *Art in Transit: Studies in the Transport of Paintings,* National Gallery of Art, Washington.

Miles, G. (1992) Object handling, in Thompson, J.M.A., (ed.), *Manual of Curatorship,* Butterworth, London, 455-458.

Morris, J.W. & Staniforth, S. (eds.) (1985) Packing of 3-dimensional objects, *UKIC Meeting on Packing Cases, Safer Transport for Museum Objects,* Preprints, London.

Pearson, V. & Burnham, E. (1979) Preparing exhibitions for travel, in Dudley, D.H. & Wilkinson, I.B. (eds.), *Museum Registration Methods,* American Association of Museums, Washington, DC, 367-88.

Piechota, D.V. & Hansen, G. (1982) The care of cultural property in transit:a case design for travelling exhibitions,, *Technology and Conservation,* 4/82, 32-46.

Preiss, L. (1980) Recommended procedures for the packing and transport of an ethnographic collection, *ICCM Bulletin,* 6, 34-30.

Pugh, F. (1978) *Handling and Packing Works of Art: A Manual Outlining the Methods Used to Pack and Handle Works of Art,* Arts Council of Great Britain, London.

Richard, M. (1984) Elements for effective packing, *The Museologist,* 45, 18-23.

Richard, M., Mecklenburg, M.F. & Merrill, R.M. (eds.) (1991) *Art in Transit: Handbook for Packing and Transporting Paintings,* National Gallery of Art, Washington.

Rowlison, E.B. (1975) Rules for handling works of art, *Museum News,* 53(7).

Rowlison, E.B. (1979) Rules for handling works of art, in Dudley, D.H. & Wilkinson, I.B. (eds.), *Museum Registration Methods,* American Association of Museums, Washington, DC, 355-66.

Serjeant, D. (1986) The protection of paintings in loan exhibitions, *Museum,* 38(4), 246-8.

Shelley, M. et al. (1987) *The Care and Handling of Art Objects: Practices in the Metropolitan Museum of Art,* Harry N. Abrams, Inc..

Sitwell, C.L (1983) Conservation problems relating to fine art exhibitions and their transport, *The Conservator,* 7.

Sitwell, C.L. (1983) Transporting exhibitions - museums must act together, *International J. of Museum Management and Curatorship*, 2(4), 355-8.

Staniforth, S. (1984) The testing of packing cases for the transport of paintings, *Preprints of the 7th Triennial Meeting of the ICOM (International Council of Museums) Committee for Conservation*, Copenhagen, 12.7.

Stolow, N. (1966) *Controlled Environment for Works of Art in Transit*, Butterworth, London.

Stolow, N. (1977) Recent developments in exhibition conservation policies and directions, *Museum*, 29(4), 192-206.

Stolow, N. (1977) The conservation of works of art and exhibitions, *Museums Journal*, 77(2), 61-62.

Stolow, N. (1979) *Conservation Standards for Works of Art in Transit and on Exhibition*, UNESCO, Paris, Museums and Monuments Series No. XVII.

Stolow, N. (1979) Conservation standards for works of art in transit and on exhibition, *Museums and Monuments*, XVII.

Stolow, N. (1979) The ideal containers for travel of humidity sensitive collections, in Dudley, D.H. & Wilkinson, I.B. (eds.), *Museum Registration Methods*, American Association of Museums, Washington, DC, 366-75.

Stolow, N. (1981) *Procedures and Conservation Standards for Museum Collections in Transit and on Exhition*, UNESCO, Paris, Protection of the Cultural Heritage. Technical Handbooks for Museums and Monuments, 3.

Stolow, N. (1987) *Conservation and Exhibitions*, Butterworths, London.

Sugden, R.P. (1946) *Care and Handling of Art Objects*, Metropolitan Museum of Art, New York.

Taylor, M. (1983) *A Manual for the Handling and Packaging of Museum Objects*, Art Gallery and Museums Association of New Zealand, Wellington.

4.16 Insurance & Indemnity

Allen, C.G. (1992) Insurance: risk management techniques: choosing what not to insure, *Museum Management & Curatorship*, 11, 322-323.

Allen, C.G. & Block, H.T. (1974) Should museums form a buyers pool for insurance?, *Museum News*, 52(6), 32-5.

Babcock, P.H. (1979) Insurance: alternative to certificates, *Museum News*, 57(5), 56-7.

Babcock, P.H. & Haack, M.J. (1981) Plain-English collections insurance, *Museum News*, 59(7), 22-5.

Cannon-Brookes, P. (1976) Towards a museum insurance consortium, *Museums Association Conference Proceedings*, 14-16.

Coutts, H. (1968) Museum security: first principles, *Museum Assistants Group (MAG) Transactions*, 7, 19-22.

Dudley, D.H. & Wilkinson, I.B. (1979) Insurance, in Dudley, D.H. & Wilkinson, I.B. (eds.), *Museum Registration Methods,*, American Association of Museums, Washington, DC, 139-50.

HM Government (1980) *National Heritage Act*, HMSO, London.

Jocelyn, Viscount (1976) Problems of museum insurance and security, *Museums Association Conference Proceedings*, 16-18.

Landais, H. (1974) Museums and insurance, *ICOM (International Council of Museums) News*, 27(3/4), 79-82.

Malaro, M.C. (1993) The anatomy of a loan, *Museum International.* (178(2)) 51-54.

Mills, P.C. (1979) Insurance: are fine art premiums out of line?, *Museum News*, 57(5), 54-5.

Mitchell, R. (1988) *Insurance for independent Museums*, 2nd edition, AIM, Ellesmere Port.

Monreal, L. (1974) Notes on insurance, *ICOM (International Council of Museums) News*, 27(3/4), 76-9.

Museums Association (1978) *An Approach to Museum insurance*, Museums Association Information Sheet No 23.

Nauert, P. & Black, C.M. (1979) *Fine Art Insurance*, Association of Art Museum Directors, Washington, DC.

Office of Arts & Libraries (1980) *Government Indemnity Scheme: National Heritage Act 1980: Indemnity Arrangements for Local Museums, Galleries, and other Non-governmental Bodies*, Office of Arts & Libraries, London.

Pfeffer, I. (1974) Strategies for insurance cost reduction in museums, *ICOM (International Council of Museums) News*, 27(3/4), 82-5.

Pfeffer, I. & Uhr, E.B. (1974) The truth about art museum insurance, *Museum News*, 52(6), 23-31.

Smith, S.E. (1993) Insurance planning, *History News*, 48(1), 18-37.

Stolow, N. (1987) *Conservation and Exhibitions*, Butterworth, London.

Turk, F. J. (1987) How are the nations museums coping with the insurance crisis?, *Museum News*, 66(1), 51-4.

Vance, D. (1969) A proposed standard insurance policy, *Museum News*, 48(1), 21-6.

Waddell, G. (1971) Museum storage, *Museum News*, 49(5), 14-20.

Ware, M. (1988) *Museum Collecting Policies and Loan Agreements*, AIM Guideline 14, Association of Independent Museums.

Williams, R. (1974) Selective bibliography, *ICOM (International Council of*

Museums) News, 27(3/4), 87.

Williams, R. (1977) The management of risks associated with the property of museums, *Museums Journal*, 77(2), 59-60.

4.17 Disaster Planning

Alsford, D. (1984) Fire Safety in Museums, *Muse*, 2(2).

American Association of Museums (1987) *Planning for Emergencies: A Guide for Museums*, American Association of Museums, Washington DC.

Anderson, H. & McIntyre, J.E. (1985) *Planning Manual for Disaster Control in Scottish Libraries and Record Offices*, National Library of Scotland, Edinburgh.

Andrew, J.A. (1989) Fire fighters, *Museum News*, 68(5), 68-72.

Association of Art Museum Directors (1987) *Planning for Emergencies*, Committee on Museum Operations.

Babcock, P.H. (1990) Ready for the Worst, *Museum News*, 69(3), 50-4.

Boggeman, K.A. (1987) *Fire Prevention*, International Council of Museums, Paris.

Boylan, P.J. (1993) *Review of the Convention for the Protection of Cultural Property in the Event of Armed Conflict (The Hague Convention of 1954)*, UNESCO.

Department of National Heritage (1993) *Fire Protection Measures for Royal Palaces*, HMSO, London.

Douglas, R.M. (1989) Fire prevention and control in museums, *SAMAB: Southern African Museums Association Bulletin*, 18(5), 195-210.

East Midlands Museums Service (1991) *The Museum & Record Office Emergency Manual*, East Midlands Museums Service, Nottingham.

Faulk, W. (1991) How the J. Paul Getty Museum plans and prepares for major emergencies, *Ali-aba, Legal Problems of Museum Administration*, 20-22 March, Philadelphia.

Faulk, W. (1993) Are you ready when disaster strikes?, *History News*, 48(1), 5-11.

Federal Emergency Management Agency (1992) Emergency preparedness and response, *Conservation*, 7(1), 10-11.

Feilden, B.M. (1987) *Between Two Earthquakes*, J. Paul Getty Museum, California.

Felix, N.B. (1993) A test of strength, *History News*, 48(1), 12-15.

Fenner, G.J. (1982) Artifacts under pressure - effects of Halon gas release on a collection, *Curator*, 25(2), 85-90.

Fielden, B.M. (1982) Museum management and national disasters,

International J. of Museum Management and Curatorship, 1(3), 231-35.

Fire Protection Association (1990) *Heritage Under Fire*, Fire Prevention Association.

Forston, J. (1990) *Disaster Planning and Recovery: A How to Do It Manual for Librarians and Archivists*, Neal-Schuman.

Garfield, D. (1990) Out of harms way, *Museum News*, 69(3), 67-70.

Getty Conservation Institute (1992) Cultural heritage under fire, *Conservation*, 7(1), 12-14.

Gibson, J.A. & Reay, D. (1980) Drying rare old books soaked by flood water, *Museums Journal*, 80(3), 147-148.

Ginell, W.S. (1990) Making it quake-proof, *Museum News*, 69(3), 60-3.

Harp, D.L. (1980) Intumescent paint:a useful component of fire protection, *Technology and Conservation*, 6(1), 30-1.

Hensley, J. R. (1987) Safeguarding museum collections from the effects of earthquakes, *Curator*, 30(3), 199-205.

Hume, I. (1993) Structural first aid after a disaster, *English Heritage Scientific and Technical Review*, 2, 6-7.

Hunter, J.E. (1986) Museum disaster preparedness planning, in Jones, B.G. (ed.), *Protecting Historic Architecture and Museum Collections from Natural Disasters*, Butterworth, London, 211-230.

Hutchins, J. (1990) Earthquake, flood, cyclone - is your museum ready?, *Museum*, 42(3), 189-90.

Jones, A. (1990) No surprises, please, *Museum News*, May/June, 64-6.

Jones, B.G. (1986) Experiencing loss, in Jones, B.G. (ed.), *Protecting Historic Architecture and Museum Collections from Natural Disasters*, Butterworth, London, 3-13.

Jones, B.G. (1990) Litany of losses, *Museum News*, 69(3), 56-8.

Jones, B.G. (ed.) (1986) *Protecting Historic Architecture and Museum Collections from Natural Disasters*, Butterworth, London.

Kemp, (1983) Disaster assistance - bibliography, *Technology and Conservation*, 8(2), 25-7.

Lachs, M. (1985) Museums and the horrors of war, *Museum*, 37(3), 167-168.

Landi, S. (1992) *The Textile Conservator's Manual*, 2nd edition, Butterworth-Heinemann, London.

Lein, H.L. (1982) Protecting museums from threat of fire, *Curator*, 25(2), 91-6.

Lindbolm B.C. & Motylewski, K. (1993) *Disaster Planning for Cultural Institutions*, American Association for State and Local History, Technical Leaflet.

Marsden, J. (1993) Be prepared for disasters to paintings, *Conservation News*, 50, 22-23.

Martin, J.H. (ed.) (1977) *The Corning Flood:Museum Under Water*, Corning Museum of Glass, Corning, New York.

Mathieson, D.F. (1983) Hurricane preparedness - establishing workable policies for dealing with storm threats, *Technology and Conservation*, 8(2), 28-9.

Matthai, R.A. (ed.) (1978) *Protection of Cultural Properties During Energy Emergencies*, American Association of Museums, Washington DC.

McGiffen, G.E. (1993) Sharing the risk, *History News*, 48(1), 16-19.

Meister, P. (ed.) (1991) *1991 Disaster Preparedness Seminar Proceedings*, Southeastern Museums Conference.

Musgrove, S.W. (1984) A new look at fire protection, *Museum News*, 62 (6).

National Fire Protection Association (1985) *Protection of Museums and Museum collections*, NFPA, Batterymarsh Park, Quincy, Maryland.

National Fire Protection Association (1991) *Recommended Practice for the Protection of Museums and Museum Collections*, No. 911, Quincy, Massechusetts.

Nelson, C. (1991) *Protecting the Past from Natural Disasters*, National Trust for Historic Preservation.

Noblecourt, A. (1958) *Protection of Cultural Property in the Event of Armed Conflict*, Museums & Monuments No. 8, UNESCO, Paris.

O'Connell, M. (1983) Disaster planning - writing and implementing plans for collections holding institutions, *Technology and Conservation*, 8(2), 18-24.

Page, H. & Ladds, M. (1993) Disaster issue, *North of England Museums Service (NEMS) News*, 37.

Pozzi, E. (1985) Earthquake resistant measures in Naples, *Museum*, 37(2), 122.

Roberts, B. *et al.* (1988) An account of the conservation and preservation procedures following a fire at the Huntingdon Library and Art Gallery, *Journal of the American Institute for Conservation*, 27(1), 1-31.

Rorimer, J.J. (1950) *Survival: The Salvage and Protection of Art in War*, Abelard, New York.

Roth, E. (1991) Museums begin to assess the fallout from the Gulf War, *Museum News*, 3, 22-24.

Schmidt, J.D. (1985) Freeze drying of historic/cultural properties - a valuable process in restoration and documentation, *Technology and Conservation*, 1/85, 20-26.

Schur, S.E. (1980) Fire protection at Mount Vernon; incorporating modern fire safety systems into an historic site, *Technology and Conservation*, 5(4), 18-24.

Society of Industrial Emergency Service Officers (1987) *Guide to Emergency Planning*, Paramount, Borehamwood.

Solley, T.T., Williams, J. & Baden, L. (1987) *Planning for Emergencies: A Guide for Museums*, Association of Art Museum Directors, Washington, DC.

Teichman, J.L. (1991) Selected materials on disaster planning for collections, visitors, staff and facilities, *Ali-aba, Legal Problems of*

Museum Administration, 20-22 March, Philadelphia.

Upton, M.S. & Pearson, C. (1978) *Disaster Planning and Emergency Treatment in Museums, Art Galleries, Archives and Allied Institutions*, Institute for the Conservation of Cultural Material, Canberra, 41-3.

Walsh, B. (1988) Salvage operations for water damaged collections, *Western Association for Art Conservation Newsletter*, 10(2).

Washizuka, H. (1985) Protection against earthquakes in Japan, *Museum*, 37(2), 119-27.

Wilson, J.A. (1989) Fire fighters - an automatic fire suppression system is among your museums best and safest forms of insurance, *Museum News*, 68(6), 68-71.

Zaktrager, J. (1988) Emergency planning, *SAMAB: Southern African Museums Association Bulletin*, 18(3), 121-133.

4.18 Security

Alsford, D. (1975) *An Approach to Museum Security*, Canadian Museums Association, Ottawa.

American Society for Industrial Security (1990) *Suggested Guidelines in Museum Security*, ASIS, Virginia.

Anon. (1972) Your security questions answered, questions and answers from the AAM day programme on security, *Museum News*, 50(5), 22-5.

Anon. (1985) Booty - a digest from Stolen Art Alert, *Museum*, 37(1), 52-60.

Bostick, L.A. (1977) *The Guarding of Cultural Property*, UNESCO, Technical Handbooks for Museums and Monuments, 1.

Burcaw, G.E. (1975) *Introduction to Museum Work*, American Association for State and Local History (AASLH), Nashville, Tennessee.

Burke, R.B. & Adeloye, S. (1986) *A Manual of Basic Museum Security*, ICOM (International Council of Museums), International Committee for Museum Security in liaison with Leicestershire Museums, Paris.

Burnham, B. (1978) *Art Theft, Its Scope, Its Impact and Its Control*, International Foundation for Art Research, New York City.

Burnham, B. (1987) Creating an art theft archive, *Curator*, 30(2), 113-117.

Cannon-Brookes, P. (1978) Museums and fine art transporters, *Museums Journal*, 77(4), 174-76.

Carroll, R.S. (1985) Security begins at the top, *International J. of Museum Management and Curatorship*, 4(4), 373-8.

Choudhury, A.R. (1963) *Art Museum Documentation and Practical Handling*, Choudhury & Choudhury, Hyderabad, India.

Clamen, M. (1974) Museums and the theft of works of art, *Museum*, 26(1), 10-19.

Dovey, B. (1991) Security requirements, in Ambrose, T. & Runyard, S. (eds.), *Forward Planning*, Routledge, London, 102-105.

Dovey, B. (1992) Planning for safety and security, in Lord, G.D. & Lord, B. (eds.), *The Manual of Museum Planning*, HMSO, London, 161-176.

Dovey, B. (1992) Security, in Thompson, J.M.A. *et al* (eds.), *Manual of Curatorship*, 2nd edition, Butterworth-Heinemann, Oxford, 183-190.

Fennelly, L. (1982) *Museum, Archive and Library Security*, Butterworths, London.

Francis, Sir F. (1963) Security, *Museums Journal*, 63(1/2), 28-32.

Fuss, E.L. (1980) Security in cultural institutions - advance in electronic protection techniques, *Technology and Conservation*, 1, 34-7.

Gooding, D. (1980) Card access control systems - a modern approach to improving building security, *Technology and Conservation*, 1, 44-6.

Hilbert, G.D. (1985) Protection against theft and wilful damage, *Museum*, 37(2), 115-118.

Historic Houses Association (1983) *The Security of Works of Art and Heritage Objects - Seminar Report*, Historic Houses Association.

Hoare, N. (1990) *Security for Museums*, Committee for Area Museum Councils in association with the Museums Association.

Jocelyn, Viscount (1976) Problems of museum insurance and security, *Museums Association Conference Proceedings*, 16-18.

Keck, C.K. *et al.* (1966) *A Primer on Museum Security*, (Material presented at a seminar on museum security New York, 1964), New York State Historical Association.

Keller, S.R. (1985) Taking steps towards better museum security, *Curator*, 28(1), 57-64.

Leo, J. (1980) How to secure your museum - a basic check list, *History News*, 35(6), 10-12.

Liston, D. (ed.) (1993) *Museum Security and Protection: A Handbook for Cultural Heritage Institutions*, International Committee on Museum Security, ICOM (International Council of Museums) & Routledge.

Mannings, J. (1970) Security of museums and art galleries, *Museums Journal*, 70(1), 7-9.

Museums Association (1981) *Museum Security*, Museums Association, London.

Musgrove, S.W. (1989) Keep your guard up, *Museum News*, 68(1), 68-9.

Noblecourt, A. (1964) Protection of museums against theft, *Museum*, 17(4), 170-96.

Noblecourt, A. (1974) The need for a systematic approach to the protection of museums, *Museum*, 26(1), 38-41.

O'Rourke, W.J. (1973) Magnetometers for museum theft control, *Curator*, 16(1), 56-8.

Oliver, E. & Wilson, J. (1983) *Security Manual*, Gower, Aldershot.

Pegden, N. (1974) An international meeting on security, *Museum*, 26(1), 38-

41.
Poyner, B. (1983) *Design Against Crime*, Butterworths, London.
Schroder, G.H.H. (1981) *Museum Security Survey*, ICOM (International Council of Museums), Paris.
Sportouch, G. (1974) Museum attendants, *Museum*, 26(1), 34-7.
Steward, D. (1986) A case study of a museum thief, *Museums Journal*, 86(2), 74-8.
Stolow, N. (1987) *Conservation and Exhibitions*, Butterworths, London.
Sykes, J. (ed.) (1979) *Designing Against Vandalism*, Design Council, London.
Synk, K.A. (1976) Art and artefact theft - how to protect the past, *Technology and Conservation*, 76(1), 20-2.
Turner, S. et al. (1978) Technical notes: the security of the Hancock Museum, *Museums Journal*, 77(4), 189.

5 Research

5.1 General

Able, E.H. (1992) Building upon the foundation of scholarship and research, *Museum News*, 71(1), 96.

Alexander, E.P. (1979) *Museums in Motion*, American Association for State and Local History (AASLH), Nashville, Tennessee, 157-72.

Anderson, D. (1990) What shall we do with the curators?, *Museum Management & Curatorship*, 9, 197-210.

Ballinger, C. (1990) Selling research, *Museums Journal*, 90(4), 23.

Black, C. (1980) The case for research, *Museum News*, 58(5), 51-3.

Bliss, D.E. (1959) A museum exhibit interprets basic research. Why?, *Curator*, 2(3), 212-18.

Boylan, P.J. (1988) Joint research programmes,in Ambrose, T. (ed.), *Working with Museums*, Scottish Museums Council.

Canadian Museum of Civilization (1990) Research policy, *Museum Management & Curatorship*, 9, 406-9.

Charnley, H.W. (1976) Museum research program, *ICOM (International Council of Museums) Committee of Natural History Museums*, 95-7.

Cipalla, R. (1985) The videodisc advantage, *History News*, 40(8), 18-20.

Colbert, E.H. (1958) On being a curator, *Curator*, 1(11), 7-12.

Colbert, E.H. (1960) The museum and geological research, *Curator*, 3(4), 317-26.

Collier, D. (1962) Museums and ethnological research, *Curator*, 5(4), 322-28.

Culotta, E. (1992) Museums cut research in hard times, *Science*, 256, 1268-1271.

Daifuku, H. (1960) Museums and research, *Organisation of Museums:Practical Advice*, Museums and Monuments Series No IX, UNESCO, Paris.

Earnes, J.V.H. (1969) Museums and scholarship, *Museums Journal*, 69(3), 103-105.

Evans, I. (1979) Researching your collections - natural sciences, *Museum Assistants Group (MAG) Transactions*, 15.

Farr, D. (1976) Connoisseurship and the curator, *Museums Journal*, 75(4), 161-62.

Faunce, S. (1992) Theory and practice, *Museum News*, 71(1), 36-9.

Fenton, A. (ed.) (1992) Section four: collections research, in Thompson,

J.M.A. *et al. (eds.)*, *Manual of Curatorship*, Butterworth, London, 493-574.

Fenton, W.N. (1960) The museum and anthropological research, *Curator*, 3(4), 327-55.

Ferguson, E.L. & Nason, J. (1980) Human subject rights and museum research, *Museum News*, 38(3), 44-47.

Finedelg, E. (1983) Hi-tech history, *History News*, 38(10), 23-26.

Force, R. (1975) Museum collections - access, use and control, *Curator*, 18(4), 249-55.

Hancock, E.G. (1977) The North West Collections Research Unit, *Museums Journal*, 77(4), 188-9.

International Council of Museums (1968) Museums and research /Musees et recherche, *ICOM 8th General Conference Papers*, ICOM (International Council of Museums), Cologne-Munich.

International Council of Museums (1970) Museum and research, *ICOM 8th General Conference Papers*, Munich.

Kwasnik, E. (1992) Foreign ethnographic collections research programme, *Scottish Museum News*, 8(3) & 8(4), 4 & 13.

Lindsay, G.C. (1962) Museums and research in history and technology, *Curator*, 5(3), 236-44.

Lochnan, K.A. (1982) The research function as a philosopher's stone, *Muse*, 16-23.

MacGregor, N. (1990) Scholarship and the public, *International J. of Museum Management and Curatorship*, 9(4), 361-6.

McClung Fleming, E. (1975) The place of research, in I.M.G. Quimby (ed.), *Arts of the Anglo-American Community in the 17th Century*, University Press of Virginia, Charlottesville, 1-12.

McGillivray, W.B. (1991) Museum research: axiom or oxymoron?, *Muse*, 9(2), 62-66.

Miller, A.H. (1963) The curator as a research worker, *Curator*, 6(4), 282-86.

Miller, E.H. (ed.) (1985) *Museum Collections: Their Roles and Future in Biological Research*, Occasional Paper No. 25, British Columbia Provincial Museum.

Moe, H.A. (1968) The role and obligation of museums as a scholarly resource, in Larrabee, E. (ed.), *Museums and Education*, Smithsonian Institution Press, Washington, DC, 25-34.

Montgomery, C.F. (1969) The role of the museum in research, in Ellsworth, L.F. and O'Brien, M.A. (eds.), *Material Culture:Historical Agencies and the Historian*, Book Reprint Service, Philadelphia, 204-07.

Moore, T.E. (1962) Experimental research in the natural history museum, *Museum News*, 41(4), 30-3.

Morgan, P.J. (Compiler) (1986) *A National Plan for Systematic Collections*, National Museum of Wales, Cardiff.

Mori, J.L. (1972) Revising our conceptions of museum research, *Curator*,

15(3), 189-99.

Multhauf, R.P. (1960) The research museum of the physical sciences, *Curator*, 3(4), 355-60.

Netting, N.G. (1962) Objectives of museum research in natural history, *Museum News*, 41(3), 29-34.

Neustupny, J. (1968) *Museum and Research*, National Museum, Prague.

Nyerges, A.L. (1982) Museums and the videodisc revolution:cautious involvement, *Videodisc-Videotex*, 3(4), 267-74.

Ogborn, E. (1979) Researching your collections - fine art, *Museums Assistants Group (MAG) Transactions*, 15.

Owen, D.E. (1970) Geological research for curators, *Museums Assistants Group (MAG) Transactions*, 9, 5-7.

Parr, A.E. (1958) The right to do research, *Curator*, 1(3), 70-3.

Parr, A.E. (1963) The functions of museums:research centres or show places?, *Curator*, 6(1), 20-31.

Parr, A.E. (1967) Museums research, *Museum News*, 41(7), 36-7.

Pearce, S.M. (1974) The role of the archaeological curator in the wider pattern of archaeological research: some suggestions, *Museums Journal*, 73(4), 149-51.

Perring, F.H. (1967) The requirements of the research worker in biology, *Museums Journal*, 67(2), 108-11.

Peters, J.A. & Collette, B.B. (1968) The role of timeshare computing in museum research, *Curator*, 11(1), 65-75.

Pettit, C.W. (1986) Collections research in the United Kingdom, in Light, R.B., Roberts, D.A. & Stewart, J.D. (eds.), *Museum Documentation Systems*, Butterworths, London, 221-228.

Pettit, C.W. & Hancock, E.G. (1981) Natural sciences collections research units, their origin, aims and current status, *Museums Journal*, 81(2), 73-74.

Pope-Hennessy, J. (1967) Contribution of museums to scholarship, *ICOM 7th General Conference Report*, ICOM (International Council of Museums), Paris.

Renfrew, C. (1967) The requirements of the research worker in archaeology, *Museums Journal*, 67(2), 111-113.

Rodeck, H.G. (1960) The university museum and biological research, *Curator*, 3(4), 313-316.

Rodeck, H.G. (1962) The research role of the local natural history museum, *Museum News*, 41(3), 34-37.

Select Committee on Science & Technology (1991) *Systematic Biology Research*, HMSO, London.

Stott, M.A. (1986) Videodisc:museums and the future, *Muse*, 3(4), 44-46.

Vanausdall, J. (1986) The computer as interpreter, *Museum News*, 64(3), 73-82.

Weizman, S.M. (1988) The changing role of the curator, *Muse*, Summer, 41-

43.
West, A. (1989) Lists, documents, objects: museum research and display, *Museums Journal*, 89(1), 193-7.

5.2 Environmental Recording

Association of County Archaeological Officers (1985) *County Archaeological Records - Progress and Potential*, ACAO, Taunton, Somerset.

Association of County Archaeological Officers (nd) *A Guide to the Establishment of Sites and Monuments Records*.

Benson, D. (1972) A sites and monuments record for the Oxford region, *Oxeniensia*, 37, 226-37.

Berry, R. J. (Chairman) (1988) *Biological Survey: Need and Network*, Linnean Society, London.

Black, C.C. (1978) New strains on our resources, *Museum News*, 56(3), 18-22.

Bond, C.J. (1984) The Oxfordshire sites and monuments record - a progress report, *MDA Information*, 8(4), 112-8.

Cleere, H.F. (1976) Council for British Archaeology, *Museums Association Conference Proceedings*, 21-2.

Copp, C.J.T. & Harding, P. (1985) *Biological Recording Forum 1985*, Biology Curators Group, Special Publication No.4, Bolton.

Council for British Archaeology (1975) *Report of the Working Party on Archaeological Records Made to the Royal Commission and Historical Monuments (England)*, Council for British Archaeology.

Ely, B. (1978) Job creation and biological records at Clifton Park Museum, Rotherham, *Biology Curators Group Newsletter*, 9, 11-14.

Flood. S.W. (1975) Museums as biological record centres, *Museums Journal*, 75, 27-8.

Flood. S.W. (1975) Record centres and interpretation, *Museums Journal*, 75(supplement), 32-3.

Flood, S.W. & Perring, F.H. (1978) *A Handbook for Local Biological Record Centres*, Biology Curators Group and Biological Records Centre, Institute of Terrestial Ecology, Monks Wood, Huntingdon.

Foster, R.A. (1976) Oxfordshire sites and monuments record, *Museums Association Conference Proceedings*, Museums Association, London, 22-3.

Garland, S. (ed.) (1985) Biological recording and the use of site based information, *Biology Curators Group Newsletter*, 4(2).

Grant, J. (1984) Hampshire's environmental record - marking time?, *Museum Documentaion Association Information*, 8(4), 119-20.

Greenwood, E.F. (1971) North West Biological Field Data Bank, *Museums Journal*, 71, 7-10.

Greenwood, E.F. (1976) Regional and local biological record centres, *North West Museum and Art Gallery Service Newsletter*, Autumn.

Greenwood, E.F. (1984) Biological recording and the use of site based biological information, *Museum Documentation Association Information*, 8(4), 100.

Greenwood, E.F. & Harding, P. (1982) Survey of local and regional biological record centres - analysis, *Biology Curators Group Newsletter*, 3(2), 108-14.

Harding, P. (1984) The biological records centre, *Museum Documentation Association Information*, 8(4), 102-6.

Harding, P. & Greenwood, E.G. (1981) Survey of local and regional biological record centres, *Biology Curators Group Newsletter*, 2(10), 468-87.

Harding, R.T. & Roberts, D.A. (eds.) (1986) *Biological Recording in a Changing Landscape*, National Federation for Biological Recording, Cambridge.

Hawke-Smith, C. (1984) Recording buildings of the industrial age: the Stoke on Trent historic buildings survey, *Museums Journal*, 84(3), 117-20.

Heaton, A. (1984) Site recording of the Nature Conservation Trust, *Museum Documentation Association Information*, 8(4), 107-11.

Hope, L.E. (1910) The natural history record bureau at the Carlisle Museum, *Museums Journal*, 10, 157-61.

Irwin, H.S. *et al.* (1973) *Americas Systematics Collections: A National Plan*, Association of Systematics Collections, Lawrence, Kansas, 12-13 and 35.

Johnels, A.A. (1973) Role of natural history museums in environmental recording, *Museum*, 25, 54-58.

Knell, S.J. (1991) Making rock records, *Geology Today*, 7(2), 62-66.

Lavin, J.C. & Wilmore, G.T.D. (1977) The development of the Biological Data Bank, West Yorkshire Region, *Museums Journal*, 77, 2-6.

Light, K. (1984) The development of the MDA locality application package, *Museum Documentation Association Information*, 8(4), 127-9.

Museum Documentation Association (1984) Environmental recording and museums, *Museum Documentation Association Information*, 8(4).

Perring, F.H. & Heath, J. (1975) Biological recording in Europe, *Endeavour*, 34(123), 103-07.

Pottinger, P.M. (1977) Towards an environmental record - some problems, *Museums Journal*, 77, 65-6.

Reynolds, D. (1987) The Royal Commission on the Ancient & Historical Monuments of Scotland: National Monuments Record of Scotland,

Scottish Museum News, 3(2), 2-3.

Ritchie, A. (ed.) (1975) *Biorec 75, Conference on Biological Recording in Scotland*, Dundee Museum, Dundee.

Slocombe, P.M. (1984) Documentation at the Wiltshire Buildings Record, *Museum Documentation Association Information*, 8(4), 121-6.

Somerville, A. (ed.) (1977) *A Guide to Biological Recording in Scotland*, Biological Recording in Scotland Committee, Edinburgh.

Stanley, M. (1984) The National Scheme for Geological Site Documentation, *Geological Curator*, 4(2), 95-9.

Stanley, M. (1984) The National Scheme for Geological Site Documentation and the Locality Applications, *Museum Documentation Association Information*, 8(4), 94-9.

Stansfield, G. (ed.) (1973) *Centres for Environmental Records*, Department of Adult Education, University of Leicester.

Stansfield, G. (ed.) (1984) The development of environmental recording by museums, *Museum Documentation Association Information*, 8(4), 88-93.

Stansfield, G. & Harding, P.T. (eds) (1990) *National Perspectives in Biological Recording in the UK*, National Federation for Biological Recording, Cambridge.

Stewart, J.D. (1980) *Environmental Record Centre - A Decade of Progress*, Museums Documentation Association.

Stewart, J.D. (1980) A summary of local environmental record centres, *Museums Journal*, 80, 161-64.

Whiteley, D. (1978) Vertebrate recording schemes at Sheffield Museum, *Biology Curators Group Newsletter*, 9, 17-23.

6 Communication & Exhibitions

6.1 Communication Theory

Abbey, D.S. (1986) The exhibit as educator, *Museum*, 38(3), 172-175.

Allan, D.A. (1961) Display policy in museums: a symposium, *Museums Journal*, 61(3), 191-200.

Alt, M.B. (1977) Evaluating didactic exhibits: a critical look at Shettel's work, *Curator*, 20(3), 241-58.

Alt, M.B. (1979) Improving audio-visual presentations, *Curator*, 22(2), 85-95.

Alt, M.B. & Miles, R.S. (1979) British Museum (Natural History): a new approach to the visiting public, *Museums Journal*, 78(4), 158-62.

Alt, M.B. & Shaw, K.M. (1984) Characterisation of ideal museum exhibits, *British Journal of Psychology*, 75, 25-36.

Alvarado, M., Gutch, R., & Wollen, T. (1987) *Learning the Media: an Introduction to Media Teaching,*, MacMillan Education, Hampshire and London.

Ambrose, T.M. (ed.) (1985) *Museums Are for People*, Scottish Museums Council & HMSO, Edinburgh.

American Association of Museums (1984) A new imperative for learning, *Museums for a New Century*, AAM, Washington DC, 3.

American Association of Museums(1992) *Excellence and Equity: Education and the Public Dimension of Museums*, American Association of Museums, Washington DC.

Ames, M.M. (1981) Museum anthropologists and the arts of acculturation on the Northwest coast, *British Columbia Studies*, 49, 3-14.

Ames, M.M. (1983) How should we think about what we see in a museum of anthropology?, *Transactions of the Royal Society of Canada*, IV(xxi), 93-101.

Ames, M.M. (1984/85) Bill Holm, Willie Seaweed and the problem of Northwest coast Indian "Art": a review article, *British Columbia Studies*, 64, 74-81.

Ames, M.M. (1985) De-schooling the museum: a proposal to increase public access to museums through their resources, *Museum*, 37(1), 25-31.

Ames, M.M. (1987) Free Indians from their ethnological fate, *Muse*, 5(2), 14-19.

Annis, S. (1986) The museum as a staging ground for symbolic action, *Museum*, 38, 168-171.

Anon. (1975) Museums and interpretive techniques: an interim report,

Museums Journal, 75(2), 71-5.

Anon. (1980) Adam's ancestors, Eve's in-laws: sexual relations and "Man's Place in Evolution", *Schooling & Culture*, 8, 57-62.

Arnell, V., Hammer, I. & Nylof, G. (1980) *Going to Exhibitions*, Riksutstallningar, Stockholm, Sweden.

Avery, R. and Eason, D. (1991) *Critical perspectives on media and society*, The Guilford Press, London.

Barnard, W.A. *et al.* (1980) Assessment of visual recall and recognition learning in a museum environment, *Bulletin of the Psychonomic Society*, 16, 311-313.

Barthes, R. (1973) The great family of man, *Mythologies*, Paladin, St. Albans, 100-102.

Barthes, R. (1976) *Mythologies*, Paladin, St Albans.

Barthes, R. (1977) The rhetoric of the image, *Image - Music - Text*, Fontana/Collins, 32-51.

Barthes, R. (1982) The plates of the Encyclopedia in Sontag, S. (ed.), *Barthes: Selected writings*, Fontana/Collins, 218-235.

Basile, G. (1984) For a didactic museum of conservation and restoration, *Museum*, 36, 81-84.

Baudrillard, J. (1988) The system of objects, *Art Monthly*, 115 (April), 5-8.

Belsey, C. (1980) *Critical Practice*, Methuen, London and New York.

Bennett, T. (1988) Museums and the people, in Lumley, R., (ed.), *The Museum Time Machine*, Comedia/Routledge, London, 63-86.

Bennett, T. (1989) Museums and public culture: history, theory, policy, *Media Information Australia*, 53, 57-65.

Benos, J. (1983) Variations in display methods, *Museum*, 35, 102-107.

Berger, A.A. (1982) *Media Analysis Techniques*, Sage Publications, London.

Berger, J. *et al.* (1972) *Ways of Seeing*, British Broadcasting Corporation and Penguin Books, Middlesex.

Bitgood, S. & Patterson, D. (1987) Principles of exhibit design, *Visitor Behaviour*, 2(1), 4-6.

Blackbourn, C. (1986) Visible storage, *Museum Quarterly*, Fall, 22-30.

Bleicher, E. (1967) Presentational aesthetics, *Museum News*, 46(2), 20-3.

Bott, V. (1990) Beyond the museum, *Museums Journal*, 15(1), 7-9.

Bourne, R. (1985) Are Amazon Indians museum pieces?, *New Society*, 29 September.

Boyd-Barrett, O. & Braham, P. (1987) *Media, Knowledge and Power*, Croom Helm, London/Open University.

Brawne, M. (1983) Some recent trends in museum design and the new National Archaeological Museum of Jordan, *International J. of Museum Management and Curatorship*, 2, 257-264.

Britt, S.H. (1978) *Psychological Principles of Marketing and Consumer Behaviour*, Lexington, Mass..

Brody, J. J. (1991) Meanings of things, *Museum News*, 70(6), 58-61.

Cabe, L. (1985) Living tombs, *New Internationalist*, 144, 26-27.

Cameron, D. (1968) A viewpoint: the museum as a communication system and implications for museum education, *Curator*, 11(1), 33-40.

Cameron, D.F. (1968) The museum as a communications system and implications for museum education, *Curator*, 11(1), 33-40.

Cameron, D.F. (1971) The museum, a temple or the forum?, *Curator*, 14, 11-24.

Cameron, D.F. (1982) Museums and public access: the Glenbow approach, *International J. of Museum Management and Curatorship*, 1(3), 177-96.

Cannizzo, J. (1987) How sweet it is: cultural politics in Barbados, *Muse*, Winter, 22-27.

Carr, J.R. (1986) Education everywhere for everyone at Mystic Seaport, in Ambrose, T. (ed.), *The American Museum Experience: In Search of Excellence*, Scottish Museums Council, Edinburgh, 41-58.

Caston, E. (1980) The object of my affections: a commentary on museumness, *Art Education*, 33(1), 21-24.

Chadwick, A. (1983) Practical aids to nineteenth century self-help - the museums: private collections into public institutions, in Stephens, M.cD. & Roderick, G.W. (eds.), *Samuel Smiles and Nineteenth Century Self-Help in Education*, Department of Adult Education, University of Nottingham, 47-69..

Chambers, M. (1984) Is anyone out there? Audience and communication, *Museum News*, 62(5), 47-54.

Chambers, M. (1990) Beyond 'Aha!': motivating museum visitors, in Serrell, B. (ed.), *What Research Says About Learning in Science Museums*, Association of Science - Technology Centres, Washington DC, 10-12.

Chase, R.A. (1978) The social ecology of the museums learning environment implications for environmental design and management, in Esser, A.H. and Greenbie, B.B. (eds.), *Design for Communality and Privacy*, New York.

Clifford, T. (1982) The historical approach to the display of paintings, *International J. of Museum Management and Curatorship*, 2, 93-106.

Cohen, M. *et al.* (1977) Orientation in a museum: an experimental visitor study, *Curator*, 20(2), 85-97.

Cork, R. (1979) *The Social Role of Art; Essays in Criticism for a Newspaper Public*, Gordon Frazer, London.

Csikszentmihalyi, M. (1991) Notes on art museum experiences, in Getty Centre for Education in the Arts, *Insights: Museums, Visitors, Attitudes, Expectations*, J. Paul Getty Museum, California.

Csikszentmihalyi, M. & Robinson, R.E. (1975) *Beyond Boredom and Anxiety*, Jossey-Bass, San Francisco.

Csikszentmihalyi, M. & Robinson, R.E. (1990) *The Art of Seeing: An Interpretation of the Aesthetic Encounter*, J. Paul Getty Museum and the Getty Centre for Education in the Arts, Malibu, California.

Csikszentmihalyi, M. & Rochberg-Halton, E. (1981) *The Meaning of Things: Domestic Symbols and the Self,* Cambridge University Press, Cambridge.

Cuisenier, J. (1984) Exhibiting meaning fully - the semantics of display in agricultural museums, *Museum,* 36, 30-137.

Curran, J. & Gurevitch, M. (1991) *Mass Media and Society,* Edward Arnold, London.

Dabydeen, D. (1987) High culture based on black slavery, *The Listener,* 24 September, 14-15.

De Borhegyi, S.F. (1978) Museum brainstorming: a creative approach to exhibit planning, *Curator,* 21, 217-224.

De Borhegyi, S.F. (1963) Visual communication in the science museum, *Curator,* 6(1), 45-57.

De Waard, R. J. *et al.* (1974) Effects of using programmed cards on learning in a museum environment, *Journal of Educational Research,* 67(10).

Decrosse, A. (1987) Museologie des sciences et des techniques: approches linguistiques et semiotiques, *Brises,* 10 September, 75-78.

Dick, R.E. *et al.* (1974) A summary and annotated bibliography of communication principles, *Journal of Environmental Education,* Summer, 8-12.

DiMaggio, P. & Useem, M. (1978) Social class and arts consumption: the origins and consequences of class differences in exposure to the arts in America, *Theory and Society,* 5, 141-61.

Dobbs, S.M. & Edner, E.W. (1990) Client pedagogy in our museums, *Curator,* 33(3), 217-236.

Droba, D.D. (1929) Effect of printed information on memory for pictures, *Museum News,* 7(9), 6-8.

Duncan, C. (1991) Art museums and the ritual of citizenship, in Karp, I. and Levine, D. (eds.), *Exhibiting Cultures: The Poetics and Politices of Museum Display,* Smithsonian Institution Press, Washington DC, 88-103.

Duncan, C. & Wallach, A. (1978) The Museum of Modern Art as late capitalist ritual: an iconographic analysis, *Marxist Perspectives,* Winter, 28-51.

Duncan, C. & Wallach, A., (1980) The universal survey museum, *Art History,* 3(4), 448-469.

Duncan, D. (1981) *Approaching Ontario's past - The Artifact: What Can It Tell Us About the Past?,* Ontario Historical Society, Ontario.

Elliott, P. & Loomis, J.L. (1975) *Studies of Visitor Behaviour in Museums and Exhibitions: An Annotated Bibliography Primarily in the English Language,* Office of Museum Programs, Smithsonian Institution, Washington DC.

Falk, J. (1985) Predicting visitor behaviour, *Curator,* 28(4), 249-257.

Falk, J. H. & Dierking, L. D. (1992) *The Museum Experience,* Whalesback

Books, Washington, DC.

Fine, P.A. (1963) The role of design in educational exhibits, *Curator*, 6, 37-43.

Fiske, J. (1982) *Introduction to communication studies*, Routledge, London.

Fleming, D. (1991) Second class citizens, *Museums Journal*, 91(2), 31-33.

Fleming, E. M. (1972) The period room as a curatorial publication, *Museum News*, 50(10), 39-43.

Foster, R. (1988) Reconciling museums and marketing, *Museums Journal*, 88(3), 127-130.

Gabus, J. (1965) Aesthetic principles and general planning of educational exhibitions, *Museum*, 18, 2-31,82-97.

Gamwell, L. (1990) Striking a balance, *Museum News*, 69(4), 58-62.

Gardner, J. & Heller, C. (1960) *Exhibition and Display*, New York.

Getty Centre for Education in the Arts (1991) *Insights: Museums, Visitors, Attitudes, Expectations*, J. Paul Getty Museum, California.

Gilman, B. (1978) *The Museum As An instrument of Cultural innovation*, Council of Europe, Strasbourg.

Gilmour, P (1979) How can museums be more effective in society?, *Museums Journal*, 79(3), 120-22.

Glodberg, J. (1987) Opening eyes and minds, *Museum*, 39, 40-44.

Gordon, A. (1982) The Neue Pinakothek in Munich: "making pictures live", *International J. of Museum Management and Curatorship*, 1(4), 281-302.

Griggs, S.A. (1983) Orienting visitors within a thematic display, *International J. of Museum Management and Curatorship*, 2, 119-134.

Griggs, S.A. (1984) Museums for the people, *New Scientist*, 15 November, 34-35.

Griggs, S.A. (1990) Lets empower all those who have a stake in exhibitions, *Museum News*, 69(2), 90-3.

Griggs, S.A. & Hays-Jackson, K. (1983) Visitor perceptions of cultural institutions, *Museums Journal*, 83(2/3), 121-25.

Gurevitch, M. Bennett, T., Curran, J. & Woollacott, J. (1982) *Culture, society and the media*, Routledge, London.

Gurian, E. (1981) Adult learning at Children's Museum of Boston, in Collins, Z (ed.), *Museums, Adults and the Humanities*, American Association of Museums, Washington DC, 271-296.

Gurian, E. (1992) The importance of "and", in Museum Education Roundtable, *Patterns in Practice: Selections from the Journal of Museum Education*, Museum Education Roundtable, Washington, DC, 88-89.

Ham, S.H. (1983) Cognitive psychology and interpretation: synthesis and application, *Journal of Interpretation*, 8(1), 11-28.

Ham, S.H. & Shew, D.L. (1979) A comparison of visitors and interpreters assessments of conducted interpretive activities, *Journal of*

Interpretation, 4(2), 39-44.

Hammadd, M. (1987) Semiotic reading of a museum, *Museum*, 39(2), 56-60.

Hammitt, W. F. (1981) A theoretical foundation for Tilden's interpretive principles, *Journal of interpretation*, 4(1), 9-12.

Hardt, H. (1992) *Critical communication studies - communication, history and theory in America*, Routledge, London.

Harrison, J. (1987) De-colonizing museum classification systems: a case in point - the Metis, *Muse*, Winter, 46-50.

Hartley, J. (1982) *The Politics of Pictures:The Creation of the Public in the Age of Popular Media*, Routledge, London.

Hasted, R. (1990) Museums, racism and censorship, in Baker, F. and Thomas, J. (eds.), *Writing the Past in the Present*, Saint David's College, Lampeter, 152-16.

Hayward, D.G. & Jensen, A.D. (1981) Enhancing a sense of the past : perceptions of visitors and interpreters, *The interpreter*, 12(2), 4-12.

Heath, R. L. & Bryant, J. (1992) *Human communication theory and research: concepts, contexts and challenges*, Lawrence Erlbaum Associates, New Jersey and London.

Heighton, M. (1987) Museums as community enterprises, *Museums Journal*, 87(2), 61-64.

Hodge, R. & D'Souza, W. (1979) The museum as a communicator: a semiotic analysis of the Western Australian Museum Aboriginal Gallery, Perth, *Museum*, 31(4), 251-66.

Hoek, G.J. Van Der (1971) Listen to the written word, *In the Museum in the Service of Man Today and Tomorrow*, Ninth General Conference Proceedings,ICOM (International Council of Museums), Paris, 100-12.

Home, A.L. (1980) A comparative study of two methods of conducting docent tours in arts museums, *Curator*, 23(2), 105-117.

Hooper-Greenhill, E. (1982) Some aspects of a sociology of museums, *Museums Journal*, 82(2), 69-70.

Hooper-Greenhill, E. (1987) Knowledge in an open prison, *New Statesman*, 13 February, 21-22.

Hooper-Greenhill, E. (1989) Museums in the disciplinary society, in Pearce, S. (ed.), *Museum Studies in Material Culture*, Leicester University Press, Leicester, London and New York.

Hooper-Greenhill, E. (1990) The space of the museum, *Continuum: An Australian Journal of the Media*, 3(1), 56-69.

Hooper-Greenhill, E. (1991) *Museums and the Shaping of Knowledge*, Routledge, London.

Hooper-Greenhill, E. (1991) A new communications model for museums, in Kavanagh, G. (ed.), *Museum Languages: Objects and Texts*, Leicester University Press, Leicester, London and New York, 47-61.

Horne, D. (1984) *The Great Museum*, Pluto Press, London and Sidney.

Hudson, K. (1983) *The Archaeology of the Consumer Society*, Heinemann, London.

Hudson, K. (1987) *Museums of Influence: The Pioneers of the Last 200 Years*, Cambridge University Press.

Iser, W. (1985) Interaction between text and reader, in Corner, J. and Hawthorn, J. (eds.), *Communication Studies: An Introductory Reader*, Edward Arnold, London.

James, A., Sfougaras, G. and Wheeler, R. (nd) *Evaluating Artefacts*, Centre for Multicultural Education and Museum Education, Leicestershire Museums, Arts and Records Service.

Janes, R.R. (1987) Museum ideology and practice in Canada's third world, *Muse*, Winter, 33-40.

Johnston, C. (1991) Documenting diversity, *Museums Journal*, 91(2), 29-30.

Jones, D. (1992) Dealing with the past, *Museums Journal*, 92(1), 24-27.

Jones, S. (1991) Presenting the Past: towards a feminist critique of museum practice, *The Field Archaeologist*, 14, 247-9.

Jones, S. (1991) The female perspective, *Museums Journal*, 91(2), 24-27.

Knez, E. & Wright, A.G. (1970) The museum as a communications system: an assessment of Cameron's view-point, *Curator*, 13(3), 204-12.

Kruger, H. (1984) Planning and layout of museums: the central importance of the room, *International J. of Museum Management and Curatorship*, 3, 351-356.

Lamarche, H. (1989) The museum and its vast public, *Muse*, 7(1), 58-62.

Landay, J. & Bridge, R.G. (1982) Video vs. wall-panel display - an experiment in museums learning, *Curator*, 25(1), 41-56.

Leavitt, T.W. (1967) The need for critical standards in history museum exhibits: a case in point, *Curator*, 10(2), 91-94.

Leone, M. (1983) Method as message: interpreting the past with the public, *Museum News*, 62(1), 34-41.

Lewis, J. (1991) *The Ideological Octopus: An Exploration of Television and its Audience*, Routledge, London.

MacCannell, D. (1976) *The Tourist: A New Theory of the Leisure Class*, Schocken Books, New York.

Martin-Barbero, J. (1993) *Communication, culture and hegemony*, Sage Publications, London.

McGuigan, J. (1992) *Cultural populism*, Routledge, London.

McLuhan, M. (1968) McLuhanism in the museum, *Museum News*, 46(7), 11-18.

McLuhan, M. *et al.* (1969) *Exploration of the Ways, Means and Values of Museum Communication With the Viewing Public*, Museum of the City of New York.

McManus, G. (1991) The crisis of representation in museums: the exhibition 'The Spirit Sings, in Pearce, S.M. (ed.), *Museum Economics and the Community*, New Research in Museum Studies, Vol. 2, Athlone,

London, 202-206.

McManus, P.M. (1986) Reviewing the reviewers: towards a critical language for didactic science exhibitions, *International J. of Museum Management and Curatorship*, 5(3), 213-226.

McManus, P.M. (1988) Good companions: more on the social determination of learning-related behaviour in a science museums, *International J. of Museum Management and Curatorship*, 7, 37-44.

McManus, P.M. (1988) Its the company you keep... the social determination of learning-related behaviour in a science museum, *International J. of Museum Management and Curatorship*, 6, 263-270.

McManus, P.M. (1991) Making sense of exhibits, in Kavanagh, G. (ed.), *Museum Languages: Objects and Texts*, Leicester University Press, Leicester, London and New York, 33-45.

McNeill, P. (1985) *Research Methods*, Routledge, London.

McQuail, D. (1975) *Communication*, Longman, London and New York.

McQuail, D. (1987) *Mass Communication Theory: An Introduction*, Sage Publications, London.

McQuail, D. (1992) *Media Performance - Mass Communication and the Public Interest*, Sage publications, London.

Melosch, B. & Simmons, C. (1981) From Martha Washington to Alice Paul in our nations capital, *Radical History Review*, 25, 101-113.

Miles, R.S. (1988) Museums and public culture, a context for communicating science, in P. G. Heltne & L. A. Marquardt (eds.), *Science Learning in the Informal Setting*, Chicago Academy of Sciences, Chicago, 157-169.

Miles, R.S. (1989) *Evaluation in Its Communications Context*, Technical Report no. 89-10, Centre for Social Design, Jacksonville, Alabama.

Miles, R.S. (1993) Exhibiting learning, *Museums Journal*, 93(5), 27-28.

Miles, R.S. & Tout, A.F. (1978) Human biology and the new exhibition scheme in the British Museum (Natural History), *Curator*, 21, 36-50.

Miller, G.A. (1970) *The Psychology of Communication*, Penguin, London.

Minihan, J. (1977) *The Nationalization of Culture: The Development of State Subsidies to the Arts in Great Britain*, Hamish Hamilton.

Morgan, J. & Welton, P. (1986) *See What I Mean: An Introduction to Visual Communication*, Edward Arnold, London and New York, 1-12.

Morley, D. (1980) *The 'Nationwide' Audience: Structure and Decoding*, British Film Institute, London.

Morley, D. (1992) *Television audiences and cultural studies*, Routledge, London.

Morris, B. (1986) The special demands placed upon museums by their users, *Art Gallery and Museums Association of New Zealand (AGMANZ) Journal*, Winter, 3 - 5.

Morris, R.G.M. & Alt, M.B. (1978) An experiment to help design a map for a large museum, *Museums Journal*, 77(4), 179-80.

Mounin, G. (1985) *Semiotic Praxis: Studies in Pertinence and in the Means* *and Expression of Communication*, Plenum Press, New York and London.

Museums & Galleries Commission (1992) *Quality of Service in Museums and Galleries: Customer Care in Museums - Guidelines on Implementation*, Museums and Galleries Commission, London.

Myerscough, J. (1988) *The Economic Importance of the Arts in Britain*, Policy Studies Institute, London.

Myerscough, J. (1991) Your museum in context: knowing the museum industry; the background statistics, in Ambrose, T. and Runyard, S. (eds.), *Forward Planning*, Routledge, London,, 16-24.

Nash, G. (1975) Art museums as perceived by the public, *Curator*, 18(1), 55-67.

Neal, A. (1965) Function of display: regional museums, *Curator*, 8(3), 228-34.

Neuman, R. (1991) *The future of the mass audience*, Cambridge University Press, Cambridge.

Newsom, B.Y. & Silver, A.Z. (1978) *The Art Museum As Educator*, University of California Press, Berkeley Los Angeles and London.

Nyberg, K.L. (1984) Some radical comments on interpretation: a little heresy is good for the soul, in Machlis, C.E., and Field, D.R. (eds.), *On interpretation - Sociology for interpreters of Natural and Cultural History*, Oregon State University Press, 151-156.

O'Hare, M. (1974) The audience of the Museum of Fine Arts, *Curator*, 17(2), 126-158.

O'Hare, M. (1974) The publics use of Art: visitor behaviour in an art museum, *Curator*, 17(2), 309-320.

O'Neill, M. (1987) Quantity vs. quality or what is a community museum anyway?, *Scottish Museum News*, 3(1), 5-7.

Olds, A. R. (1990) Sending them home alive, *Journal of Museum Education*, 15(1), 10-12.

Oppenheimer, F. (1983) Museums for the love of learning - a personal perspective, *Museum Studies Journal*, 1(1), 16-18.

Orrom, M. (1975) The interpretive policy and visitor centres of the Forestry Commission, *Museums Journal*, 77(4), 171-73.

Palmer, S.E. (1975) The effects of contextual scenes on the identification of objects, *Memory and Cognition*, 3(5), 519-526.

Parker, H.W. (1963) The museum as a communication system, *Curator*, 6(4), 350-60.

Parkin, A. (1980) *Systems Analysis*, Edward Arnold, London.

Parr, A.E. (1962) Marketing the message, *Curator*, 12(2), 77-82.

Parr, A.E. (1962) Some basic problems of visual education by means of exhibits, *Curator*, 5(1), 36-44.

Parr, A.E. (1973) Theatre or playground, *Curator*, 16(2), 103-06.

Patten, L.H. (1982/83) Education by design, *ICOM (International Council* *of Museums) Education,* 10, 6-7.

Patten, L.H. (1986) One view from inside: the ROMs new exhibits, 1978-1984, *Muse,* 37-40.

Peart, B. (1982) Impact of exhibit type or knowledge gain, attitudes and behaviour, *Curator,* 24(3), 220-237.

Peirson Jones, J. (1991) Cultural representation and the creation of dialogue, Paper presented to the ICOM (International Council of Museums)/Committe for Education and Cultural Action, Conference at Liverpool Museum on May 15th 1991.

Peirson Jones, J. (1992) The colonial legacy and the community: the Gallery 33 project, in Karp, I., Kreamer, C., and Lavine, S. (eds.), *Museums and Communities: Debating Public Culture,* Smithsonian Institution Press, Washington DC, 221-241.

Porter, G. (1988) Putting your house in order, in Lumley, R. (ed.), *The Museum Time Machine,* Comedia/Routledge, 102-127.

Porter, G. (1991) Partial truths, in Kavanagh, G. (ed.), *Museum Languages: Objects and Texts,* Leicester University Press, Leicester, London and New York, 101-117.

Postman, N. (1990) Museum as dialogue, *Museum News,* 69(5), 55-9.

Pouw, J.M. & Schouten, F.J. (1983) *Exhibition Design As An Educational Tool,* Reinwardt Studies in Museology No.1, Reinwardt Academy, Leiden, Netherlands.

Prince, D.R. (1983) Behavioural consistency and visitor attraction, *International J. of Museum Management and Curatorship,* 2(3), 235-247.

Report of the National Inquiry into Arts and the Community (1992) *Arts and Communities,* Community Development Foundation, London.

Roberts, L. (1990) The elusive qualities of "affect", in Serrell, B. (ed.), *What Research Says About Learning in Science Museums,* Association of Science - Technology Centres, Washington DC, 19-22.

Royal Ontario Museum (1976) *Communicating with the Museum Visitor: Guidelines for Planning,* Royal Ontario Museum, Toronto.

Ruder, W. (1984) The image in the mirror, *Museum News,* 63(2), 33-34.

Ruffins, F.D. (1979) *Mankind Discovering: Volume I. A Plan for New Galleries At the Royal Ontario Museum, Volume II. Evaluation - the Basis for Planning,* Royal Ontario Museum, Toronto.

Ruffins, F.D. (1985) The exhibition as form; an elegant metaphor, *Museum News,* 61(1).

Saumarez Smith, C. (1989) Museums, artefacts and meanings, in Vergo, P. (ed.), *The New Museology,* Reaktion Books, London, 6-21 and 205-207.

Schlereth, T.J. (1980) A perspective on criticism - guidelines for history museum exhibition reviews, *History News,* 35(8), 18-19.

Schlereth, T.J. (1981) Historic house museums: seven teaching strategies, *History News,* 33(4), 91-119.

Schlereth, T.J. (1984) Causing conflict, doing violence, *Museum News*, 63(1), 45-52.

Scottish Museum News (1987) Leisure learning programme gets underway, *Scottish Museum News*, 3(3), 17.

Screven, C.G. (1969) The museum as a responsive learning environment, *Museum News*, 47(10), 7-10.

Screven, C.G. (1974) *The Measurement and Facilitator of Learning in the Museum Environment: An Experimental Analysis*, Smithsonian Institution Press, Washington DC.

Screven, C.G. (1974) Learning and exhibits - instructional design, *Museum News*, 52(5), 67-75.

Screven, C.G. (1975) The effectiveness of guidance devices in visitor learning, *Curator*, 18(3), 219-43.

Screven, C.G. (1986) Exhibition and information centers: some principles and approaches, *Curator*, 29(2), 109-137.

Searle, A. (1984) Museums and the public interest, *Museum News*, 63(1), 53-58.

Shelton, A. (1992) Constructing the global village, *Museums Journal*, 92(8), 25-28.

Shettel, H.H. (1973) Exhibits: art form or educational medium?, *Museum News*, 52(1), 32-41.

Simpson, M. (1992) Celebration, commemoration, or condemnation?, *Museums Journal*, 92(3), 28-31.

Sorsby, B.D. & Horne, S.D. (1980) The readability of museum labels, *Museums Journal*, 80(3), 157-59.

Spalding, J. (1992) Communicating generously, *Museums Journal*, 92(2), 28-31.

Spencer, H. & Reynolds, L. (1977) *Directional Signing and Labelling in Libraries and Museums*, Readability of Print Research Unit, Royal College of Arts.

Stansfield, G. (1981) *Effective interpretive Exhibitions*, Countryside Commission for England and Wales.

Stansfield, G. (1986) Nature on display. Trends in natural history museum exhibitions, *Museums Journal*, 86(2), 97-103.

Stanton, J.E. (1983) Communication and communicators: some problems of display, *Museum*, 35(3), 159-63.

Stewart, D. (1988) Leisure learning programme - update, *Scottish Museum News*, 4(2), 2-3.

Strong, R. (1983) The museum as a communicator, *Museum*, 35(2).

Swank, S. (1992) Museums' social contract,in Museum Education Roundtable, *Patterns in Practice: Selections from the Journal of Museum Education*, Museum Education Roundtable, Washington, DC, 93-94.

Szemere, A. (1978) *The Problems of Contents, Didactics and Aesthetics of*

Modern Museum Exhibitions, Institute of Conservation and Methodology of Museums, Budapest.

Taborsky, E. (1982) The socio-structural role of the museum, *International J. of Museum Management and Curatorship*, 1, 339-345.

Thiev, H.D. & Linn, M.C. (1976) The value of interactive learning experiences, *Curator*, 19, 233-245.

Thiev, H.D. & Linn, M.C. (1984) Developing effective exhibits for the expanding role of museums, *Curator*, 27, 93-103.

Tilden, F. (1957) *Interpreting Our Heritage*, University of North Carolina Press, USA.

Tramposch, W.J. (1982) "Put there a spark" How Colonial Williamsburg trains its interpretive crew, *History News*, 37(7), 21-3.

Turner, G. (1990) *British Cultural Studies - An Introduction*, Unwin Hyman, London,.

Uzzell, D.L. (ed.) (1989) *Heritage interpretation Volume 1: the Natural and Built Environment*, Belhaven Press, London and New York.

Velarde, G. (1988) Role of honour, *Design Week*, 19 February, 17-18.

Visram, R. (1990) British history: whose history? Black perspectives on British history, in Baker, F. and Thomas, J. (eds.), *Writing the Past in the Present*, Saint David's College, Lampeter, 163-171.

Volkert, J.W. (1991) Monologue to dialogue, *Museum News*, 70(2), 46-8.

Washburne, R.F. & Wagar, J.A. (1972) Evaluating visitor response to exhibit content, *Curator*, 15(3), 248-254.

Watson, J. (1985) *What is communication studies?*, Edward Arnold, London.

Weil, S.E. (1990) Rethinking the museum, *Museum News*, 69(2), 56-61.

West, A. (1990) Museums and the real world, *Museums Journal*, 90(2), 24-6.

West, B. (1985) Danger! History at work. a critical consumers guide to the Ironbridge Gorge Museum, *Centre for Contemporary Cultural Studies*, Birmingham.

Westwood, M. (1989) Warwick Castle: safeguarding the future through service, in Uzzell, D. (ed.), *Heritage Interpretation Volume 2: The Visitor Experience*, Belhaven Press, 84-95.

Wilton, A. (1990) In museums is knowledge at risk from commercialism?, *International J. of Museum Management and Curatorship*, 9(2), 191-8.

Winner, L. (1980) Do artifacts have politics?, *Daedalus*, 109, 121-136.

Wittlin, A.S. (1968) Exhibits: interpretive, under-interpretive, mis-interpretive, in E. Larrabee (ed.), *Museums and Education*, Smithsonian Institution Press, Washington DC, 95-114.

Wittlin, A.S. (1972) The hazards of communication by exhibits, *Curator*, 14(2), 138-50.

Wolf, R.L. (1984) Enhancing museum leadership through evaluation, *Museum Studies Journal*, 1(3), 31-33.

Wright, J. & Mazel, A. (1987) Bastions of ideology: the depiction of precolonial history in the museums of Natal and Kwazulu, *SAMAB: Southern African Museums Association Bulletin*, 17(7/8), 301-310.

Zolberg, V. (1990) *Constructing a sociology of the arts*, Cambridge University Press, Cambridge.

6.2 Visitor Studies

Abbey, D.S. & Cameron, D.F. (1959) *The Museum Visitor: Survey Design*, Royal Ontario Museum, Toronto.

Abbey, D.S. & Cameron, D.F. (1960) *The Museum Visitor 2: Survey Results*, Royal Ontario Museum, Toronto.

Abbey, D.S. & Cameron, D.F. (1961) *The Museum Visitor 3: Supplementary Studies*, Royal Ontario Museum, Toronto.

Alt, M.B. (1980) Four years of visitor surveys at the British Museum (NH) 1976-79, *Museums Journal*, 80(1), 10-19.

Alt, M.B. (1983) Visitors attitudes to two old and two new exhibitions at the British Museum (NH), *Museums Journal*, 83(2/3), 145-150.

Alvin, G. & Griffenhagen, G. (1957) Psychological studies of museum visitors and exhibits at the US National Museum, *The Museologist*, 64, 1-6.

Arber, A.J.N. (1975) A survey of visitors to the Rouault exhibition at Manchester City Art Gallery, *Museums Journal*, 75(1), 5-8.

Arnell, V., Hammer, I. & Nylof, G. (1976) *Going to Exhibitions*, Riksutstallningar/ Swedish travelling exhibition, Stockholm, Sweden.

Arts Council (1991) *RSGB Omnibus Arts Survey: Report on a Survey of Arts and Cultural Activities in Gb*, Research Surveys of Great Britain Arts Council, London.

Arts Council (1991) *Target Group Index*, British Market Research Bureau/ Arts Council, London.

Barnett, V. (1991) *Sample Survey: Principles and Methods*, Edward Arnold, London.

Beer, V. (1987) Great expectations: do museums know what visitors are doing?, *Curator*, 30(3), 206-215.

Belgian National Committee of the International Council of Museums (1968) *Le Musée Et Son Public*, ICOM, Brussels.

Bitgood, S. (1988) Problems in visitor circulation, *Visitor Studies -1988:Theory, Research and Practice - Proceedings of the First Annual Visitor Studies Conference*, Proceedings of the First Annual Visitor Studies Conference, Centre for Social Design, Jacksonville State University, 155-170.

Bitgood, S. (1989) *Visitor Studies: Theory, Research and Practice, 2*, Centre for Social Design, Jacksonville, Alabama.

Blud, L.M. (1990) Social interacting and learning in family groups visiting a museum, *International J. of Museum Management and Curatorship*, 9(1), 43-52.

Blud, L.M. (1990) Sons and daughters - observation on the way families interact during a museum visit, *International J. of Museum Management and Curatorship*, 9(3), 257-272.

Bourdieu, P. (1980) Class and culture: the work of Bourdieu, *Media, Culture and Society*, 2(3).

Bourdieu, P., Darbel, A. & Schnapper, D. (1991) *The Love of Art: European Art Museums & Their Public*, Polity Press (English Translation).

British Tourist Authority (1991) *Sightseeing in the UK: A Survey of the Usage and Capacity of the United Kingdom's Attractions for Visitors*, BTA/ETB Research Services, London.

British Tourist Authority & Countryside Commission (1969) *Historic Houses Survey*, Countryside Commission, Cheltenham.

Budd, M. (1987) Pilot visitor survey at Perth, *Scottish Museum News*, 3(4), 16-17.

Cameron, D.F. & Abbey, D.S. (1961) Museum audience research, *Museum News*, 40(2), 34-8.

Capstick, B. (1985) Museums and tourism, *International J. of Museum Management and Curatorship*, 41, 365-372.

Census Research Unit (1980) *People in Britain: A Census Atlas*, CRU with Office of Population Censuses and Surveys and General Register Office, HMSO, London.

Cohen, M.S. (1977) Orientation in a museum: an experimental visitor study, *Curator*, 20, 85-97.

Cone, C. (1978) Space, time and family interaction: visitor behaviour at the Science Museum of Minnesota, *Curator*, 21(3), 245-258.

Coneybeare, C. (1991) *Museum Visitor Surveys: A Practical Guide*, Area Museum Council for the South West,Taunton.

Coutts, H. (1971) The antiquities gallery of Dundee Museum, *Museums Journal*, 70(4), 173-74.

Cruickshank, G. (1972) Jewry Wall Museum, Leicester: trial by questionnaire, *Museums Journal*, 72(2), 65-7.

De Borhegyi, S.F. & Hanson, I. (1964) Chronological bibliography of museum visitor surveys, *Museum News*, 42(6), 39-41.

De Borhegyi, S.F. & Hanson, I. (1968) Chronological bibliography of museum visitor surveys, in Larrabee, E. (ed), *Museums and Education*, 239-251.

Digby, P.W. (1974) *Visitors to Three London Museums*, HMSO, London.

Digby, P.W. (1975) Some results from a survey of visitors to three London museums, *Museum Assistants Group (MAG) Transactions*, 11, 20-5.

DiMaggio, P. *et al.* (1978) *Audience Studies of the Performing Arts and Museums*, National Endowment for the Arts.

DiMaggio, P. & Useem, M. (1978) Social class and arts consumption, *Theory and Society*, 5(March), 141-46.

Dixon, B., Courtney, A. & Bailey, R. (1974) *The Museum and the Canadian Public*, Arts and Culture Branch, Department of the Secretary of State, Toronto.

Doughty, P.S. (1968) The public of the Ulster Museum: a statistical survey, *Museums Journal*, 68(1), 19-25.

Draper, L. (ed.) (1977) *The Visitor and the Museum*, American Association of Museums, Washington DC.

Du Bery, T. (1991) Why don't people go to museums?, *Museum Development*, March, 25-27.

Eckstein, J. & Feist, A. (1992) *Cultural Trends 1991*, Policy Studies Institute, London, 70-79.

Eisenbeis, M. (1972) Elements for a sociology of museums, *Museum*, 24(2), 110-19.

English Tourist Board (1981) *Sightseeing in 1980*, English Tourist Board Socio-economic Research Unit, November.

English Tourist Board (1982) *Visitors to Museums Survey 1982*, Report by the English Tourist Board Market Research Department and NOP Market Research Ltd, London.

English Tourist Board (1982) Museums and tourism: entertain or inform?, *Tourism in England*, 41, 8-11.

English Tourist Board (1984) *National Tourism Facts*, English Tourist Board, London.

English Tourist Board (1987) *Sightseeing in 1986*, English Tourist Board, London.

Erwin, D. (1971) The Belfast public and the Ulster museum: a statistical survey, *Museums Journal*, 70(4), 175-79.

Falk, J.H. (1982) The use of time as a measure of visitor behaviour and exhibit effectiveness, *Museum Roundtable Reports: The Journal of Museum Education*, 7(4), 22-28.

Falk, J.H. (1985) Predicting visitor behaviour, *Curator*, 28(4), 249-257.

Falk J. H. (1988) Museum recollections, *Visitor Studies -1988:Theory, Research and Practice - Proceedings of the First Annual Visitor Studies Conference*, 61-65.

Falk J. H. (1991) Analysis of the behavior of family visitors in natural history museums: the National Museum of Natural History, *Curator*, 34(1), 44-50.

Frankfort-Nachmias, C. & Nachmias, D. (1992) *Research Methods in the Social Sciences*, Edward Arnold, London.

Gardiner, C. & Burton, A. (1987) Visitor survey at the Bethnal Green

Museum of Childhood: two viewpoints, *International J. of Museum Management and Curatorship*, 6(2), 155-164.

Gardner, A. (1986) Learning from listening, *Museum News*, 64(3), 40-44.

Greater London Arts (1990) *Arts in London: A Qualitative Research Study*, Greater London Arts.

Greater London Arts (1990) *Arts in London: A Survey of Attitudes of Users and Non-Users*, Greater London Arts.

Greene, J.P. (1978) A visitor survey at Norton Priory Museum, *Museums Journal*, 78(1), 7-9.

Griggs, S.A. & Alt, M.B. (1982) Visitors to the British Museum (NH) in 1980 and 1981, *Museums Journal*, 82(3), 149-56.

Griggs, S.A. & Hays-Jackson, K. (1983) Visitors perceptions of cultural institutions, *Museums Journal*, 83(2/3), 121-26.

Harris, N. (1990) Polling for opinions, *Museum News*, 69(5), 46-54.

Harvey, B. (1987) *Visiting the National Portrait Gallery: A Report of a Survey of Visitors to the National Portrait Gallery*, Office of Population Censuses and Surveys, Social Survey Division, HMSO.

Harvey, L. & MacDonald, M. (1993) *Doing sociology*, The Macmillan Press, London.

Hay, B. (1987) Who needs research? Part 2, *Scottish Museums News*, 3(3), 12-15.

Hayward, D.G. & Larkin, J.W. (1983) Evaluating visitor experiences and exhibit effectiveness at Old Sturbridge Village, *Museum Studies Journal*, 1(2).

Heady, P. (1984) *Visiting Museums: A Report of a Survey of Visitors to the Victoria & Albert, Science and National Railway Museums for the Office of Arts and Libraries*, Office of Population Censuses and Surveys, HMSO, London.

Heinich, N. (1988) The Pompidou Centre and its public: the limits of a utopian site, in Lumley, R. (ed.), *The Museum Time Machine*, Comedia.

Helsby, D. (1990) Putting people into boxes can be useful, *Environmental Interpretation*, July, 12-13.

Henley Centre & (1983) *Leisure Futures*, Henley Centre for Forecasting.

Higginbotham, J.B. & Cox, K.K. (1979) *Focus Group Interviews - A Reader*, American Marketing Association, Chicago.

Hodd, M.G. (1986) Getting started in audience research, *Museum News*, 64(3), 24-31.

Hood, M.G. (1983) Staying away - why people choose not to visit museums, *Museum News*, 61(4), 50-57.

Hooper-Greenhill, E. (1985) Art gallery audiences and class constraints, *Bullet*, 5-8.

Hooper-Greenhill, E. (1988) Counting visitors or visitors who count, in Lumley, R. (ed.), *The Museum Time Machine*, Routledge, London, 213-232.

Hooper-Greenhill. E. (1994) *Museums and Their Visitors*, Routledge, London.

Housen, A. (1987) Three methods for understanding museum audiences, *Museum Studies Journal*, 2(4), 41-49.

Hudson, K. (1975) *A Social History of Museums*, Macmillan Press.

Jensen, K.B. & Jankowski, N.W. (1991) *A Handbook of Qualitative Methodologies for Mass Communication Research*, Routledge, London.

Johnson, D.A. (1969) Museum attendance in the New York Metropolitan region, *Curator*, 12(3), 201-30.

Jowell, R. *et al.* (eds.) (1986) *British Social Attitudes, the 1986 Report*, Gower Publishing Company.

Klein, R. (1974) Who goes to museums?, *Illustrated London News*, 27-9 April.

Koran, J.J. *et al.* (1986) The relationship of age, sex, attention and holding power with two types of science exhibit, *Curator*, 29(3), 227-236.

London Museums Service (1991) *Dingy Places with Different Kinds of Bits: An Attitudes Survey of London Museums Amongst Non-Visitors*, Area Museum Service for South Eastern England.

Loomis, R.J. (1973) Please, not another visitor survey, *Museum News*, 52(2), 21-6.

Mann, P. (1974) Surveys of the Trust, *National Trust*, 21, 20-1.

Mann, P. (1986) *A Visitor to the British Museum (1982-1983)*, British Museum Occasional Paper 64, British Museum.

Market and Opinion Research International (1982) *Visitors to the Royal Academy*, Market and Opinion Research International.

Mason, T. (1974) The visitors to Manchester Museum - a questionnaire survey, *Museums Journal*, 73(4), 153-56.

Mass Observation (UK) Ltd (1978) *National Trust Visitors Survey Part I.*

McWilliams, B. & Hopwood, J. (1973) The public of Norwich Castle Museum, *Museums Journal*, 72(4), 153-56.

Melton, A.W. (1972) Visitor behaviour in museums: some early research, *Environmental Design Human Factors*, 14(5), 393-403.

Merriman, N. (1989) The social basis of museum and heritage visiting, in Pearce, S. (ed.), *Museum Studies in Material Culture*, Leicester University Press, Leicester, London and New York.

Merriman, N. (1991) *Beyond the Glass Case: The Past, the Heritage and the Public in Britain*, Leicester University Press, Leicester, London and New York.

Middleton, V. (1990) *New Visions for Independent Museums in the UK*, Association of Independent Museums.

Middleton, V. (1991) The future demand for museums 1990-2001, in Kavanagh, G. (ed.), *The museums profession: internal and external relations*, Leicester University Press, Leicester, London and New York, 137-159.

Miles, R.S. (1986) Museum audiences, *International J. of Museum Management and Curatorship*, 5(1), 73-80.

Miles, R.S. & Alt, M.B. (1979) British Museum (NH): a new approach to the visiting public, *Museums Journal*, 78, 158-162.

Mills, S. (1976) Tourism - opportunity or threat, *Museums Association Conference Proceedings*, 30-32.

Millward Brown (1991) *Galleries and Museums Research Digest*, British Market Research Bureau, London.

Morris, B. (1986) The special demands placed upon museums by their users, *Art Gallery and Museums Association of New Zealand (AGMANZ) Journal*, Winter, 3-5.

Munley, M.E. (1992) Back to the future: a call for coordinated research programs in museums, in Museum Education Roundtable, *Patterns in Practice: Selections from the Journal of Museum Education*, Museum Education Roundtable, Washington, DC, 196-203.

Murray, C.H. (1932) How to estimate a museums value, *Museums Journal*, 31(12), 527-31.

Myerscough, J. (1986) *Facts About the Arts 2*, Policy Studies Institute, London.

New York State Museum (1968) *An Evaluation of the Museums Visitors Programme*, New York State Museum, Albany.

Nichols, P. (1991) *Social Survey Methods: A Fieldguide for Development Workers*, Oxfam, Oxford.

Nichols, S. K. (1990) *Visitor Surveys: A User's Manual*, American Association of Museums, Washington DC.

Nissel, M. (1983) *Facts About the Arts*, Policy Studies Institute, London.

O'Hare, M. (1975) Why do people go to museums? The effects of prices and hours on museum utilization, *Museum*, 27(3), 134-46.

Office of Population Censuses Surveys (1979) General household survey 1977, *Leisure*, HMSO, London.

Office of Population Censuses Surveys (1984) *Government Statistics - A Brief Guide to Sources*, Government Statistical Service.

Owen, D.E. (1970) Are national museums in the provinces necessary? A brief survey of Manchester visitors to London museums, *Museums Journal*, 70(1), 29-30.

Prague, R.H. (1974) The university museum visitor survey project, *Curator*, 17(3), 207-12.

Prince, D.R. (1983) Behavioural consistency and visitor attraction, *International J. of Museum Management and Curatorship*, 2(3), 235-47.

Prince, D.R. (1990) Factors influencing museum visits - an empirical evaluation of audience selection, *International J. of Museum Management and Curatorship*, 9(2), 149-168.

Prince, D.R. & Higgins, B. (1992) *The Public View: The Findings of the 1991/92 Study of the Perception and Use of Leicestershire Museums,*

Arts and Records Service, Prince Research Consultants Limited.

Pring, I. (1988) Museums: a market for development, *Interactive Media International*, 2 May, 62-64.

Research Surveys of Great Britain (1991) *RSGB Omnibus Arts Survey: Report on a survey on arts and culutral activities in G.B.*, Arts Council of Great Britain, London.

Robbins, J.E. & Robbins, S.S. (1981) Museum marketing: identification of high, moderate, and low attendee segments, *Journal of the Academy of Marketing Science*, 9(1), 66-75.

Robinson, E.S. (1928) *The Behaviour of the Museum Visitor*, Publication of the American Association of Museums No. 5, Washington, DC.

Ruder, W. (1984) The image in the mirror, *Museum News*, 63(2), 18-19.

Runcorn Development Corporation (1980) *Survey of Visitors to Norton Priory Museum*, RDC.

Ryan, C. (1991) *Recreational tourism - A social science perspective*, Routledge, London.

Scottish Museums Council (1986) *Public Attitudes to Scottish Museums*, Scottish Museums Council.

Scottish Office (1981) *A Survey of Visitors to the Scottish National Museums and Galleries*, Central Research Unit Papers, June.

Screven, C.G. (1979) Bibliography on visitor research, *Museum News*, 58(3), 59-88.

Selwood, S. (1991) *Investigating Audiences: Audience Surveys in the Visual Arts - A Resource Pack for Art Administrators*, Art and Society, London.

Serrell, B. (1977) Survey of visitor attitude and awareness at an aquarium, *Curator*, 20, 48-52.

Serrell, B. (1980) Looking at zoo and aquarium visitors, *Museum News*, 59(3), 36-41.

Settle, R.B., Alrock, P. & Belch, M. (1979) Social class determinants of leisure activity in Wilkie, W. (ed.), *Advances in Consumer Behaviour 6*, Association for Consumer Research, 139-145.

Slattery, M. (1986) *Official Statistics*, Tavistock.

Smyth, M. & Ayton, B. (1985) *Visiting the National Maritime Museum: A Report of a Survey of Visitors*, Office of Population Censuses Survey/HMSO.

Sobel, M.G. (1980) Do the blockbusters change the audience?, *Museums Journal*, 80(1), 25-7.

Stevens, T. (1987) Visitors - who cares? The welcome approach, *Environmental Interpretation*, July, 5.

Stewart, J.H. (1972) A museum and its visitors, *Studies in Adult Education*, 4, 46-56.

Susie Fisher Group (1990) *Bringing History and the Arts to a New Audience: Qualitative Research for the London Borough of Croydon*, The Susie Fisher Group, London.

Touche Ross (1989) *Museum Funding and Services - the Visitor's Perspective*, Report of a survey carried out by Touche Ross Management Consultants.

Trevelyan, V. (ed.) (1991) *"Dingy Places With Different Kinds of Bits": An Attitudes Survey of London Museums Amongst Non-Visitors*, London Museums Service.

Walsh, A. (ed.) (1991) *Insights: Museums, visitors, Attitudes, Expectations - A Focus Group Experiment*, Getty Centre for Education and the Arts and The J. Paul Getty Museum.

Wells, C.H. (1971) *Smithsonian Visitor*, (a survey in the National Museum of History and Technology and the National Museum of Natural History), Smithsonian Institution, Washington, DC.

Wilson, G. (1991) Planning for visitors, *Museum Economics and the Community*, New Research in Museum Studies, Vol. 2, Athlone, London, 89-117.

Wilson, G. & Worcester, R.M. (1988) The role of research in the planning process of the Royal Armouries, *Museums Journal*, 88(1), 37-40.

Wood, R. (1990) Museum learning: a family focus, *Journal of Education in Museums*, 11, 20-23.

Zygulski, K. (1974) *Reception of Paintings in Polish Museums (a qualitative analysis)*,, Polish National Committee of ICOM (International Council of Museums), Poznan-Warsaw.

Zygulski, K. (1977) *The Public in the Martyrdom Museum in Oswiecim (a sociological study)*, Polish National Committee of ICOM (International Council of Museums), Poznan-Warsaw.

6.3 Language & Texts

Barrass, R. (1978) *Scientists Must Write*, Science Paperbacks, London.

Bitgood, S. (1989) Deadly sins revisited: a review of the exhibit label literature, *Visitor Behaviour*, 4(3), 4-13.

Bitgood, S. (1989) The role of evaluation in the development of exhibit labels, *Visitor Behaviour*, 4(3), 16.

Bloch, M.J. (1968) Labels, legends and legibility, *Museum News*, 47, 13-17.

Borun, M. & Miller, M. (1980) To label or not to label?, *Museum News*, 58, 64-7.

Carter, J. (1993) How old is this text?, *Environmental Interpretation*, 8(2), 10-11.

Cohen, D.F. (1990) Words to live by, *Museum News*, 69(3), 76-80.

Cohen, D.F. (1993) Matter of interpretation (labels), *Museum News*, 72(6),

14-16.

Conway, M.F. (1972) Exhibit labelling: another alternative, *Curator*, 15, 161-66.

Coxall, H. (1990) Museum text as mediated message, *Women Heritage and Museums (Wham), Newsletter*, 14, 15-21.

Coxall, H. (1991) How language means: an alternative view of museums text', in Kavanagh, G. (ed.), *Museum Languages: Objects and Texts*, Leicester University Press, Leicester, London and New York, 83-99.

Coxall, H. (1991) Museum text: accessibility and relevance, *Journal of Education in Museums*, 12, 9-10.

Coxall, H. (1991) The Spertus Museum of Judaica: Chicago, in Pearce, S.M. (ed.), *Objects of Knowledge*, New Research in Museum Studies, Vol. 1, Athlone, London, 211-214.

Coxall, H. (1993) Writing between the lines, *Environmental Interpretation*, 8(2), 5-7.

Devenish, D. (1990) Labelling in museum display, *International J. of Museum Management and Curatorship*, 9(1), 63-72.

Ekarv, M. (1987) Combating redundancy - writing texts for exhibitions, *Exhibitions in Sweden*, 27/28, 1-7.

Fairclough, N. (1989) *Language and Power*, Longman, London and New York.

Fairclough, N. (ed.) (1992) *Critical Language Awareness*, Longman, London and New York.

Fruitman, M.P. & Dubro, L.S. (1979) Writing effective labels, *Museum News*, 57, 57-61.

Gowers, Sir E. (1977) *The Complete Plain Words*, Penguin.

Hartley, J. (1978) *Designing Instructional Text*, Kegan Paul, London.

Holmes, J. (1992) *An Introduction to Sociolinguistics*, Longman, London.

Hull, T.G. & Jones, T. (1961) *Scientific Exhibits*, Springfield, Illinois.

Kanel, V. & Tamir, P. (1991) Different labels - different learnings, *Curator*, 34(1), 18-30.

Kress, G. & Hodge, R. (1979) *Language As Ideology*, Routledge and Kegan Paul, London.

Lewin, R.A. (1975) Labelling, *Museum*, 27, 90-1.

McManus, P.M. (1990) Watch your language! People do read labels, in Serrell, B. (ed.), *What Research Says About Learning in Science Museums*, Association of Science - Technology Centres, Washington DC, 4-6.

Miller, J.R. & Kintsch, W. (1980) Readability and recall of short prose passages: a theoretical analysis, *Journal of Experimental Psychology: Human Learning and Memory*, 6, 335-354.

Miller, S. (1990) Labels, *Curator*, 33(2), 85-9.

Patten, L.H. (1982/83) Education by design, *ICOM (International Council of Museums) Education*, 10, 6-7.

Punt, B. (1989) *Doing It Right: A Workbook for Improving Exhibit Labels*, Brooklyn Children's Museum.

Rickards, J.P. & Denner, P.R. (1978) Inserted questions as a guide to reading text, *Instructional Science*, 7, 313-346.

Serrell, B. (1979) A plan for writing interpretive signs, *Curator*, 22(4), 299-302.

Serrell, B. (1983) *Making Exhibit Labels: AStep-By-Step Guide*, American Association for State and Local History, Nashville, Tennessee.

Serrell, B. (1988) Making better layered labels, AAZPA Annual Conference Proceedings.

Sherman, J.L. (1976) Contextual information and prose comprehension, *Journal of Reading Behaviour*, 8, 369-379.

Shettel, H.H. (1975) *A Flesch Readability Analysis of the Labels of the Contemporary African Art Exhibition*, American institute of Research, Washington, DC.

Sorsby, B.D. & Horne, S.D. (1980) The readability of museum labels, *Museums Journal*, 80(3), 157-159.

Spender, D. (1980) *Man Made Language*, Routledge and Kegan Paul, London.

Various (1989) Exhibit labelling (special issue), *Visitor Behavior*, 4(3).

Weiner, G. (1963) Why Johnny can't read labels, *Curator*, 6, 143-56.

Williams, L.A. (1960) Writing design and preparation, *Curator*, 3, 26-42.

Wilson, D.W. & Medina, D. (1972) *Exhibit Labels: A Consideration of the Content*, American Association for State and Local History (AASLH), Nashville, Tennessee, Technical Leaflet 60.

Wilson, D.W. & Medina, D. (1976) Text panels and labels, *Communicating With the Museum Visitor*, Royal Ontario Museum, Toronto, 131-39.

6.4 Exhibition Theory and Practice

Airlie, S. (1985) The Emperors warriors, *Museums Journal*, 85, 144-5.

Alt, M.B. & Griggs, S.A. (1984) Psychology and the museum visitor, in Thompson, J.M.A. *et al. (ed.)*, *Manual of Curatorship*, Butterworths, London, 386-393.

Andrews, M. (1986) Museum design - a team effort, *Museums Journal*, 86(3), 105-8.

Anon. (1993) A writing checklist, *Environmental Interpretation*, 8(2), 21.

Barbean, L. & Swain, R. (1982) Exhibition policy and programmes, in Johnson, M. & Smith, F.K. (eds.), *Art Gallery Handbook*, Ontario Association of Art Galleries, Toronto, 97-102.

Baynes, K. (1992) Lessons from the Art Machine, *Museum Development*, February, 29-39.

Becket, McD. (1972) The total design concept, *Museum News*, 51(1), 15-16.

Belcher, M. (1970) The role of the designer in the museum, *Museums Journal*, 70(2), 63-6.

Belcher, M. (1972) Second design conference, *Museums Journal*, 72(2), 58-63.

Belcher, M. (1978) Chairman's address, *Designers/Interpreters Newsletter*, 2(1), 3-5.

Belcher, M. (1983) A decade of museum design and interpretation: a personal view, *Museums Journal*, 83(1), 53-60.

Belcher, M. (1991) *Exhibitions in Museums*, Leicester University Press, Leicester, London and New York.

Belcher, M. (1992) Communicating through museum exhibitions, in Thompson, J.M.A. *et al. (eds.)*, *Manual of Curatorship*, Butterworth, London, 649-659.

Bell, J. (1991) Planning for interactive galleries, *Muse*, Spring, 24-29.

Benes, J. (1983) Variations in display methods, *Museum*, 35, 102-7.

Bennet, T. (1988) The exhibitionary complex, *New Formations*, 4, 73-102.

Bergman, E. (1971) Exhibits that flow, *Curator*, 14(4), 278-86.

Bergman, E. (1976) Exhibits, *Curator*, 19(2), 157-61.

Bergman, E. (1977) Making exhibits - a reference file, *Curator*, 20(3), 227-37.

Bertram, B. (1982) *Display Technology for Small Museums*, Museums Association of Australia (NSW Branch) and Division of Cultural Activities, Premiers Department, Sydney.

Bevleant, A. (1990) The museum of art as a participatory environment, *Curator*, 33(1), 31-9.

Boyer, P. (1982) Real things and short term displays: a museum survival course, *Kalori*, 59 & 60, 12-15.

Brain, C.K. (1979) The narrative concept in museum display, *SAMAB: Southern African Museums Association Bulletin*, 13(3), 90-4.

Buckland, G. (1978) Problems associated with temporary displays, *SAMAB: Southern African Museums Association Bulletin*, 13(1), 2-4.

Burns, W.A. (1969) Museum exhibition: do-it-yourself or commercial, *Curator*, 12, 160-67.

Center for Environmental Interpretation (1983) *Design, interpretation and Computers*, Centre for Environmental Interpretation, Manchester.

Chabot, N. J. (1990) A man called Lucy: self reflection in a museum exhibit, in Baker, F. and Thomas, J. (eds.), *Writing the past in the present*, St. David's University College, Lampeter, 138-142.

Chadbourne, C. (1991) A tool for storytelling, *Museum News*, 70(2), 39-43.

Ciulla, V. & Montgomery, C.F. (1977) The curator and the designer, *Museum News*, 55(4), 31-7.

Clearwater, W. (1980) How to make mannequins, *History News*, 35(12), 36-9.

Coen, L.H. & Wright, A.G. (1975) The interpretive function in museum work, *Curator*, 18(4), 281-86.

Conway, W. (1972) Increasing the life of graphic materials, *Museum News*, 50, 28-31.

Coutts, H. (1986) Profile of a blockbuster, *Museums Journal*, 86, 23-26.

Curtis, J.C. (1978) Clio's dilemma: to be a muse or to be amusing, in Quimby, I.M.G. (ed.), *Material Culture and the Study of American Life*, Norton, New York, 201-18.

Davidson, B., Heald, C.D. & Hein, G.E. (1991) Increased exhibit accessibility through multisensory interaction, *Curator*, 34(4), 273-290.

Davis, G. & Hurt, W. (1973) Designs of modular exhibit units, *Curator*, 16(2), 158-69.

Dawson, J. (1981) *Prints and Printmaking*, Phaidon Press.

De Borhegyi, S.F. (1978) Museum brainstorming - a creative approach to exhibit planning, *Curator*, 21(3), 217-24.

Dean, D. (1994) *Museum Exhibition: Theory and Practice*, Routledge, London.

Densley, M. (1978) Report of designers/interpreters in museums, *Museums Journal*, 78(3), 131-32.

Diamond, J., Bond, A. & Hirumi, A. (1989) Desert explorations - a video disc exhibit designed for flexibility, *Curator*, 32(3), 161-173.

Eagar, M. (1961) Light typing on dark backgrounds, *Museums Journal*, 61, 180-83.

Eden, P. (1978) The listening post, a new audio guide device, *Museums Journal*, 78, 119-22.

Elliott, W.M. (1975) Design briefing procedures, *Area Service Magazine*, 27, 19-22.

Floyd, C. (1981) Exhibit designers talk about their work, *History News*, 36(3), 40-3.

Fowler, H.W. (1983) A bluegrass blockbuster, *Museum News*, 61(4), 19-25.

Frostick, E. (1991) Worth a Hull lot more, *Museums Journal*, 91(2), 33-5.

Gaiber, M. (1984) Cooperation within museum work: the team approach to exhibition development, *Museum Studies Journal*, 1(3), 20-22.

Gardner, J. (1965) Communicating ideas, *Museums Journal*, 65(2), 131-36.

Gatacre, E.V. (1976) The limits of professional design, *Museums Journal*, 76(3), 93-9.

Gleadowe, T. (1977) *Organising Art Exhibitions*, Arts Council of Great Britain, London.

Hall, M. (1987) *On Display: a Design Grammar for Museum Exhibitions*, Lund Humphries, London.

Hancocks, A. (1987) Museum exhibition as a tool of social awareness, *Curator*, 30(3), 181-192.

Hartman, S.G. (1976) A design for a short-term display system, *Curator*, 19(2), 130-36.

Hayward, G.D. & Larkin, J.W. (1983) Evaluating visitor experiences and exhibit effectiveness at Old Stanbridge Village, *Museum Studies Journal*, 1(2), 42-51.

Hebditch, M. (1970) Briefing the designer, *Museums Journal*, 70(2), 67-8.

Holleman, W. (1981) Some considerations in the design and planning of exhibits, *SAMAB: Southern African Museums Association Bulletin*, 14(6), 247-56.

Howell, D.B. (1971) A network system for the planning, designing, construction and installation of exhibits, *Curator*, 14(2), 100-08.

Jenkins, I. (1986) Greek and Roman Life at the BM, *Museums Journal*, 86, 67-69.

Jones, J. (1992) Museum computers: design innovations, *Curator*, 35(3), 225-236.

Karp, I. & Lavine, S.D. (eds.) (1991) *Exhibiting Cultures, the Poetics and Politics of Museum Display*, Smithsonian Institution Press, Washington DC.

Kelly, F.S. (1973) Setting the stage for exhibits, *Museum News*, 52(1), 42-5.

Kentley, E. & Neagus, D. (1989) *Writing on the Wall: A Guide for Presenting Exhibition Text*, National Maritime Museum, London.

Kirrane, S. and Hayes, F. (1993) Do it yourself, *Museums Journal*, 93(2), 28-30.

Klein, L. (1986) *Exhibits: Planning and Design*, Madison Square Press, New York.

Lane, M. (ed.) (1981) Advice to the beginning designer: a symposium, *Curator*, 24(3), 203-12.

Little, D.B. (1967) The misguided mission, a disenchanted view of art museums today, *Curator*, 10(3), 221-26.

Loughbrough, B. (1982) The Canal Museum of Nottingham; setting up the display: the design brief, *Museums Journal*, 82(1), 5-8.

Lyons, D.J. & Allen-Grimes, A.W. (1985) A new labelling method, *Curator*, 28, 85-86.

Matthews, G. (1991) *Museums and Art Galleries: A Design and Development Guide*, Butterworth, London.

Mayo, R.B. (1971) A strategy for exhibitions, *Museum News*, 49, 30-3.

McCabe, G. (1973) Circulating temporary exhibitions, *Museums Journal*, 72(4), 159-60.

McManus, P.M. (1989) Oh, yes, they do: how museum visitors read labels and interact with exhibit texts, *Curator*, 32(3), 174-189.

Meggs, P.B. (1983) *A History of Graphic Design*, Viking Art History.

Miles, R.S. (1985) Exhibitions: Management, for a change, in Cossons, N. (ed.), *The Management of Change in Museums*, National Maritime Museum, London, 31-34.

Miles, R.S. (1986) Lessons in Human Biology testing a theory of exhibit design, *International J. of Museum Management and Curatorship*, 5, 227-240.

Miles, R.S. (1993) Exhibiting learning, *Museums Journal*, 93(5) 27-28.

Miles, R.S., Alt, M.B. & Gosling, D.C. (1988) *The Design of Educational Exhibits*, 2nd edition, Routledge.

Miles, R.S. & Tout, A.F. (1979) Outline of a technology for effective science exhibits, *Special Papers in Palaeontology*, 22, 209-24.

Millard, J. (1992) Art history for all the family, *Museums Journal*, 92(2), 32-33.

Miller, L.G. (1963) The industrial designer: new member of the museum team, *Curator*, 6(2), 187-90.

Milwaukee Public Museum (1979) *Not Built in a Day*, Milwaukee Public Museum, Milwaukee.

Molson, K.M. & Post, J.J. (1966) Some methods of presenting exhibit information at the National Aviation Museum, *Curator*, 9, 146-50.

Murray, J. (1991) Costume display in 10 easy steps - a guide for the busy curator, *Scottish Museum News*, Winter, 17-18.

Neal, A. (1976) *Exhibits for the Small Museum - A Handbook*, American Association for State and Local History (AASLH), Nashville, Tennessee.

Neal, A. (1977) *Labels Exhibits for the small museum*, American Association for State and Local History (AASLH), Nashville, Tennessee, 11-16.

Nicholson, T.D. (1973) The Hall of Man in Africa at the American Museum of Natural History, *Curator*, 16(1), 5-24.

North, F.J. (1957) *Museum Labels*, Handbook for Curators, Museums Association, London.

O'Neill, M. (1990) Cheap and cheerful: techniques for temporary displays, *Scottish Museum News*, Spring, 17-19.

Olofsson, U.K. (1973) Temporary and travelling exhibitions, *Museums, Imagination and Education*, Museums and Monuments Series, No 15, UNESCO, Paris.

Ontario Ministry of Citizenship and Culture (nd) *Developing an Exhibition Policy*, Museum Notes for Community Museums in Ontario, 9, Ministry of Citizenship and Culture.

Osborn, D.J. (1971) Dressing the naked cage, *Curator*, 16(3), 194-99.

Palmer, A.M. (1978) Through the glass case: the curator and the object, in Quimby, I.M.G. (ed.), *Material and Culture and the Study of American Life*, Norton, New York, 219-44.

Parker, A.C. (1966) *A Manual for History Museums*, AMS Press inc., New York.

Parr, A.E. (1958) A time and place for experimentation in museum design, *Curator*, 1(4), 36-40.

Parr, A.E. (1962) Some basic problems of visual education by means of exhibits, *Curator*, 5(1), 36-44.

Patten, L. H. (1982/3) Education by design, *ICOM (International Council of Museums) Education*, 10, 6-7.

Penny, L.J. (1978) Design and aesthetics, *SAMAB: Southern African Museums Association Bulletin*, 13(1), 22-4.

Prince, D.R. & Schadla-Hall, R.T. (1985) The image of the museum: a case study of Kingston upon Hull, *Museums Journal*, 85(1), 39-45.

Prochnak, M. (1990) Multimedia is the Message, *Museums Journal*, 90(8), 25-27.

Reynolds, L. (1977) Directional signing and labelling in museums, *Museum Assistants Group (MAG) Transactions*, 14, 11-16.

Reynolds, L. & Spencer, H. (1977) *Directional Signing and Labelling in Libraries and Museums: A Review of Current Theory and Practice*, Readability of Print Research Unit, Royal College of Art, London.

Riksutstallningar (1976) *Going to Exhibitions*, Swedish Travelling Exhibitions, Sweden.

Robinowitz, R. (1991) Exhibit as canvas, *Museum News*, 70(2), 34-7.

Rolfe, W.D. (1969) A rapid method for producing enlarged exhibit labels, *Museums Journal*, 68, 162-64.

Royal Ontario Museum (1976) *Communicating With the Museum Visitor: Guidelines for Planning*, Royal Ontario Museum, Toronto.

Rudkin, E.B. (1979) A sign for all seasons: from writers clipboard to zoo exhibit, *Curator*, 22(4), 303-09.

Schadla-Hall, R.T. & Davidson, J. (1982) Its very grand but who's it for? - Designing archaeology galleries, *Museums Journal*, 82(3), 171-75.

Schaeffer, M.W. (1965) The display function of the small museum, *Curator*, 8(2), 103-18.

Schlereth, T.J. (1978) It wasn't that simple, *Museum News*, 56(3), 36-44.

Schlereth, T.J. (1980) Collecting ideas and artifacts: common problems of history museums and history texts, in Schlereth, T.J. (ed.), *Artifacts and the American Past*, American Association for State and Local History (AASLH), Nashville, Tennessee, 207-21.

Schouten, F. (1983) Target groups and displays in museums, *Reinwardt Studies in Museology, 1. Exhibition Design As an Educational Tool*, 3-11.

Schouten, F. (1987) Psychology and exhibit design: a note, *International J. of Museum Management and Curatorship*, 6(3), 259-62.

Schroeder, F. (1976) Designing your exhibits: seven ways to view an artifact, *History News*, 31(11), American Association of State and Local History (AASLH), Nashville, Tennessee, Technical Leaflet 91.

Screven, C. G. (1986) Exhibitions and information centres: some principles and approaches, *Curator*, 29(2), 109-137.

Seale, W. (1979) *Recreating the Historic House Interior*, American Association for State and Local History (AASLH), Nashville,

Tennessee.

Serrell, B. (1983) *Making Exhibit Labels - A Step by Step Guide*, American Association for State and Local History (AASLH), Nashville, Tennessee.

Silver, S. (1982) Almost everyone loves a winner - a designer looks at the blockbuster era, *Museum News*, 61(2), 24-35.

Silverman, L. (1991) Tearing down walls, *Museum News*, 70(6), 62-64.

Skramstad, H.K., Jnr. (1978) Interpreting material culture: a view from the other side of the glass, in Quimby, I.M.G. (ed.), *Material Culture and the Study of American Life*, Norton, New York.

Society of Industrial Artists and Designers (1980) *Working With Your Designer - A General Guide to a Designers Service*, Society of Industrial Artists and Designers (SIAD), London.

Society of Industrial Artists and Designers (1981) *Working Together - Guidelines for Designers Working With Other Professionals*, Society of Industrial Artists and Designers (SIAD), London.

Stansfield, G. (1986) Nature on Display: Trends in Natural History Exhibitions, *Museums Journal*, 86, 97-103.

Tyler, D. & Dickenson, V. (1977) *A Handbook for the Travelling Exhibitionist*, Canadian Museums Association, Ottawa.

UNESCO (1963) *Temporary and Travelling Exhibitions*, (bibliography) Museums and Monuments Series, No 10, UNESCO, Paris.

Vandell, K.D., Barry, T.E., Starling, J.D. & Seid, B. (1979) The arts and the local economy: the impact of "Pompeii AD 79", *Curator*, 22(3), 199-215.

Velarde, G. (1976) An exhibition is as good as, *Report of Meeting of ICOM (International Council of Museums) Natural History Committee*, Ottawa.

Velarde, G. (1988) Directions for Designers, *Museums Journal*, 84(4), 181-184.

Velarde, G. (1992) Exhibition design, in Thompson, J.M.A. *et al.* (eds.), *Manual of Curatorship*, Butterworth, London, 660-669.

Ward, P.R. (1979) *In Support of Difficult Shapes*, British Columbia Provincial Museum, Victoria.

West, M. (1982) The communications dilemma - trends in museum display techniques, *Kalori*, 59/60, 63-4.

Wetmore, R. (1965) Curator and designer, *Museums Journal*, 65(1), 48-53.

Wetmore, R. (ed.) (1972) Designers in the museum, *The Designer*, 3-14.

Wetzel, J. (1972) An interview with Paul J. Smith, *Museum News*, 50(6), 15-19.

Wetzel, J. (1972) Three steps to exhibit success, *Museum News*, 50(6), 20-1.

Witteborg, L.P. (1958) Design standards in museum exhibits, *Curator*, 1(1), 29-41.

Witteborg, L.P. (1983) Exhibit planning, *History News*, 38(6), 21-4.

Witteborg, L.P. (1992) *Good Show! a Practical Guide for Temporary Exhibitions*, Smithsonian Institution Travelling Exhibition Service, Washington DC.

Works, D. (1991) The good, the bad and the unknown: computers in exhibits, *Muse*, Spring, 40-45.

Yorks & Humberside Federation of Museums & Art Galleries (1980) *Design in Museums*, YHFMAG, Leeds.

6.5 Exhibition Evaluation

Alt, M.B. & Morris, R.G.M. (1979) The human biology exhibition at the Natural History Museum, *Bulletin of the British Psychological Society*, 32, 273-78.

Alt, M.B. & Shaw, K.M. (1984) Characteristisation of ideal museum exhibits, *British Journal of Psychology*, 75, 25-36.

Alter, P. (1988) Exhibit evaluation: taking account of human factors, *Curator*, 31(3), 167-177.

Ambrose, T.M. (ed.) (1986) *The American Museum Experience: In Search of Excellence*, HMSO/Scottish Museums Council.

Anon. (1990) Monitoring and evaluation: the techniques, *Environmental Interpretation*, 7, 16-17.

Arnell, V., Hammer, I. & Nylof, G. (1980) *Going to Exhibitions*, Riksutstallningar, Swedish travelling exhibition, Stockholm.

Badman, T. (1990) Small scale evaluation, *Environmental Interpretation*, 7, 20-21.

Bitgood, S. *et al.* (1986) Formative evaluation of case exhibit, *Curator*, 29(2), 85-92.

Blackmore, S., Lee, T.R. & Turnbull, A.M. (1975) *Exhibitions: An Annotated Bibliography*, Department of Psychology, University of Surrey.

Borun, M. (1977) *Measuring the Immeasurable - A Pilot Study of Museum Effectiveness*, Association of Science - Technology Centers, Washington, DC.

Borun, M. (1977) Exhibit evaluation: an introduction, *The Visitor and the Museum*, The 1977 Program Planning Committee of the American Association of Museums, Seattle, Washington.

Borun, M. (1989) Assessing the impact, *Museum News*, 68(3), 36-40.

Borun, M. & Miller, M. (1980) *Whats in a Name: A Study of the Effectiveness of Explanatory Labels in a Science Museum*, Franklin Institute Science Museum and Planetarium & Association of Science-

Technology Centers, Washington, DC.

Braverman, B. (1988) Empowering visitors: focus group interviews for art museums, *Curator*, 31(1), 43-52.

Burcaw, G.E. (1980) Can history be too lively?, *Museums Journal*, 80(1), 5-7.

Burns, W.A. (1969) Museum exhibition: do-it-yourself or commercial?, *Curator*, 12, 160-67.

Cohen, M.S. (1974) *The State of the Art of Museum Visitor Orientation - A Survey of Selected Institutions*, Office of Museum Programs, Smithsonian Institution, Washington DC.

De Borhegyi, S.F. (1964) Some thoughts on anthropological exhibits in natural history museums in the United States, *Curator*, 7, 121-27.

Diamond, J. (1986) The behaviour of family groups in museums, *Curator*, 29(2), 139-154.

Eason, L.P. & Linn, M.C. (1976) Evaluation of the effectiveness of participatory exhibits, *Curator*, 19(1), 45-62.

Elliott, P. & Loomis, R.J. (1975) *Studies of Visitor Behaviour in Museums and Exhibitions - An Annotated Bibliography*, Office of Museum Programs, Smithsonian Institution, Washington DC.

Falk, J.H. (1983) A cross-cultural investigation of the novel field trip phenomenon: National Museum of Natural History, New Delhi, *Curator*, 26(4), 315-23.

Falk, J.H. *et al.* (1985) Auditing visitor behaviour, *Curator*, 24(4), 249-258.

Fruitman, M.P. & Du Bro, L.S. (1979) Writing effective labels, *Museum News*, 57(3), 57-61.

Gardner, T. (1986) Learning from listening - museums improve their effectiveness through visitor studies, *Museum News*, 64(3), 40-82.

Greenglass, D & Abbey, D.S. (1981) An analysis of visitors responses to objects in a travelling exhibition, *Curator*, 24(3), 181-88.

Griggs, S.A. (1981) Formative evaluation of the exhibits at the British Museum (Natural History), *Curator*, 24(3), 189-201.

Griggs, S.A. (1983) Orientating visitors within a thematic display, *International J. of Museum Management and Curatorship*, 2, 119-34.

Griggs, S.A. (1983) The predictive validity of formative evaluation of exhibits, *Museum Studies Journal*, 31-41.

Griggs, S.A. (1984) Evaluating exhibitions, in Thompson, J.M.A. *et al.* (eds.), *Manual of Curatorship*, Butterworth, London, 412-23.

Griggs, S.A. (1990) Perceptions of traditional versus new style exhibitions at the Natural History Museum, London, *ILVS Review: A Journal of Visitor Behavior*, 1(2), 78-90.

Griggs, S.A. (1992) *Evaluating Museum Displays*, Committee of Area Museum Councils Museum Factsheet, Committee of Area Museum Councils, Cirencester.

Griggs, S.A. & Hays-Jackson, K. (1983) Visitors perceptions of cultural institutions, *Museums Journal*, 83(2/3), 121-25.

Harlen, W., Van Der Waal, A. & Russell, T. (1986) *Evaluation of the Pilot Phase of the Liverpool Interactive Technology Centre*, Centre for Research and Development in Primary School Science and Technology, Department of Education, Liverpool University.

Harvey, L. & MacDonald, M. (1993) *Doing Sociology*, MacMillan.

Hayward, D.G. & Larkin, J.W. (1983) Evaluating visitor experiences and exhibit effectiveness at Old Stourbridge Village, *Museum Studies Journal*, 1(1), 42-51.

Helsby, D. (1990) Putting people into boxes can be useful, *Environmental Interpretation*, 7, 12-13.

Herbert, M.E. (1981) The water pushes it and the wheel turns it, *Curator*, 24(1), 5-18.

Hicks, E.C. (1986) An artful science: a conversation about exhibit evaluation, *Museum News*, 64(3), 32-39.

Hood, M. (1986) Getting started in audience research, *Museum News*, 64(3), 25-31.

Jarrett, J.E. (1986) Learning from developmental testing of exhibits, *Curator*, 29(4), 295-306.

Kissiloff, W. (1969) How to use mixed media in exhibits, *Curator*, 12, 83-95.

Kool, R. (1985) The effect of label design on exhibit effectiveness, *Muse*, 3(2), 32-7.

Koran, J.J. *et al.* (1986) The relationship of age, sex and holding power with two types of science exhibits, *Curator*, 29(3), 227-236.

Korn, R. (1989) Introduction to evaluation: theory and methodology, in Berry, N. and Mayer, S. (eds.), *Museum education, history, theory and practice*, National Art Education Association, USA, 219-238.

Lakota, R.A. (1973) *The Efficacy of Three Visitor Learning Support Systems in an Art Museum*, Office of Museum Programs, Smithsonian Institution, Washington DC.

Lakota, R.A. (1976) Techniques to improve exhibit effectiveness in Royal Ontario Museum, *Rom Communicating With the Museum Visitor*, Royal Ontario Museum, Toronto, 245-79.

Landay, J. & Bridge, R.G. (1982) Video as wall panel displays - an experiment in museum learning, *Curator*, 25(1), 41-56.

Leavitt, T.W. (1967) The need for critical standards in history museum exhibits: a case in point, *Curator*, 10(2), 91-4.

Lehmbruck, M. (1974) Psychology: perception and behaviour, *Museum*, 27, 191-204.

Linn, M.C. (1976) Exhibit evaluation - informed decision making, *Curator*, 19, 291-302.

Lockett, C. (1991) Ten years of exhibit evaluation at the Royal Ontario Museum (1980-1990), *ILVS Review: a Journal of Visitor Behavior*, 2(1),

19-47.

Loomis, R.J. (1987) *Museum Visitor Evaluation: New Tool for Management,* American Association for State and Local History, Nashville, Tennessee.

Marsh, J.S. (1986) *National and Cultural Heritage Interpretation Evaluation,* Interpretation Canada, Ottawa.

McNamara, P.A. (1988) Visitor-tested exhibits, in Bitgood,S., Roper, J.T. Jr. and Benefield, A. (eds.), *Visitor Studies -1988:Theory, Research and Practice - Proceedings of the First Annual Visitor Studies Conference,* Centre for Social Design, Jacksonville, Alabama, 150-154.

Melton, A.W. (1935) *Problems of Installation in Museums of Art,* American Association of Museums, New Series No 14, Washington, DC.

Miles, R.S. (1984) Assessing the effectiveness of exhibits, *Museums Association Conference Proceedings,* 11-12.

Miles, R.S. & Alt, M.B. (1979) British Museum (Natural History): a new approach to the visiting public, *Museums Journal,* 78, 158-62.

Miles, R.S. & Tout, A.F. (1978) Human biology and the new exhibition scheme in the British Museum (Natural History), *Curator,* 21, 36-50.

Miles, R.S. & Tout, A.F. (1991) Impact of research on the approach to the visiting public at the Natural History Museum, London, *International J.of Science Education,* 13(5), 534-549.

Munley, M.E. (1986) Asking the right questions: evaluation and the museum mission, *Museum News,* 64(3), 18-23.

Nicol, E. (1969) *The Development of Validated Museum Exhibits,* Bureau of Research, United States Department of Health, Education and Welfare, Washington, DC.

Parsons, L.A. (1965) Systematic testing of display techniques for an anthropological exhibit, *Curator,* 8, 167-89.

Peirson Jones, J. (ed.) (1993) *Gallery 33: A Visitor Survey,* Department of Archaeology and Ethnograhy, Birmingham Museums and Art Gallery.

Porter, J. (1982) Mobile exhibition services in Great Britain: a survey of their practice and potential, *Museums Journal,* 82(3), 135-37.

Porter, M.C.D. (1938) *Behaviour of the Average Visitor in the Peabody Museum of Natural History, Yale University,* American Association of Museums, New Series No 16, Washington, DC.

Prince, D.R. (1982) Countryside interpretation: a cognitive evaluation, *Museums Journal,* 82(3), 165-70.

Prince, D.R. (1992) Approaches to summative evaluation, in Thompson J.M.A. *et al. (eds.), Manual of Curatorship,* Butterworth, London, 690-701.

Richeson, D.R. (ed.) (1979) *Western Canadian History: Museum Interpretations,* Mercury Series History Division Paper No 27, National Museum of Man, Ottawa.

Rider, P.E. (1981) *The History of Atlantic Canada,* Mercury Series History

Division Paper No 32, National Museum of Man, Ottawa.

Robinson, E.S. (1925) *The Behaviour of the Museum Visitor*, American Association of Museums, New Series No 5, Washington, DC.

Royal Ontario Museum (1976) *ROM Communicating With the Museum Visitor*, Royal Ontario Museum, Toronto.

Rubenstein, R. (1988) The use of focus groups in audience research, *Visitor Studies -1988: Theory, Research and Practice - Proceedings of the First Annual Visitor Studies Conference*, 180-188.

Schlereth, T.J. (1980) A perspective on criticism. Guidelines for history museum exhibition reviews, *History News*, 35(8), 18.

Schlereth, T.J. (1980) American material culture technique: historical museum exhibit review, in Schlereth, T.J. (ed.), *Artifacts and the American Past*, American Association for State and Local History (AASLH), Nashville, Tennessee, 233-37.

Screven, C.G. (1976) Exhibit evaluation: a goal-referenced approach, *Curator*, 19(4), 271-290.

Screven, C.G. (1978) A critical look at a critical look: the response to Alt's critique of Shettel's work, *Curator*, 20(4), 329-46.

Screven, C.G. (1986) Exhibitions and information centres: some principles and approaches, *Curator*, 24(2), 109-138.

Screven, C.G. (1988) Formative evaluation: conceptions and misconceptions, in Bitgood,S., Roper, J.T. Jr. and Benefield, A. (eds.), *Visitor Studies -1988: Theory, Research and Practice - Proceedings of the First Annual Visitor Studies Conference*, Centre for Social Design, Jacksonville, Alabama, 73-81.

Screven, C.G. & Giraudy, D. (1991) The Musee Picasso-Antibes Project, *ILVS Review: A Journal of Visitor Behavior*, 2(1), 116-117.

Shettel, H.H. (1977) Exhibits - art form or educational medium, *Museum News*, 52(1), 32-41.

Shettel, H.H. *et al.* (1968) *Strategies for Determining Exhibit Effectiveness*, American Institutes for Research, Pittsburgh.

Shettel, H.H. & Reilly, P.C. (1965) *An Evaluation of the Existing Criteria for Judging the Quality of Science Exhibits*, American Institutes for Research, Pittsburgh.

Sorsby, B.D. & Horne, S.D. (1980) The readability of museum labels, *Museums Journal*, 80(3), 157-60.

Stansfield, G. (1981) *Effective Interpretive Exhibitions*, Countryside Commission, Cheltenham.

Stevenson, A. & Bryden, M. (1991) The National Museums of Scotland's 1990 Discovery Room: an evaluation, *Museum Management & Curatorship*, 10, 24-36.

Stevenson, J. (1991) The long-term impact of interactive exhibits, *International J.of Science Education*, 13(5), 521-531.

Taylor, J.B. (1963) *Science on Display: A Study of the United States Science*

Exhibit, Seattle Worlds Fair, 1962, Institute for Sociological Research, University of Washington, Seattle.

Wedge, E.F. (1976) *Nefertiti Graphiti - Comment on an Exhibition*, Brooklyn Museum, New York.

Weiss, R. & Boutourline, S. (1963) The communication value of exhibits, *Museum News*, 42(3), 23-7.

Wolf, R.L. (1980) A naturalistic view of evaluation, *Museum News*, 58(4), 39-45.

Wolf, R.L. (1984) Enhancing museum leadership through evaluation, *Museum Studies Journal*, 1(3), 31-3.

Wolf, R.L. *et al.* (1979) *East Side West Side, Straight Down the Middle - a Study of Visitor Perceptions of Our Changing Land, the Bicentennial Exhibit, National Museum of Natural History*, Office of Museum Programs, Smithsonian Institution, Washington, DC.

Wolf, R.L. *et al.* (1979) *The Pause That Refreshes: A Study of Visitor Reactions to the Discovery Corners in the National Museum of History and Technology, Smithsonian Institution*, Office of Museum Programs, Smithsonian Institution, Washington DC.

Wolf, R.L. & Tymitz, B.C. (1977) *Things to Consider When Evaluating Museum Programs*, Indiana Center for Evaluation.

Wolf, R.L. & Tymitz, B.C. (1978) *Whatever Happened to the Giant Wombat: An Investigation of the Impact of the Ice Age Mammals and Emergence of Man Exhibit, National Museum of Natural History, Smithsonian Institution*, Office of Museum Programs, Smithsonian Institution, Washington, DC.

Wolf, R.L. & Tymitz, B.C. (1979) *Do Giraffes Ever Sit? A Study of Visitor Perceptions at the National Zoological Park, Smithsonian Institution*, Office of Museum Programs, Smithsonian Institution, Washington, DC.

Wolf, R.L. & Tymitz, B.C. (nd) *A Preliminary Guide for Conducting Naturalistic Evaluation in Studying Museum Environments*, Office of Museum Programs, Smithsonian Institution, Washington, DC.

Wright, S. (1990) Your visitors have something to say, *Environmental Interpretation*, July, 8-10.

Yalow, E.S. *et al.* (1980) Improving museums through evaluation, *Curator*, 23(4), 275-86.

Zyskowski, G. (1983) A review of literature on the evaluation of museum programs, *Curator*, 26(2), 121-28.

7 Museum Education

7.1 Educational Role of Museums

Adams, C. (ed.) (1981) History and social sciences teachers centre review: visits and field studies, *Clio*, Inner London Education Authority, Spring.

Adams, G. (1984) Museum and school links in London - past and future, *Museums Journal*, 84(2), 57-61.

Adams, G. (1989) *Museums and Galleries: A Teachers Handbook*, Hutchinson..

Alston, D. *et al.* (1979) Art and education, *Oxford Art Journal*, 3 (Special issue).

Ambrose, T.M. (1987) *Education in Museums: Museums in Education*, Scottish Museums Council.

Ambrose, T.M. (ed.) (1985) *Museums Are for People*, HMSO/Scottish Museums Council.

American Association of Museums (1971) *Museums and the Environment: A Handbook for Education*, American Association of Museums, Washington DC.

American Association of Museums (1972) *Museums: Their New Audience*, American Association of Museums, Washington DC.

American Association of Museums (1984) *Museums for a New Century*, American Association of Museums, Washington, DC.

Ames, M.M. (1985) De-schooling the museum: a proposal to increase public access to museums and their resources, *Museum*, 145, 25-31.

Anderson, D, (1989) Museum education, marketing and sponsorship, in Hooper-Greenhill, E., (ed.), *Initiatives in Museum Education*, Department of Museum Studies, University of Leicester, 24-25.

Anderson, D.C. (1973) Project ETW: an exemplary school museum program, *Curator*, 16(2), 141-57.

Anon. (1987) Meeting the GCSE challenge, *North of England Museum Service News*, 16, 6-7.

Bestall, J.M. (1970) What can museums offer?, *Adult Education*, 42(5), 315-19.

Blyth, J. (1988) *Primary Bookshelf: History 5-9*, Hodder and Stoughton, London.

Brown, M. (1982) One museum's drama experience, *Museums Journal*, 81(4), 208-09.

Cameron, D.F. (1980) Reaction and over-reaction to the museum's expanding role in education, *Museum News*, 46(6), 27-30.

Campbell, G. (1992) Beyond the classroom wall, in Greeves, M. and Martin, B. (eds.), *Chalk, Talk and Dinosaurs: Museums and Education in Scotland*, Scottish Museums Council and Moray House Institute, Edinburgh, 26-28.

Canadian Museums Association (1989) Museums and education, *Muse*, 7(2).

Capernos, Z. & Patterson, D. (1992) Chalk and cheese, in Greeves, M. and Martin, B. (eds.), *Chalk, Talk and Dinosaurs: Museums and Education in Scotland*, Scottish Museums Council and Moray House Institute, Edinburgh, 35-37.

Cart, G., Harrison, M. & Russell, C. (1952) *Museums and Young People*, ICOM (International Council of Museums), Paris.

Carter, G. (1984) Educational services in Thompson, J.M.A. *et al. (eds.)*, *Manual of Curatorship*, Butterworths, London, 435-447.

Carter, P.G. (1984) *Education in Independent Museums*, AIM Guideline No 6, Association of Independent Museums.

Chadwick, A.F. (1980) *The Role of the Museum and Art Gallery in Community Education*, University of Nottingham.

Chapman, L.H. (1982) The future and museum education, *Museum News*, 60(6), 48-56.

Clarke, P. (1992) Peter Clarke, in Hooper-Greenhill, E. (ed.), *Working in Museum and Gallery Education - 10 Career Experiences*, Department of Museum Studies, University of Leicester, 14-15.

Clausen, S.K. (1979) Commission for environmental interpretation and education, Denmark, *Museums Journal*, 79(2).

Cooper, C. & Latham, J. (1985) *The Market for Educational Visits to Tourist Attractions*, Dorset Institute of Higher Education.

Council for Museums & Galleries in Scotland (1970) *Report on Museums and Education*, Council for Museums and Galleries in Scotland.

Council for Museums & Galleries in Scotland (1981) *Museum Education Scotland - A Directory*, CMGS, Edinburgh.

Danilov, V.J. (1975) Science museums as education centres, *Curator*, 18(2), 87-108.

Department of Education and Science (1971) *Museums in Education*, Education Survey No 12, London, HMSO.

Department of Education and Science (1971) *Museums in Education*, Education Survey,12, HMSO, London..

Department of Education and Science (1985) Report by HM Inspectors on a survey of the use of museums made by some schools in the North West, carried out 17-21 June 1985, *HMI Report*, 20/87.

Department of Education and Science (1985) Report by HM Inspectors on a survey of the use some Hertfordshire schools make of museum services, carried out 1-4 July 1985, *HMI Report*, 40/86.

Department of Education and Science (1986) *A Survey of the Use Some*

Hertfordshire Schools Make of Museum Services, DES 40/86.

Department of Education and Science (1986) Report by HM Inspectors on a survey of the use some Oxfordshire schools and colleges make of museum services, carried out Sept-Nov 1986, *HMI Report*, 312/87.

Department of Education and Science (1986) Report by HM Inspectors on a survey of the use some schools in six local education authorities make of museum services, carried out June, 1986, *HMI Report*, 53/87.

Department of Education and Science (1987) *A Survey of How Some Schools in Five Local Education Authorities Made Use of Museum Loan Services*, DES 290/87.

Department of Education and Science (1987) *A Survey of the Use of Museums Made by Some Schools in the North West*, DES 20/87.

Department of Education and Science (1987) *A Survey of the Use Some Oxfordshire Schools and Colleges Made of Museum Services*, DES 312/87.

Department of Education and Science (1987) *A Survey of the Use Some Schools in Six Local Education Authorities Make of Museum Services*, DES 53/87.

Department of Education and Science (1987) *Report by HM Inspectors on a Survey of the Use Some Pupils and Students With Special Educational Needs Make of Museums and Historic Buildings*, DES 4/88.

Department of Education and Science (1987) Report by HM Inspectors on a survey of how some schools in five LEAs made use of museum loan services, carried out Spring,1987, *HMI Report*, 290/87.

Department of Education and Science (1987) Report by HM Inspectors on a survey of the use some pupils and students with special education needs make of museums and historic buildings, *HMI Report*, 4/88.

Department of Education and Science (1988) A survey of the use of museums and galleries in GCSE courses, *HMI Report*, 369/88.

Department of Education and Science (1988) A survey of the use of museums in adult and community education, *HMI Report*, 7/88.

Department of Education and Science (1988) A survey of the use schools make of museums for learning about ethnic and cultural diversity, *HMI Report*, 163/89.

Department of Education and Science (1989) *National Curriculum - From Policy to Practice*, HMSO, London.

Department of Education and Science (1989) *The Curriculum from 5-16*, 2nd edition, Curriculum Matters 2, HMSO.

Department of Education and Science (1989) A survey of the use schools make of museums across the curriculum, *HMI Report*, 340/89.

Dewey, J. (1979) *Experience and Education*, Collier Macmillan Publishers, London.

Divall, P. (1989) Museum education - a new ERA?, *Museums Journal*, 89(2), 23-24.

Durbin, G. (1988) Education at the Royal Palaces, *Remnants*, 5, 10-11.

Durbin, G., Morris, S. & Wilkingson, S. (1990) *A Teachers Guide to Learning from Objects*, English Heritage.

Edwardes, Y. (1987) Museums must decide: hands-on or hands-off, *Muse*, 5,1, 18-23.

Eisner, E.W. & Dobbs, S.M. (1986) Museum education in twenty American art museums, *Museum News*, 65(2), 42-49.

Elder, B. (1981) Drama for interpretation, *History News*, 36(7), 9-11.

Fairley, J. (1977) *History Teaching Through Museums*, Longmans, London.

Fertig, B. (1982) Historians, artefacts, learners: the history museum as educator, *Museum News*, 60(6), 57-61.

Frese, H.H. (1957) The living museum: educational work in the National Museum of Ethnography, Leiden, *Museum*, 10(4), 294-96.

Goodhew, E. (1988) *Museums and the Curriculum*, Area Museums Service for South Eastern England, London.

Goodhew, E. (1988) *Museums and the New Exams*, Area Museums Service for South Eastern England, London.

Greenaway, F. (1966) The Science Museum, *Adult Education*, 39(2), 82-5.

Group for Education in Museums Multi-cultural education and museums, *Journal of Education in Museums*, 7.

Group for Education in Museums Museums and environmental education, *Journal of Education in Museums*, 3.

Group for Education Services in Museums (1975) *Museums As an Influence on the Quality of Life*, British National Committee of ICOM (International Council of Museums), Group for Educational Studies in Museums.

Gurian, E. (1982) Museums relationship to education, *Museums and Education*, Danish ICOM (International Council of Museums)/Committee for Education and Cultural Action, Copenhagen, Denmark.

Hale, J. (1968) Museums and the teaching of history, *Museum*, 21(1).

Hall, C. (1981) Grandma's attic or Aladdin's cave: museum education services for children, *Studies in Education No 27*, New Zealand Council for Education Research, Wellington (Deslandes Ltd.), New Zealand.

Hall, J. (1992) Museum education: adapting to a changing South Africa, *Journal of Education in Museums*, 12, 10-14.

Hames, R. (1987) Appaldurcombe - in song and tale, *Remnants*, 3, 20-21.

Hamilton, M. (1974) Museum educational work in the Netherlands, *Museums Journal*, 74(2), 75.

Hansen, T.H. (ed.) (1984) The museum as educator, *Museum*, 36(4).

Harrison, M. (1967) *Changing Museums - Their Use and Misuse*, Longmans, London.

Harrison, M. (1967) Group visits to museums, *Visual Education*, London, 4-6.

Harrison, M. (1973) *Museums and Galleries*, Routledge and Kegan Paul, London.

Heath, A. (1975) Excursions to sites and monuments as sources of knowledge, *Museum*, 31(3).

Hein, G. E. (ed.) (1990) *Journal of Museum Education*, 15(1) Museum Education Roundtable, Washington, DC.

Hein, H. (1987) The museum as teacher of theory: a case history of the Exploratorium vision section, *Museum Studies Journal*, 2(4), 30-40.

Hooper-Greenhill, E. (1987) Museum education comes of age, *Journal of Education in Museums*, 8, 6-8.

Hooper-Greenhill, E. (1987) Museums in education: towards the twenty-first century, in Ambrose, T. (ed.), *Museums in Education: Education in Museums*, Scottish Museums Council & HMSO, Edinburgh, 39-52.

Hooper-Greenhill, E. (1988) Museums in education: working with other organisations, *Working With Museums*, HMSO/Scottish Museums Council.

Hooper-Greenhill, E. (1991) *Museum and Gallery Education*, Leicester University Press, Leicester, London and New York.

Hooper-Greenhill, E. (1992) Museum education, in Thompson, J.M.A. *et al. (ed.)*, *Manual of Curatorship*, 2nd edition, Butterworths, Cambridge, 670-689.

Hooper-Greenhill, E. (1993) Museum education: past, present and future, in Miles, R. & Zavala, L. (ed.), *Towards the Museum of the Future: European Perspectives*, Routledge, London.

Hooper-Greenhill, E. (ed.) (1989) *Initiatives in Museum Education*, Department of Museum Studies, University of Leicester.

Hooper-Greenhill, E. (ed.) (1992) *Working in Museum and Gallery Education: 10 Career Experiences*, Department of Museum Studies, University of Leicester.

International Council of Museums (1956) *Museums and Teachers*, ICOM (International Council of Museums), Paris.

International Council of Museums (1978) *Museums as Educational Instruments, Selective Bibliography 1970-78*, ICOM (International Council of Museums), Paris.

Jeaunot-Vignes, B. (1976) Collecting material for an ethnographical exhibition. an experiment conducted by the Ecomuseum of Le Creusot-Montceau-les-Mines, *Museum*, 28(3), 163-70.

Jensen, N. (ed.) (1982) Children, teenagers and adults in museums, a developmental perspective, *Museum News*, 60(5), 25-30.

Keatch, S. (1987) Cloots, creels and claikin - drama on display, in Ambrose. T. (ed.), *Education in Museums, Museums in Education*, Scottish Museums Council, 77-84.

Lacey, T.J. & Agar, J. (1980) Bringing teachers and museums together, *Museum News*, 58(4), 50-5.

Lamarche, H. (1989) Educators on museums and education, *Muse*, 7(2), 16-3.

Lavionova, E. (1968) The aesthetic education of children, *Museum*, 21(1), 45-7.

Lawson, I. & Coulter, S. (1981) Scottish museums and education, *Omnigatherum*, February, Council for Museums and Galleries in Scotland.

Lefroy, J.A. (1967) Museums and educational institutions, *Museums Journal*, 67(2).

Lewis, B.N. (1980) The museum as an educational facility, *Museums Journal*, 80(3), 151-5.

London-Morris, H. (1992) What's the Catch? Report on the first UK conference on the use of drama in museums, *Museums Journal*, 92(8) Supplement.

Mainstone, M. (1967) The place of the museum in education, *Athene*, 2(7).

Marcouse, R. (1961) *The Listening Eye: Teaching in an Art Museum*, HMSO, London.

Marcouse, R. (1968) The role of education in museums, *Museums Journal*, 68(3).

McCabe, G. (1970) Museum educational work in Holland, *Museums Journal*, 69(4), 167-68.

McCabe, G. (1972) Museum educational work in Poland, *Museums Journal*, 72(1), 20-1.

McCabe, G. (1975) Museums in Sweden, *Museums Journal*, 74(4), 175-76.

Measham, T. (1973) Tate - kidsplay - a participatory experience for little children,, *Museums Annual*, 5, 39-42.

Measham, T. (1974) Creative appreciation - an exercise in collaboration between the Cockpit Theatre and the Tate Gallery, *Contact*, 14.

Measham, T. (1974) Kidsplay II 1974 at the Tate Gallery, London, *Museums Annual*, 6, 42-4.

Mesallam, M. (1971) Educational work: the collective responsibility of all museum personnel, *The Museum in the Service of Man Today and Tomorrow*, ICOM (International Council of Museums), Paris, 157-66.

Miles, H. (1986) *Museums in Scotland*, Museums and Galleries Commission, HMSO, London.

Moffat, H. (1988) Museums and schools, *Museums Bulletin*, 28(5), 97-98.

Moffat, H. (1989) Museums and the Education Reform Act, *Museums Journal*, 89(2), 23-24.

Moore, D. (1976) In search of the past: a travelling exhibition for schools, *Museums Journal*, 76(2), 60-2.

Morris, S. (1985) Museum Studies - a mode three CSE course at the National Portrait Gallery, *Journal of Education in Museums*, 6, 37-40.

Morris, S. & Wilkinson, S. (1992) What are the differences between 'objects' and 'documents' as historical sources and what is the value of using objects?', *Journal of Education in Museums*, 13, 24-28.

Munley, M.E. (1986) Educational excellence for American museums, *Museum News*, 65(2), 51-57.

Museums Association (1971) *Museums in Education*, Museums Association Report No 1, amended edition.

Museums Association (1975) *Museum Education Services*, Museums Association Information Sheet No 1,3rd edition.

Museums Association (1982) Working party - museums in education, *Museums Journal*, 81(4), 236-39.

National Institute of Adult Education (1956) *Museums and Adult Education*, National Institute of Adult Education, London.

Newsom, B.Y. & Silver, A.Z. (1978) *The Art Museum As Educator*, Council on Museums & Education in the Visual Arts, University of California Press.

Olofsson, U.K. (ed.) (1979) *Museums and Children*, UNESCO, Paris.

Ontario Ministry of Citizenship and Culture (1985) *Developing an Interpretation and Education Policy for the Museum*, Museum Notes - Practical Information on Operating a Community Museum, 11, Ministry of Citizenship and Culture.

Park, G.S. (1989) The employment of education officers in New Zealand museums: a report on progress, *Art Gallery and Museums Association of New Zealand (AGMANZ) Journal*, 20(3), 6-8,30.

Paterson, I. (1987) Approaches for implementing change, *Journal of Education in Museums*, 8, 30-32.

Paterson, I. (1989) Museum education and liaison with local education authorities, in Hooper-Greenhill, E. (ed.), *Initiatives in Museum Education*, Department of Museum Studies, University of Leicester, 5-7.

Pittman, N. (1991) Writing a museum education policy: introductory remarks, *Group for Education in Museums Newsletter*, 43(Autumn), 22-24.

Pond, M. (1984) Recreating a trip to York in Victorian times, *Teaching History*, 39, 12-16.

Ripley, S.D. (1968) Museums and education, *Curator*, 11(3), 183.

Rodger, L. (1987) Museums in education: seizing the market opportunities, in Ambrose, T. (ed.), *Education in Museums, Museums in Education*, Scottish Museums Council, Edinburgh, 27-38.

Romp, H. (1979) An eye for the cockpit, *Cockpit Arts Workshop*, Inner London Education Authority.

Rowley, C. (1977) Painting it. the colour workshop at the National Gallery, *Museums Journal*, 76(4), 153-54.

Schlereth, T.J. (ed.) (1980) *Artifacts and the American Past*, American Association for State and Local History (AASLH), Nashville, Tennessee.

Schools Council (1972) *Pterodactyls and Old Lace: Museums in Education*,

Schools Council, London.

Sekers, D. (1977) The educational potential of the museum shop, *Museums Journal*, 76(4), 146-47.

Sekules, V. (1984) A small child could do it? The University of East Anglia Collection of Abstract Art and Design - an experiment in gallery education, *Museums Journal*, 84, 125-127.

Shorland-Ball, R. (1989) Managing museums for learning, in Hooper-Greenhill, E. (ed.), *Initiatives in Museum Education*, Department of Museum Studies, University of Leicester, 26-27.

Shortland, M. (1987) No business like show business, *Nature*, 328(16th July).

Siliprandi, K. (1990) Museum education - the state of pay, *Museums Journal*, 90(3), 14.

Silver, A.Z. (1973) The new education wing, Cleveland Museum of Art, *Museum*, 25(4), 229-41.

Simpson, M. (1989) Visions of other cultures, current practices in Dutch museum education, *Journal of Education in Museums*, 10, 31-36.

Standing Commission on Museums and Galleries (1973) *Ninth Report, 1969-73*, chapter 3 and appendices on National and Provincial Museums, HMSO.

Standing Commission on Museums and Galleries (1978) *Tenth Report, 1973-77*, Appendices on National and Provincial Museums, HMSO.

Standing Committee for Museum Services in Hertfordshire (1987) *Museum Education in Hertfordshire: A Development Plan*, Hertfordshire Museums.

Stevens, T. (1981) Dramatic approaches to museum education, *Journal of Education in Museums*, 2, 30-33.

Stevens, T. (1987) Change: a constant theme, *Journal of Education in Museums*, 8, 15-17.

Stevenson, J. (1987) The philosophy behind Launchpad, *Journal of Education in Museums*, 8, 18-20.

Stokstad, M. (ed.) (1982) *Museums, Humanities and Educated Eyes*, University of Kansas, Lawrence, Kansas.

Suina, J. H. (1992) Museum multicultural education for young learners, in Museum Education Roundtable, *Patterns in Practice: Selections from the Journal of Museum Education*, Museum Education Roundtable, Washington, DC, 179-184.

Supplee, C. (1974) Museum on wheels, *Museum News*, 53(2), 27-36.

Sutton, R. (1989.) Marketing new education programmes - the Ferrymead experience, *Art Gallery and Museums Association of New Zealand (AGMANZ) Journal*, 20(3), 9-10.

Taylor, W.W. (1973) Museums in education - a progress report, *Museums Journal*, 73(3), 101-02.

Thomas, G. (ed.) (1989) Museums and education, *Art Gallery and Museums*

Association of New Zealand (AGMANZ) Journal, 20(3).

Thompson, C. (nd) Looking at pictures: the unwitting rules of the game, *Athene*, 63, 18-19.

Thompson, J. (1980) Cities in decline. Museums and the urban programme 1969-79, *Museums Journal*, 79(4), 188-90.

UNESCO (1973) *Museums, Imagination and Education*, UNESCO Museums and Monuments Series, No 15, Paris.

Van Balgooy, M. (1990) Hands-on or hands-off? The management of collections and museum education, *Curator*, 33(2), 90-118.

Vygotsky, L.S. (1933) Play and its role in the mental development of the child, in Bruner, J. S., Jolly, A., and Sylva, K. (eds), 1976, *Play: Its Role in Development and Evolution*, Penguin Books, Harmondsworth, Middlesex, 537-554.

Washburn, W.E. (1964) Museum responsibilities in adult education, *Curator*, 7(1), 33-8.

Webb, C. D. (1986) Museums in search of income, Ambrose, T. (ed.), *The American Museum Experience: In Search of Excellence*, Scottish Museums Council & HMSO, Edinburgh, 75-83.

Wilkinson, G. (1978) The integration of a successful education department with the overall work of the Museum Service in Bradford, *Museums Journal*, 77(4), 86.

Williams, A. (1981) *A Heritage for Scotland - Scotland's National Museums and Galleries: the Next 25 Years*, HMSO, Glasgow.

Winterbotham, N. (1987) The dark towers of Newstead Abbey, *Journal of Education in Museums*, 7, 7-9.

Wittlin, A.S. (1970) *Museums: In Search of a Usable Future*, Massachussetts Institute of Technology Press.

Wright, C.W. (1973) Education, *Provincial Museums and Galleries*, (The Wright Report), HMSO.

Zetterburg, H. (1969) *Museums and Adult Education*, Hugh Evelym, for ICOM (International Council of Museums), Paris.

Zyl, S. Van (1987) A policy for museum education, *SAMAB: Southern African Museums Association Bulletin*, 17(5), 193-199.

Zyl, S. Van (1987) Setting standards for museum education: developing a policy, *SAMAB: Southern African Museums Association Bulletin*, 17(6), 270-277.

7.2 Museum Education Theory

Abler, T.S. (1965) *Traffic Pattern and Exhibit Design: A Study of Learning* *in the Museum*, Milwaukee Public Museum, Milwaukee.

Adams, C. & Miller, S. (1982) Museums and the use of evidence in history teaching, *Teaching History*, 34(October).

Alexander, E.P. (1974) *Museums and How to Use Them*, Batsford, London.

Ambach, G.M. (1986) Museums as places of learning, *Museum News*, 65(2), 35-41.

Ambrose, T.M. (ed.) (1987) *Education in Museums: Museums in Education*, Scottish Museums Council & HMSO, Edinburgh.

Anderson, D. (1989) Learning history in museums, *International J. of Museum Management and Curatorship*, 8, 357-368.

Anon. (1967) The influence of museums on education, *Museums Journal*, 67(1), 60.

Belland, J.C. & Searles, H. (1986) Concept learning in the museum, *Curator*, 29, 85-91.

Berry, N. & Mayer, S. (1989) *Museum Educaton: History, Theory and Practice*, National Art Education Association, Virginia, USA.

Booth, J.H., Krockover, G.H. & Woods, P.R. (1982) *Creative Museum Methods and Educational Techniques*, Charles C. Thomas, Springfield, Illinois.

Bosdet, M. & Durbin, G. (1989) *Museum Education Bibliography 1978-1988*, Group for Education in Museums.

Brice, P. (1971) Establishing a teaching museum, *Teaching History*, 2(6), 112-16.

Brooks, J.A.M. (1956) A study of children's interests and comprehension at a science museum, *British Journal of Psychology*, 47, 175-82.

Bruner, J. (1960) *The Process of Knowing*, Vintage Books, New York.

Bruner, J. (1962) *On Knowing: Essays for the Left Hand*, Belknap, Cambridge, MA.

Bruner, J. (1966) *Towards a Theory of Instruction*, Norton and Co. New York.

Caston, E. (1979) An interdisciplinary approach to education, *Museum News*, 57(4), 50-3.

Chase, R.A. (1975) Museums as learning environments, *Museum News*, 54(1), 37-43.

Cole, P. (1984) Piaget in the galleries, *Museum News*, 63, 9-15.

Cole, P. R. (1985) Dewey and the galleries: educational theorists talk to museum educators, *The Museologist*, 48, 12-14.

Deetz, J. (1981) The link from object to person to concept in Collins, Z.W. (ed.), *Museums, Adults and the Humanities - A Guide for Educational Programming*, American Association of Museums, Washington DC, 24-34.

Delahaye, M. (1987) Can children be taught how to think?, *The Listener*, 22 October, 14.

Dyer, M. (1986) *Heritage Education Handbook*, Heritage Education Trust.

Endter, E.A. (1975) Museum learning and the performing arts, *Museum News*, 53(9), 34-7.

Falk, J.H. (1983) Time and behaviour as predictors of learning, *Science Education*, 67, 267-276.

Farmelo, G. (1992) Drama on the galleries, in Durant, J. (ed.), *Museums and the Public Understanding of Science*, Science Museum in association with the Committee on the Public Understanding of Science, London.

Feher, E. & Rice, K. (1985) Development of scientific concepts through the use of interactive exhibits in a museum, *Curator*, 28(1), 35-46.

Fines, J. (1983) Starters: using objects from museums, *Museums Journal*, 83(2/3), 131-34.

Floyd, C. (1980) Education at old economy: programs that children can understand, *History News*, 35(3), 12-.

Floyd, C. (1981) Drama for training, *History News*, 36(7), 17-19.

Fry, H. (1987) Worksheets as museum learning devices, *Museums Journal*, 86(4), 219-224.

Gardner, H. (1983) *Frames of Mind*, Paladin Books, London.

Gardner, H. (1990) Developing the spectrum of human intelligences, in Hedley, C., Houtz, J., and Barratta, A. (eds.), *Cognition, Curriculum and Literacy*, Ablex Publishing Corporation, New Jersey, USA.

Gardner, H. (1993) *The Unschooled Mind: How Children Think and How Schools Should Teach*, Fontana, London.

Gathercole, P. (1979) Education and new museum displays: an ethnographic view, *Museums Journal*, 78(4).

Gillies, P.A. & Wilson, A.W. (1982) Participatory exhibits: is fun educational?, *Museums Journal*, 82(3), 131-34.

Greenglass, D. (1986) Learning from objects in a museum, *Curator*, 29(1), 53-66.

Greeves, M. & Martin, B. (1992) *Chalk, Talk and Dinosaurs: Museums and Education in Scotland*, Scottish Museums Council and Moray House Institute, Edinburgh.

Group for Education in Museums Education in art galleries, dramatic approaches, *Journal of Education in Museums*, 2.

Group for Education in Museums International edition I, *Journal of Education in Museums*, 4.

Group for Education in Museums International edition II, *Journal of Education in Museums*, 5.

Group for Education in Museums Museum education today, *Journal of Education in Museums*, 8.

Group for Education in Museums Training edition, *Journal of Education in Museums*, 6.

Hall, N. (ed.) (1984) *Writing and Designing Interpretive Materials for Children*, Centre for Environmental Interpretation, Manchester.

Hennigar-Shuh, J. (1982) Teaching yourself to teach with objects, *Journal* *of Education*, 7(4), 8-14.

Hepler, S. (1978) A visit to the seventeenth century: history as language experience, *Language Arts*, 56(2), 126-131.

Hooper-Greenhill, E. (1981) Why bother? Learning in the museum, *Clio, History and Social Sciences Teachers Centre Review: Visits and Field Studies Issue*, 4-5, Inner London Education Authority, Spring.

Hooper-Greenhill, E. (1983) Some basic principles and issues relating to museum education, *Museums Journal*, 83(2/3), 127-30.

Hooper-Greenhill, E. (1988) The art of memory and learning in the museum: museum education and the GCSE, *International J. of Museum Management and Curatorship*, 2, 129-137.

Hooper-Greenhill, E. (1991) Learning and teaching with objects, *Actes Du Colloque: A Propos Des Recherches Didactiques Au Musee*, La Societe des Musees Quebecois, Quebec, Canada, 48-52.

Hooper-Greenhill, E. (1992) Object lessons for schools, in Greeves, M. and Martin, B. (eds.), *Chalk, Talk and Dinosaurs: Museums and Education in Scotland*, Scottish Museums Council and Moray House Institute, Edinburgh, 9-15.

Hooper-Greenhill, E. (ed.) (1989) *Initiatives in Museum Education*, Department of Museum Studies, University of Leicester.

Hooper-Greenhill, E. (ed.) (1991) *Writing a Museum Education Policy*, Department of Museum Studies, University of Leicester.

Husbands, C. (1992) Objects, evidence and learning: some thoughts on meaning and interpretation in museum education, *Journal of Museum Education*, 13, 1-3.

Kurylo, L. (1976) On the need for a theory of museum learning, *Gazette*, 9(3), 20-4.

Marcouse, R. (1974) *Using Objects*, (Schools Council), Van Nostrand Reinhold Company.

Mathai, R.A. & Deaver, N.E. (1976) Child-centred learning, *Museum News*, 54(4), 15-19.

Matthias, D.C.J. (1988) The art museum as a teaching resource, *International J. of Museum Management and Curatorship*, 7(1), 57-61.

McManus, P.M. (1985) Worksheet-induced behaviour in the British Museum (NH), *Journal of Biological Education*, 19(3), 237-242.

Morris, S. (1989) *A Teachers Guide to Using Portraits*, English Heritage, London.

Museum Education Association of Australia (1977) *Museum Education Training*, Museum Education Association of Australia, Sydney.

Museum Education Roundtable (1984) *Museum Education Anthology, Perspectives on Informal Learning: a Decade of Roundtable Reports, 1973-1983*, Museum Education Roundtable, Washington, DC.

Museum Education Roundtable (1992) *Patterns in Practice: Selections from the Journal of Museum Education*, Museum Education Roundtable,

Washington, DC.

Nichols, S.K. (ed.) (nd) *Museum Education Anthology 1973-1983: Perspectives on Informal Learning - a Decade of Roundtable Reports,* American Association of Museums, Washington DC.

Novacek, M. (1990) Research and Education in Natural History Museums: the need for commitment, *International J. of Museum Management and Curatorship,* 9(4), 352-358.

Oppenheimer, F. (1973) Teaching and learning, *American Journal of Physics,* 41, 1310-1313.

Owen, D. (1991) *A New South African Challenge: Teaching History in Multi-Cultural Schools,* Albany Museum New History Series, 1, Albany Museum, Grahamstown, South Africa.

Patten, L.H. (1982-3) Education by design, *Education,* 10 ICOM Committee for Education and Cultural Action, 6-8.

Phillips, D. (1982) Experiments in visual education: the automatic art gallery and surprises, *Museums Journal,* 82(1), 11-14.

Pollock, S. (1983) Out and about - an inside view of education at the Natural History Museum in London, *Journal of Biological Education,* 17(2), 119-22.

Pond, M. (1983) School history visits and Piagetian theory, *Teaching History,* 37, 3-6.

Porter, J. & Martin, W. (1985) Learning from objects, *Museums Journal,* 85(1), 35-38.

Pouw, P. & Schouten, F. (eds.) (1983) *Exhibition Design As an Educational Tool,* Reinwardt Studies in Museology No 1, Reinwardt Academy, Leiden, Netherlands.

Rebetez, P. (1970) *How to Visit a Museum,* Council of Europe, Strasbourg.

Regue, B. (1978) From object to idea, *Museum News,* 56(3), 45-7.

Sadler, T. & Morris, B. (eds.) (1989) *Museum Educators Think Aloud on Educational Philosphy,* Quoll Enterprises, South Australia.

Schools Council (1974) *Learning from Trails: Project Environment,* Schools Council, London.

Screven, C.G. (1969) The museum as a responsive learning environment, *Museum News,* 47(10), 7-10.

Southern African Museums Association (1989) *Museum Education and Communication: Guidelines for Policy and Practice,* Albany Museum for the Southern African Museums Association.

Szemere, S. (1978) *The Problems of Contents: Didactics and Aesthetics of Modern Museum Exhibits,* Institute of Conservation and Methodology of Museums, Budapest.

Taylor, A.P. (1973) Children and artifacts: a replacement for textbook learning, *Curator,* 16(1), 25-9.

Wolins, I.S. (1983) Educating in the museum with television, *Museum Studies Journal,* 1(2).

7.3 History of Museum Education

Adams, G. (1984) Museum and school links in London - past and future, *Museums Journal*, 84(2), 57-61.

Airey, V. (1978) United Kingdom of Great Britain and Northern Ireland, in Olofsson, U.K. (ed.), *Museums and Children*, UNESCO.

Allan, D.A. (1949) *Museums and Education*, Royal Society of Arts, London.

Andrews, B.R. (1908) Museums of education, *Teachers College Record (New York)*, 9 September, 195-292.

Anon. (1901-2) Children and museums, *Museums Journal*, 171.

Anon. (1915) Discussion on museums in relation to education, *Museums Journal*, 15, 138-40.

Anon. (1916) Liverpool Museum and elementary school children, *Museums Journal*, 16, 3-4.

Anon. (1919) Report of a conference between representatives of the Board of Education and a committee of the Museums Association on the proposed transfer of museums to the local education authorities, *Museums Journal*, 19, 123-9.

Bateman, J. (1984) The control and financing of museum education services in Great Britain, *Museums Journal*, 84(2), 51-56.

Bell, B., Hitchin, M. & Taylor, C. (1933) History teaching in Manchester Museums, and its relationship to school work, *History*, July, 131-138.

Board of Education (1931) *Museums and the Schools: Memorandum of the Possibility of Increased Co-operation Between Public Museums and Public Educational Institutions*, Educational pamphlets, 87, HMSO, London.

British Association for the Advancement of Science (1920) Final report of the Committee on Museums in relation to education, *Report of the British Association for the Advancement of Science 1920*, London, 267-80.

Bryant, M.E. (1961) *The Museum and the School*, Historical Association Leaflet No 6.

Busse, F. (1880) Object-teaching: principles and methods, *American Journal of Education*, 30, 417-450.

Calkins, N.A. (1880) Object-teaching: its purpose and province, *Education*, 1, 165-172.

Chadwick, A. (1983) Practical aids to nineteenth century self help - the museums: private collections into public institutions, in Stevens, M.D. & Roderick, G. W. (eds.), *Samuel Smiles and Nineteenth Century Self-Help in Education*, Department of Adult Education, University of Nottingham, 47-69.

Derbyshire County Council (1957) *Museum Service: Twenty-One Years 1936-1957*, Derbyshire County Council Education Committee.

Derbyshire County Council Education Committee (1967) *Museum Service 1966-1967*, Derbyshire County Council.

Durbin, G. (1983) A museum in the Great War, *Museums Journal*, 82(2/3), 168-70.

Elliot, B.J. (1977) Museums and history teaching: the early experience, *History of Education Society Bulletin*, 20, 41-45.

Group for Education in Museums (1980-1) History of museum education in UK, *Journal of Education in Museums*, 1/2.

Group for Education in Museums (1980-81) *Journal of Education in Museums*.

Group for Educational Services in Museums (1975) *Museums As an Influence on the Quality of Life, Proceedings of an International Conference Held in Britain 6-11 April 1975*, Group for Educational Services in Museums.

Harrison, M. (1942) Thoughts on the function of museums in education, *Museums Journal*, 42(3), 53.

Harrison, M. (1950) *Museum Adventure: The Story of the Geffrye Museum*, University of London, London.

Harrison, M. (1954) *Learning Out of School*, Educational Supply Association, London.

Harrison, M. (1967) *Changing Museums - Their Use and Misuse*, Longmans, London.

Harrison, M. (1970) *Learning Out of School: A Teachers Guide to the Educational Use of Museums*, Ward Locke Educational.

Harrison, M. (1985) Art and Philanthropy: T.C. Horsfall and the Manchester Art Museum, in Kidd, A.J. and Roberts, K. W. (eds.), *City, Class and Culture*.

Haward, L. (1918) Discussion in Howarth, E. (ed.), *Educational Value of Museums and the Formation of Local War Museums, Report of the Proceedings of the Conference Held in Sheffield, October, 1917*, 33-42.

Heath, A. (1976) Civil War co-operation, *Inner London Education Authority Contact*, 4(32), 16-20.

Hooper-Greenhill, E. (1988) The art of memory and learning in the museum: museum education and GCSE, *International J. of Museum Management and Curatorship*, 7, 129-37.

Hooper-Greenhill, E. (1992) The past, the present and the future: museum education from the 1790s to the 1990s, *Journal of Education in Museums*, 12, 1-3.

Howarth, E. (1913-14) Presidential Address, *Museums Journal*, 13, 42.

Howarth, E. (1914) The museum and the school, *Museums Journal*, 14, 282.

Howarth, E. (ed.) (1918) *Educational Value of Museums and the Formation of Local War Museums*, Report of the proceedings of the conference held in Sheffield, October, 1917.

Hunter, K. (1986) *Golden Jubilee of the Museum School Service: 1936-*

1986, North Hertfordshire Museums.

International Council of Museums Committee for Education (1956) *Museums and Teachers*, ICOM (International Council of Museums), Paris.

John, D. D. (1950) *The Museums School Service*, National Museum of Wales, Cardiff.

Kavanagh, G. (1988) The First World War and its implications for education in British museums, *History of Education*, 17(2), 163-176.

Leicestershire Museums (1976) *Museums and the Handicapped*, Leicester.

Lowe, E.E. (1928) *A Report on American Museum Work*, Carnegie U.K. Trustees.

MacDonald, S. (1986) For "Swine of Discretion": Design for living: 1884, *Museums Journal*, 86(3), 123-130.

Marcouse, R. (1961) *The Listening Eye - Teaching in an Art Museum*, Victoria and Albert Museum.

Markham, S.F. (1938) *A Report on the Museums and Art Galleries of the British Isles*, Carnegie UK Trustees, Dunfermline.

Martin, R. F. (1918) Report on school picture collections in Aberdeen, in Howarth, E. (ed.), *Educational Value of Museums and the Formation of Local War Museums*, Report of the proceedings of the conference held in Sheffield, October, 1917.

McCabe, G. (1975) *Museums in Education: The Educational Role of Museums in the United Kingdom*, MA Thesis, University of Sheffield.

Miers, Sir H.A. (1928) *A Report on the Public Museums of the British Isles*, Carnegie United Kingdom Trust, Edinburgh.

Miers, Sir H.A. (1929) *Museums and Education*, Royal Society of Arts, London.

Moore, D. (1973) Children in a museum, *Amgueddfa*, 13.

Moore, D. (1982) Thirty years of museum education: some reflections, *International J. of Museum Management and Curatorship*, 1(3), 213-30.

Moore, K. (1991) Feasts of reason? Exhibitions at the Liverpool Mechanics Institution in the 1840s, in Kavanagh, G. (ed.), *Museum Languages: Objects and Texts*, Leicester University Press, Leicester, London and New York, 155-177.

Mullen, B. H. (1918) Scheme for scholars visiting the Salford museums in Howarth, E. (ed.), *Educational Value of Museums and the Formation of Local War Museums*, Report of the proceedings of the conference held in Sheffield, October, 1917.

Museums Association (1967) *Museum School Services*, prepared by the Group for Educational Services in Museums, London.

Museums Association (1971) *Report on Museums in Education*, No 1, London.

Ogilvie, F. G. (1919) *Report on the Sheffield City Museums*, Educational Pamphlet No. 34.

Porter, J. (1982) Mobile exhibition services in Great Britain: a survey of their practice and potential, *Museums Journal*, 82(3), 135-138.

Rees, P. (1981) A mobile for the teacher, *Ournal of Education in Museums*, 2, 26-29.

Rich, E. M. (1936) *Survey of Museums and Galleries in London*, London County Council, publication number 3172.

Rosse, Earl of (1963) *Survey of Provincial Museums and Galleries*, Standing Commission of Museums and Galleries, HMSO, London, (appendix E).

Sahasrabudhe, P. (1965.) *A Childrens Museum for India*, Department of Museology, University of Baroda.

Schools Council (1972) *Pterodactyls and Old Lace: Museums in Education*, Evans/Methuan, London.

Smythe, J.E. (1966) *The Educational Role of the Museums and Field Centres in England from 1884*, MA Thesis, University of Sheffield.

Stephens, M.D. and Roderick, G.W. (1983) Middle-class Nineteenth century self-help - the Literary and Philosophical societies, in Stephens, M. D. and Roderick, G. W. (eds.), *Samuel Smiles and Nineteenth Century Self-Help in Education*, Department of Adult Education, University of Nottingham, 16-46.

Stevens, F. (1919) *Some Account of the Educational Work at the Salisbury Museum, 1916-1919*, Salisbury Museum.

Thompson, S. (1951) *Educational Experiment 1941-1951*, Corporation of the City of Glasgow.

Weston, R. (1939) American museums and the child, *Museums Journal*, 39(2), 93-116.

Whitehead, P.J.P. (1970) Museums in the history of geology part 1, *Museums Journal*, 70(2), 55-57.

Winstanley, B. (1966) *Children and Museums*, Blackwell, Oxford.

Wittlin, A.S. (1949) *The Museum: Its History and Its Task in Education*, Routledge and Kegan Paul, London.

Wright, C.W. (1973) *Provincial Museums and Galleries*, HMSO, London.

7.4 Museum Education & Children

Andrews, K. & Asia, C. (1979) Teenagers attitudes about art museums, *Curator*, 22(3), 224-32.

Balling, J.D. & Falk, J.H. (1980) A perspective on field trips: environmental effects on learning, *Curator*, 23(4), 229-240.

Barnes, D.R. (1988) Teaching empathy with the help of theatre-in-education, *Welsh Historian*, Spring, 19-20.

Berry, N.W. (1979) Positive peer pressure, *Museum News*, 57(4), 29-34.

Brooks, J.A.M. (1956) A study of children's interests and comprehension at a science museum, *British Journal of Psychology*, 47, 175-182.

Brown, T. (1990) Kids as constituents, *Museum News*, 69(5), 72-74.

Cantrell, R.A. (1979) *An Evaluation of Museum Objects As Classroom Teaching Aids*, MSc Dissertation, University of Leicester.

Carlisle, R.W. (1985) What do school children do at a science centre, *Curator*, 28(1), 27-34.

Cheetham, F.W.(ed.) (1967) *Museum School Services*, Museums Association, London.

Cox, A. (1979) Teaching through museums, *Contact*, 11 (11 September).

Department of Education and Science & the Office of Arts and Libraries (1990) *Arts and Schools*, Central Office of Information, 5/90.

Durbin, G. (1989) Improving worksheets, *Journal of Education in Museums*, 10, 25-30.

Edeiken, L. R. (1992) Children's museums: the serious business of wonder, play and learning, *Curator*, 35(1), 21-27.

Evans, R.M. (1975) Museums, children and skills, *Amgueddfa*, 19(Spring), 19-25.

Fairclough, J. (1980) Heveningham Hall, midsummer 1790: a Suffolk schools project, *Museums Journal*, 80(1), 8-9.

Fairclough, J. (1982) Heveningham and after, *Journal of Education in Museums*, 3, 3-4.

Fairclough, J. & Redsell, P. (1985) *Living History: Reconstructing the Past With Children*, English Heritage.

Falk, J.H. & Balling, J.D. (1980) The school field trip: where you go makes the difference, *Science and Children*, 17(6), 6-8.

Falk, J., Martin, W. & Balling, J. (1978.) The novel field-trip phenomena: adjustment to novel settings interferes with task learning, *Journal of Research in Science Teaching*, 15(2), 127-134.

Feber, S. (1987) The Boston Children's Museum, *International J. of Museum Management and Curatorship*, 6, 63-73.

Fines, J. (1983) Starters - using objects from museums, *Museums Journal*, 83(2/3), 131-34.

Fry, H. (1987) Worksheets as museum learning devices, *Museums Journal*, 86(4), 219-225.

Gardner Smith Associates (1990) *School Visits to the Tower of London and Royal Armouries and to Other Heritage Sites and Museums*, Trustees of the Royal Armouries, London.

Glodberg, J. (1987) Opening eyes and minds, *Museum*, 39(1), 40-44.

Gortzak, H.J. (1981) The museum, children and the third world, *Museum*, 33(1), 51-6.

Greenglass, D. (1986) Learning from objects in a museum, *Curator*, 29(1), 53-66.

Hall, C. (1981) *Grandmas Attic or Aladdins Cave: Museum Education Services for Children,* New Zealand Council for Education Research, Wellington.

Heine, A. (1979) Making glad the heart of childhood, *Museum News,* 58(2), 23-5.

Hooper-Greenhill, E. (1988) The art of memory and learning in the museum: museum education and GCSE, *International J. of Museum Management and Curatorship,* 7, 129-137.

Ironbridge Gorge Museum (1987) *The GCSE and Museums: A Handbook for Teachers,* Ironbridge Gorge Museum.

Jones, L. S. & Ott, R. (1983) Self-study guides for school-age students, *Museum Studies Journal,* 1(1), 37-45.

Lawson, I. (1987) Standard grade and Scottish museums, *Museums Journal,* 87(2), 110-112.

Mathai, R.A. & Deaver, N.E. (1976) Child-centred learning, *Museum News,* 54(4), 15-19.

Mellors, M. (1982) Horniman Museum and Primary Schools, *Journal of Education in Museums,* 3, 19.

Millar, S. (1987) An opportunity to be grasped, *Museums Journal,* 82(2), 104-106.

Millar, S. (1989) Pre-vocational education and museums in Hooper-Greenhill, E. (ed.), *Initiatives in Museum Education,* Department of Museum Studies, University of Leicester, 14-15.

Millar, S. & Duston, C. (1982) Stepping back three hundred years: the Young National Trust Theatre Sixth Form Day at Montacute, *Teaching History,* 33, 32-4.

Moffat, H. (1988) Museums and schools, *Museums Bulletin,* 28(3), 97-98.

Moran, F. (1987) New opportunities for museums with the new curriculum, *Journal of Education in Museums,* 8, 23-25.

Museums Association (1987) GCSE and Museums, *Museums Journal,* 87(1).

National Curriculum Council (1990) *The National Curriculum: A Guide for Staff of Museums, Galleries, Historic Houses and Sites.*

O'Connell, P. & Alexander, M. (1979) Reaching the high school audience, *Museum News,* 58(2), 50-56.

Pennington, D.L. (1982) Two courses: the Afro-American; the Black woman in Stokstad, M. (ed.), *Museums, Humanities and Educated Eyes,* University of Kansas, 197-201.

Sahasrabudhe, P. (1968) The object, the child and the museum, *Museum,* 21(1), 51-4.

Siliprandi, K. (1987) Playgroups and museums, *Journal of Education in Museums,* 8, 13-14.

Spiller, E.M. (1917) The children's holidays at the Victoria and Albert Museum, 1917-18, *Museums Journal,* 17, 177-80.

Stillman, D. *et al.* (1983) A focus for the inter-disciplinary curriculum, *Museum News*, 61(6), 48-51.

Tanner, K. (1987) Cookworthy Museum and GCSE: a case study, *Museums Journal*, 87(2), 107-109.

Taylor, J. (1984) Primary education and local museums in Cumbria, *Museums Journal*, 84(3), 129-134.

Thomas, O. (1983) *Teaching With Overseas Artifacts*, Oxfordshire Development Education Unit, Oxford Polytechnic.

Whincop, A. (1987) GCSE for curators, *Museums Journal*, 87(2), 39-40.

Whincop, A. (1987) GCSE for curators, *Museums Journal*, 87(1), 3-5.

Whitechapel Art Gallery (1989) *Artists and Schools: The Whitechapel's Education Programme With East London Schools.*

Wolfe, G. (1987) Multi-cultural work in a mono-cultural resource, *Journal of Education in Museums*, 7, 20-23.

Woodward, S. (1989) School visits to "Gold of the Pharaohs", *Scottish Museum News*, 5(3), 3-5.

7.5 Museum Education & Adults

Adkin, G. (1981) *The Arts and Adult Education*, Advisory Council for Adult and Continuing Education.

Berger, J. *et al.* (1972) *Ways of Seeing*, Harmondsworth, Penguin.

Bown, L. (1987) New needs in adult and community education, in Ambrose, T. (ed.), *Education in Museums; Museums in Education*, HMSO/Scottish Museums Council, 7-18.

Chadwick, A.F. (1980) *The Role of the Museum and Art Gallery in Community Education*, Nottingham University Press.

Collins, Z.W. (ed.) (1981) *Museums, Adults and the Humanities - A Guide for Educational Programming*, American Association of Museums, Washington DC.

Cropley, A.J. (1980) *Towards a System of Life-Long Education*, UNESCO and Pergamon Press, London.

Durbin, G. (1987) Practical courses for teachers, *Journal of Education in Museums*, 8, 4-5.

Gabianelli, V.J. (1974) A place to learn, *Museum News*, 53(4), 28-32.

Gooding, J. (1985) How do you begin? Museum work with undergraduates and initial teacher training students in British and American institutions, *Journal of Education in Museums*, 6, 8-10.

Graetz, L. (1981) Houston: a steady hand and a peaceful heart, *Museum News*, 59(5), 33-5.

Grinder, A.L. & McCoy, S. (1985) *The Good Guide: A Sourcebook for Interpreters, Docents and Tour Guides*, Ironwood Press, Arizona.

Jackson, T. (1989) Reaching the community: modern art and the new audience in Hooper-Greenhill, E. (ed.), *Initiatives in Museum Education*, Department of Museum Studies, University of Leicester, 16-18.

Jessup, F.W. (ed.) (1969) *Lifelong Learning*, Pergamon Press, Oxford.

Jones, D. (1987) Exhibition review: "Hidden Peoples of the Amazon", *Museum Ethnographers Newsletter*, 20, 103 -110.

Jones, G.H. *et al.* (1966) The centre idea - student participation, *Adult Education*, 39.

Jones, S. & Major, C. (1986) Reaching the public: oral history as a survival strategy for museums, *Oral History Journal*, 14(2), 31-38.

Kelly, T. (1970) *A History of Adult Education in Great Britain*, Liverpool University Press.

Knox, A.B. (1981) Adults as learners, *Museum News*, 59(5), 24-9.

Marra, P. (1983) Self-study guides for the adult art museum visitor, *Museum Studies Journal*, 1(1), 37, 43-45.

Millas, J.G. (1973) Museums and life-long education, *Museum*, 35(3), 157-164.

Rogers, J. (1979) *Adults Learning*, Oxford University Press.

Rogers, J. (ed.) (1969) *Teaching on Equal Terms*, BBC, London.

Sudely, Lord, (1913) The public utility of museums, *The Nineteenth Century*, LXXIV, 1219.

Washburn, W.E. (1964) The museums responsibility in adult education, *Curator*, 7(1).

Zetterberg, H.L. *et al.* (1971) *Museums and Adult Education*, ICOM (International Council of Museums), Paris.

Zygulski, K. (1971) The museum and the adult, *The Museum in the Service of Man Today and Tomorrow*, Ninth General Conference Papers, ICOM (International Council of Museums), Paris, 125-36.

7.6 Evaluation of Museum Education Programmes

Ames, P.J. (1991) Measuring a museum's merits, in Kavanagh, G. (ed.), *The Museums Profession: Internal and External Relations*, Leicester University Press, Leicester, London and New York, 57-68.

Belland, J.C. & Searles, H. (1986) Concept learning in the museum, *Curator*, 29(2), 85-92.

Boggs, D.L. (1977) Visitor learning at the Ohio Historical Center, *Curator*,

20, 205-14.

Gillies, P.A. & Wilson, A.W. (1982) Participatory exhibits: is fun educational?, *Museums Journal*, 82(3), 131-34.

Greenglass, D. (1986) Learning from objects in a museum, *Curator*, 29(1), 53-66.

Hein, G.E. (1979) Evaluation in open classrooms: emergence of a qualitative methodology in Meisels, S. (ed.), *Special Education and Development*, Baltimore, University Park Press.

Hein, G.E. (1982) Evaluation of museums programs and exhibits, in Hansen, T.H. (ed.), *Museums and Education*, Danish ICOM (International Council of Museums)/Committee for Education and Cultural Action, Copenhagen, Denmark.

Korn, R. (1989) Introduction to evaluation: theory and methodology, in Berry, N. and Mayer, S. (ed.), *Museum Education: Theory and Practice*, The National Art Education Association, USA, 219-238.

Lucas, A.M., McManus P. & Thomas, G. (1986) Investigating learning from informal sources: listening to conversations and observing play in science museums, *European Journal of Science Education*, 8(4), 341-352.

Otto, J. (1979) Learning about "neat stuff": one approach to evaluation, *Museum News*, 58(2), 38-45.

Pond, M. (1985) The usefulness of school visits - a study, *Journal of Education in Museums*, 6, 32-36.

Rees, P. (1990) Education, evaluation and exhibitions: an outline of current thought and work on Merseyside, *Journal of Education in Museums*, 11, 9-12.

Screven, C.G. (1969) The museum as a responsive learning environment, *Museum News*, 47, 7-10.

Screven, C.G. (1974) *The Measurement and Facilitation of Learning in the Museum Environment*, Smithsonian Institution Press, Washington DC.

Screven, C.G. (1974) Learning and exhibits - instructional design, *Museum News*, 52(5), 67-75.

Screven, C.G. (1975) The effectiveness of guidance devices on visitor learning, *Curator*, 18, 219-43.

Screven, C.G. (1977) Learning in the museum environment, *Designers /Interpreters Newsletter*, 1(1), 13-15.

Screven, C.G. (1984) Educational evaluation and research in museums and public exhibits: a bibliography, *Curator*, 27, 147-165.

Walden, T.A. (1967) The alternatives in a survey of methods of providing educational services in museums, *Museums Journal*, 67(2), 141.

Walker, C.B. (1984) The kind of response that art can have, *Museum News*, 63(1), 36-44.

Zyskowski, G. (1983) A review of the literature on the evaluation of museum programs, *Curator*, 26, 121-128.

8 Museum Services - Provision & Development

8.1 Museums & Communities

Abbey-Livingston, D. (nd) *Volunteers in Your Organisation*, Ministry of Culture and Recreation, Toronto, Ontario.

Anderson, J.M. (1986) Something special: a museum folk arts program as community outreach, *Museum News*, 64(3), 50-57.

Angle, R.H. (1982) Liability or asset? How to make membership programs work, *Museum News*, 60(5), 31-4.

Arjona, M. *et al.* (1982) Museum development and cultural policy: aims, prospects and challenges, *Museum*, 34(2), 72-81.

Ball, M. (1979) Museum friends, *Arts Review*, 21(9), 239.

Banaigs, C. (1984) Curators, teachers and pupils: partners in creating an awareness of modern art, *Museum*, 36, 190-194.

Barnett, C. (1977) The Friends of the Tate Gallery, London, *Museum*, 29(1), 8-9.

Beardsley, D.G. (1975) Helping teachers to use museums, *Curator*, 18, 192-199.

Beevers, L., Moffat, S., Clark, H. & Griffiths, S. (1988) *Memories and Things: Linking Museums and Libraries With Older People*, WEA South East Scottish District, Edinburgh.

Belgrave, R. (1986) Southampton's Caribbean heritage: an analysis of the oral history project carried out by Southampton Museums 1983-1984, *Archaeological Objectivity in Interpretation*, Volume 3, World Archaeological Congress, 1-7 September, Southampton.

Beraud-Villars, M.J. (1977) Reflections and advice for the establishment of a society of friends, *Museum*, 29(1), 44-45.

Bhavnani, M. (1981) Museum highlights tours, *Curator*, 24(3), 213-20.

Bleick, C. (1980) The volunteer in art education: the art museum docent, *Art Education*, 33(1), 19-20.

Boniface, P. & Fowler, P. (1993) *Heritage and tourism in the global village*, Routledge, London.

Booth, J.H., Krockover, G.H. & Woods, P.R. (1982) *Creative Museum Methods and Educational Techniques*, Charles C. Thomas, Springfield, Illinois.

Boralevi, A. (1980) *Third International Conference of Friends of Museums*, Libreria Editvice Fiorentina, Florence.

Bradshaw, M.C. (1973) *Volunteer Docent Programs*, American Association for State and Local History, Nashville, Tennessee.

British Association of Friends of Museums (1981) *How to Form a Friends Society for Your Local Museum or Art Gallery*, BAFM.

Burgard, R. (1983) Culture co-operation - the new frontier, *Museum News*, 61(6), 20-29.

Butler, B. H. & Sussman, M. B. (1989) *Museum Visits and Activities for Family Life Enrichment, Marriage and Family Review*, 13(3/4).

Carnegie, E. (1992) Women's pictures, *Scottish Museum News*, 8(1), 8-9.

Carr, D. (1990) The adult learner in the museum, in Solinger, J.W. (ed.), *Museums and Universities: New Paths for Continuing Education*, National University Continuing Education Association, American Council on Education, and MacMillan Publishing Company, New York, 3-37.

Carr, J. R. (1986) Education everywhere for everyone at Mystic Seaport, in Ambrose, T. (ed.), *The American Museums Experience; in Search of Excellence*, Scottish Museums Council & HMSO, 41-58.

Chadwick, A. & Hooper-Greenhill, E. (1985) Volunteers in museums and galleries: a discussion of some of the issues, *Museums Journal*, 84(4), 177-178.

Chesley, K.L. (1967) How to develop a basic membership program by mail, *Museum News*, 46(1), 31.

Chesley, K.L. (1967) How to develop a basic membership program by mail, *Museum News*, 46(2), 28.

Coaldrake, M. (1986) *The Museums of Australia in the Community*, MA Thesis, University of Leicester, Department of Museum Studies.

Compton, M.S. (1965) A training program for museum volunteers, *Curator*, 8, 294.

Cone, C. (1978) Space, time and family interaction: visitor behaviour at the science museum of Minnesota, *Curator*, 21(3), 245-258.

Copeland, T. (1991) *A Teachers Guide to Maths and the Historic Environment*, English Heritage, London.

Cossons, N. (1973) The Ironbridge community service project, *Museums Journal*, 73(3), 104-106.

Diamond, J. (1986) The behaviour of family groups in science museums, *Curator*, 29, 139-154.

Dodd, J. (1992) Whose museum is it anyway?, *Journal of Education in Museums*, 13, 31-33.

Fay, P. (1974) Why NADFAS? the work of the National Association of Decorative and Fine Art Societies, *Museums Journal*, 73, 164.

Flint, L. (1959) Educational standards and volunteer performance, *Curator*, 2, 101.

Fraser, J. (1991) Do you have any Teacher's Packs?, *Scottish Museum News*, 7(4), 3-4.

Fraser, P. & Visram, R. (1988) *The Black Contribution to History*, Geffrye Museum, London.

Graham, F.P. (1965) Defining limitations of the volunteer worker, *Curator*, 8, 291.

Gribble, M.G. (1977) The use of volunteers, *Area Service Magazine (AMSSEE)*, 30, 7.

Group for Educational Services in Museums (1975) *Museums As an Influence on the Quality of Life*, British National Committee of ICOM (International Council of Museums), Group for Educational Studies in Museums.

Haase, D. (1986) The people tapestry, *Scottish Museum News*, 2(3), 5-6.

Hadley, R. & Scott, M. (1980) *Time to Give? Retired People As Volunteers*, The Volunteer Centre.

Hall, J.H. & McGray, K. (1977) The volunteer as everyman... woman and child, *Museum News*, 56(1), 27.

Harrison, R.F. (1978) Swedish travelling exhibitions, Riksutstallningar, *Museums Journal*, 78(1), 15-18.

Harvey, E.D. & Freidberg, B. (eds.) (1972) *A Museum for the People: Neighborhood Museums - A Report from the Brooklyn Muse Seminar, (New York, 1972)*, Arno Press, New York.

Hefferman, I. & Schnee, S. (1981) Brooklyn: building a new museum audience, *Museum News*, 59(5), 31-2.

Heffernan, I. & Schnee, S. (1980) *Art, the Elderly and a Museum*, Brooklyn Museum.

Heine, A. (1965) The care and feeding of volunteer staff members, *Curator*, 8, 287.

Hemmings, S. (1992) Chinese Homes, *Journal of Education in Museums*, 13, 33-34.

Hiemstra, R. (1981) The state of the art, in Collins, Z. (ed.), *Museums, Adults and the Humanities*, American Association of Museums, Washington, DC, 61-72.

Hill, T. & Nicks, T. (1992) *Turning the Page: Forging New Partnerships Between Museums and First Peoples*, Assembly of First Nations and Canadian Museums Association.

Hodgeson, J. (1986) Teaching teachers, *Museum News*, 64(5), 28-35.

Holtzhauer, H. (1971) The teacher and trainee teacher, *The Museum in the Service of Man Today and Tomorrow*, Ninth General Conference Papers, ICOM (International Council of Museums), Paris, 172-82.

Hood, M. G. (1989) Leisure criteria of family participation and nonparticipation in museums, in Butler, B. H. and Sussman, M. B. (eds.), *Museum Visits and Activities for Family Life Enrichment, Marriage and Family Review*, 13(3/4), 151-170.

Hutch. S. (ed.) (1983) *Volunteers: Patterns, Meanings and Motives*, The Volunteer Centre.

Jones S. & Major. C. (1986) Reaching the public: oral history as a survival strategy for museums, *Oral History Journal*, 14(2), 31-38.

Karp, I., Kreamer, C. M. & Lavine, S. D. (eds.) (1992) *Museums and Communities: Debating Public Culture*, Smithsonian Institution Press, Washington DC.

Kempff, K. (1981) Associations of friends - friend or foe?, *SAMAB: Southern African Museums Association Bulletin*, 14(8), 346-53.

Kropf, M. B. & Wolins, I.S. (1989) How families learn: considerations for program development', in Butler, B. H. and Sussman, M. B. (eds.), *Museum Visits and Activities for Family Life Enrichment, Marriage and Family Review*, 13(3/4), 75-86.

Leichter, H.J., Hensel, K. & Larsen, E. (1989) Families and museums: issues and perspectives, in Butler, B. H. and Sussman, M. B. (eds.), *Museum Visits and Activities for Family Life Enrichment, Marriage and Family Review*, 13(3/4), 15-50.

Linsley, S. (1975) Volunteer activity in industrial preservation, *Museums Journal*, 75(12).

MacDonald, S. (1990) Telling white lies, *Museums Journal*, 90(9), 32-33.

Martinello, M.L. & Cook, G.E. (1983) Preparing community volunteers for museum education, *Curator*, 16, 37-57.

Mattingley, J. (1984) *Volunteers in Museums and Galleries*, The Volunteer Centre.

Mawson, D. (1982) *The Role of Museum Friends and Volunteers*, British Association of Friends of Museums, London.

Measham, T. (1986) Voluntary Guide Training, *Museums Australia*, 4-8.

Meltzer, P.J. (1989) Help them help you, *Museum News*, 68(2), 60-2.

Millar, S. (1991) *The Management of Volunteers in Museums*, HMSO, London.

Millar, S. (1991) Policy planning for volunteers, in Ambrose, T. & Runyard, S. (eds.), *Forward Planning*, Routledge, London,, 112-116.

Monreal, L.A. (1972) Societies of museum friends: an attempt to define them, *ICOM (International Council of Museums) News*, 25(2), 96-9.

Morgan, W.L. (1968) A survey of American museum docent programmes, *Museum News*, 46(10), 28.

Newbery, E. (1987) Something for all the family, *Journal of Education in Museums*, 8, 9-10.

Nicholson, J. (1985) The museum and the Indian community: findings and orientation of the Leicestershire Museums Service, *Museum Ethnographers Newsletter*, 19, 3-14.

Nicholson, T.D. (1983) Volunteer employment at the American Museum of Natural History, *Curator*, 26, 241-253.

O'Connell, P. (1987) How to develop effective teacher workshops, *History News*, 42(3), 19-34.

O'Neill, M. (1987) Quantity vs. quality or what is a community museum anyway?, *Scottish Museum News*, 3(1), 5-6.

O'Neill, M. (1990) Springburn: a community and its museums', in Baker, F.

and Thomas, J. (eds.), *Writing the Past in the Present*, Saint David's College, Lampeter, 114-126.

O'Neill, M. (1991) The Open Museum, *Scottish Museum News*, 7(4), 6-7.

Osher, E. (1973) Training and motivation of volunteers, *ICOM (International Council of Museums) News*, 25(4), 226.

Paine, S. (1985) The art classroom in the training of art and design teachers, *Journal of Education in Museums*, 6, 15-19.

Paine, S. (1989) Museums as resources in the education and training of teachers in Hooper-Greenhill, E. (ed.), *Initiatives in Museum Education*, Department of Museum Studies, University of Leicester, 28-29.

Payson, H.S. (1967) Volunteers - priceless personnel for the small museum, *Museum News*, 45(6), 18.

Peirson Jones, J. (1985) Responding to a multi-cultural society: which Africa? Which Arts?, *Museum Ethnographers Group Newsletter*, 19, 15-25.

Peirson Jones, J. (1992) Multiculturalism incarnate, *Museums Journal*, 92(1), 32-33.

Pirie, V. (1992) Representation of the people, *Museums Journal*, 92(8), 29-30.

Pitman-Gelles, B. (1983) Beyond outreach, museums and community organisations, *Museum News*, 61(6), 36-41.

Plant, A. (1992) Expression and engagement, *Journal of Education in Museums*, 13, 12-15.

Prestwich, P. (1982) Notes & Comments: the World Federation of Friends of Museums, Fourth Congress held in Birmingham, 14-19 June 1981, *International J. of Museum Management and Curatorship*, 1, 65-76.

Prestwich, P. (1983) Museums, friends and volunteers: a delicate relationship, *International J. of Museum Management and Curatorship*, 2(2), 171-76.

Prince, D.R. (1985) Museum visiting and unemployment, *Museums Journal*, 85(2), 85-90.

Reeve, J. (1983) Museum materials for teachers, in Hall, N. (ed.), *Writing and Designing Interpretive Materials for Teachers*, Conference papers, Manchester Polytechnic, October.

Reeve, J. (1987.) Multi-cultural work at the British Museum, *Journal of Education in Museums*, 7, 27-32.

Reeves, P. (1975) Conserving tapestries with volunteer energy, *Curator*, 18, 182.

Reibel, D.B. (1971) The volunteer - nuisance or saviour?, *Museum News*, 49(7), 28.

Reibel, D.B. (1974) The use of volunteers in museums and historical societies, *Curator*, 17(1), 16-26.

Reid, C.G.R. (1993) The Roadshow, *Geology Today*, 9(4), 147-153.

Riviere, G.H. *et al. (1*973) The museum as a monitoring instrument,

Museum, 25(1/2), 26-59.

Robertson, A.G. *et al. (1*973) The museum and the community, *Museums Journal*, 73(3), 100-06.

Robinson, A. & Toobey, M. (1989) Reflections to the future, *Museums Journal*, 89(7), 27-29.

Schlereth, T.J. (1984) Object knowledge: every museum visitor an interpreter, in Nichols, S.K. (ed.), *Museum Education Anthology 1973-1983*, American Association of Museums, Washington DC, 108-117.

Scottish Museum News (1987) Leisure learning programme gets underway, *Scottish Museum News*, 3(3), 17.

Seidelman, J.E. (1965) Importance of volunteer placement, *Curator*, 8, 299.

Sekules, V. (1984) A small child could do it? The University of East Anglia Collection of Abstract Art & Design, *Museums Journal*, 84(3), 124-128.

Selby, R.L. (1977) Byelaws for volunteer groups, *Museum News*, 56(1), 21.

Senior, P.A. (1982) Voluntary guides at the Johannesburg Art Gallery, *SAMAB: Southern African Museums Association Bulletin*, 15(1), 34-40.

Sharpe, T. & Howe, S.R. (1982) Family expeditions - the museum outdoors, *Museums Journal*, 82(3), 143-147.

Siliprandi, K. (1987) Playgroups and museums, *Journal of Education in Museums*, 8, 13-14.

Silvester, J.W.H. (1977) An education function built into a new technical museum, *Museums Journal*, 77(3), 134.

Silvester, J.W.H. (1978) Are contemporary cultural needs being met by museums?, *Museum News (National Heritage, London)*, 14, 13-15.

Simpson, M. (1987) Multi-cultural education and the role of the museum, *Journal of Education in Museums*, 7, 1-6.

Smith, N. (1991) Exhibitions and audiences: catering for a pluralistic public, in Kavanagh, G. (ed.), *Museum Languages: Objects and Texts*, Leicester University Press, Leicester, London and New York, 119-133.

Smith, N. (1991) Museum images of a multi-cultural society, in Kavanagh, G. (ed.), *Museum Languages: Objects and Texts*, Leicester University Press, Leicester, London and New York.

Solinger, J.W. (1990) *Museums and Universities: New Paths for Continuing Education*, National University Continuing Education Association, American Council on Education, and MacMillan Publishing Company, New York.

Spruit, R. (1982) Ethnic minorities in a museum, *Museums and Education*, Danish ICOM (International Council of Museums)/Committee for Education and Cultural Action, 65-68.

Stewart, D. (1988) Leisure learning programme - update, *Scottish Museum News*, 4(2), 2-3.

Straus, E.S. (1977) Volunteer professionalism, *Museum News*, 56(1), 24.

Stubbings, P. (1981) *New Resources for Old Tasks: Disabled People As Volunteers*, The Volunteer Centre.

Sudely, Lord (1912) The public utility of museums, *Museums Journal*, 11, 271.

Swanger, J.L. (1985) Museums and the teaching of teachers, *Museum Studies Journal*, 2(1), 31-34.

Swanger, J.L. (1985) Teaching teachers to use museums, *Museum Studies Journal*, 2(1), 31-34.

Swauger, J.L. (1973) Is there life after retirement?, *Museum News*, 52(3), 31.

Swauger, J.L. (1977) Examining a delicate balance, *Museum News*, 56(1), 15.

Taborsky, E. (1978) The museum and the community, *ICOM (International Council of Museums) Education*, 8, 36.

Teruggi, M. (1973) The round table of Santiago, (Chile), *Museum*, 25(3), 129-133.

Thompson, J. (1972) A Bradford project in community involvement, *Museums Journal*, 71(4).

Tinker, A. (1992) *Elderly People in Modern Society*, Longman, London and New York.

Trade Union Congress (1982) *Working Party on the Arts*, TUC.

Trenbeth, R.P. (1967) Buildings from strength through the membership approach, *Museum News*, 46(1), 24-9.

Tresidder, G. (1977) Museum training and the volunteer, *Museum News*, 11, 10.

Trivulzio, A. (1990) Volunteers and the role of the museum for schools, the handicapped and hospitals, *International J. of Museum Management and Curatorship*, 9(3), 273-280.

Vodden, D.F. & Blench, B.R.J. (1971) Museum work in a college of education, *Teaching History*, 2(5), 15-20.

Volunteer Centre (1977) *Guidelines for the Relationship Between Volunteers and Paid Non- Professional Workers*, Volunteer Centre.

Volunteer Centre (1978) *Working With Volunteers: Recruitment and Selection*, Volunteer Centre.

Warden-Swifen, B.R. (1980) Friends of museums - their organisation and policy, *Museums Bulletin*, 20(9), 163.

Watson, G.G. (1975) Museums and the community, *Museums Journal*, 75(3).

Wilson, M. (1976) *The Effective Management of Volunteer Programs*, Volunteer Management Associates, Colorado.

Winterbotham, N. (1993) Happy hands-on, *Museums Journal*, 93(2), 30-31.

Wittmann, O. (1967) A museum serves its community: Toledo's pioneer educational programme, *Museums Journal*, 67(2).

Wolins, I.S. (1990) Teaching the teachers, *Museum News*, 69(3), 71-75.

World Federation of Friends of Museums (1987) The friends of museums of Argentina make the arts and collections of their country known,

Museum, 39(2), 120-121.

8.2 Children's Museums

Cleaver, (1988) *Doing Children's Museums: A Guide to 225 Hands-On Museums*, Williamson Publishing, Vermont.

Gurian, E. (1981) Adult learning at Children's Museum of Boston, in Collins, Z. (ed.), *Museums, Adults and the Humanities*, American Association of Museums, Washington, DC, 271-296.

Lantos, L. (1993) Naive eyes - The Children's Art Foundation, *Museum News*, 72(6), 40-41.

LeBlanc, S. (1993) Lost Youth: Museums, teens and the "Youth Alive" project., *Museum News*, 72(6), 44-54.

Lewin, A.W. (1989) Children's museums: a structure for family learning, in Butler, B. H. and Sussman, M. B. (eds.), *Museum Visits and Activities for Family Life Enrichment, Marriage and Family Review*, 13(3/4), 51-73.

Lewis, R.K. (1993) Serious play: Children's Museum of Houston, *Museum News*, 72(6), 36-9.

Sterling, P.V. (1993) Young and promising, *Museum News*, 72(6), 42-43.

Thomas, G. (1992) How Eureka! The Children's Museum responds to visitors' needs, in Durant, J. (ed.), *Museums and the Public Understanding of Science*, Science Museum in Association with the Committee on the Public Understanding of Science, London, 88-93.

8.3 Special Needs Provision

Alphen, J.V. (1982) Handling a cathedral, *International J. of Museum Management and Curatorship*, 1(4), 347-56.

Arts Council (1989) *Arts and Disability Checklist: A Quick Reference Guide for Arts Officers on Arts and Disability Issues*.

Attenborough, R. (1985) *Arts and Disabled People*, Carnegie UK Trust and the Centre for Environment for the Handicapped.

Bartlett, J.E. (1955) Museums and the blind, *Museums Journal*, 54, 283-287.

Bateman, P. (1988) Handling sessions at the Museum of Mankind, in Royal National Institute for the Blind, *Talking Touch: Report of a Seminar on* *the Use of Touch in Museums and Galleries Held at the RNIB on 29th February, 1988*, 10-15.

Bizaguet, E. (1991) Sufferers from defective hearing and the new techniques for communication, Fondation de France and ICOM, *Museums Without Barriers*, Routledge, London, 156-159.

Bouchauveau, G. (1991) Reception services for the deaf at the Cite des Sciences et de l'Industrie at La Villette in Paris, in Foundation de France and ICOM, *Museums Without Barriers*, Routledge, London, 160-162.

Bowden, O.H. (1966) Special exhibition for the benefit of blind persons arranged in the Natal Museum, *SAMAB: Southern African Museums Association Bulletin*, 8(9), 362-64.

Calhoun, S.N. (1974) On the edge of vision, *Museum News*, 52(7), 36-41.

Callow, K.N. (1974) Museums and the disabled, *Museums Journal*, 74(2), 70-2.

Carnegie Council (1988) *After Attenborough: Arts and Disabled People - Carnegie Council Review*, Carnegie United Kingdom Trust.

Charlton, J.A. (1933) The showing of museums and art galleries to the blind, *Museums Journal*, 33(3), 85-99.

Coles, P. (1983) *Please Touch: An Evaluation of the Please Touch Exhibition at the British Museum*, Committee of inquiry into Arts and Disabled People/Carnegie UK Trust.

Corbishley, M. (1987) The past replayed, *Remnants*, 5, 5-8.

Deas, C. (1913) The showing of museums and art galleries to the blind, *Museums Journal*, 13(3), 85-109.

Deas, C. (1927) Museums and the blind, *Museums Journal*, 27(2), 39-40.

Delaney, C. (1983) *Public Participation: Museums in the Community With Special Reference to Disadvantaged Groups*, Museums Association Conference Proceedings, 25-6.

Earnscliffe, J. (1992) *In Through the Front Door: Disabled People and the Visual Arts - Examples of Good Practice*, Arts Council of Great Britain, London.

Feeley, J. (1985) The "Listening Eye" tours for the deaf in San Francisco Bay Area Museums, *Museum Studies Journal*, 2(1), 36-49.

Ford-Smith, J. (1988) Touch facilities, *In Royal National Institute for the Blind*, Talking Touch: report of a seminar on the use of touch in museums and galleries held at the RNIB on 29th February, 1988, 24-26.

Foundation De France & International Council of Museums (1991) *Museums Without Barriers*, Routledge, London.

Groff, G. & Gardner, L. (1989) *What Museum Guides Need to Know: Access for Blind and Visually Impaired Visitors*, American Foundation for the Blind, New York, USA.

Grosbois, L.P. (1991) Ergonomics and museology, in Foundation de France and ICOM, *Museums Without Barriers*, Routledge, London, 60-69.

Hartley, E. (nd) *Art and Touch Education for Visually Handicapped People*,

University of Leicester, Department of Adult Education.

Hartley, E. (ed.) (1986) *Touch and See: Sculpture by and for the Visually Handicapped in Practice and Theory*, University of Leicester, Department of Adult Education.

Haseltine, J.L. (1966) Please touch, *Museum News*, 45(2), 11-16.

Heath, A. (1976) The same, only more so: museums and the handicapped visitor, *Museums Journal*, 76(2), 56-8.

Heath, A. (1977) Handicapped students and museums, *Museum Education Training*, Museum Education Association of Australia, Sydney, 5-9.

Hellman, R. & Hellman, E. (1961) A nature trail for the blind, *Museum News*, 39(9), 24-5.

Henrikson, H.C. (1971) Your museum: a resource for the blind, *Museum News*, 50(2), 26-8.

Hunt, G. & McLeod, J. (1977) *Museums: A Community Resource for the Handicapped*, Museum Education Association of Australia, Sydney.

International Council of Museums (1969) The Mary Duke Biddle gallery for the blind, *ICOM (International Council of Museums) Annual Museums Education & Cultural Action*, 1, 23-4.

James, D. (1988) Organizing visits for the physically handicapped, *Remnants*, 5, 9.

Keen, C. (1981) Everyone should have one: a practical policy for the disabled visitor, *Museums Bulletin*, 20(10), 177-78.

Keen, C. et al. (1984) Visitor services and people with a disability, *Museums Journal*, 84(1), 33-38.

Kelly, E. (1982) New services for the disabled in American museums, *Museums Journal*, 82(3), 157-60.

Kenney, A.P. (1974) Museums from a wheelchair, *Museum News*, 53(4), 14-17.

Kinsey, W.T. (1960) A museum exhibit for the blind, *Seer*, 51-4.

Kinsey, W.T. (1961) That the blind may see, *Museum News*, 39(9), 26-9.

Kirby, W. (1991) Paintings and visually impaired people', in Fondation de France and ICOM, *Museums Without Barriers*, Routledge, London, 118-121.

Leicestershire Museums (1976) *Museums and the Handicapped*, Leicester.

Moore, G. (1968) Displays for the sightless, *Curator*, 11(4), 292-96.

Museums & Galleries Commission (1992) *Guidelines on Disability for Museums and Galleries in the United Kingdom*, Museums and Galleries Commission, London.

Museums & Galleries Disability Association (1987) *Museums - Opening the Door to Disabled People*, Report of a seminar held at the Merseyside Maritime Museum.

Museums & Galleries Disability Association (1988) *Disability Design Museums*, Museums and Galleries Disability Association and Group of Designers and Interpreters in Museums.

National Trust (1984) *Facilities for the Disabled and Visually Handicapped*, National Trust.

O'Malley, C. (1976) Museum education and the gifted child: thoughts after a conference, *Museums Journal*, 76(3), 5-9.

Ontario Ministry of Culture and Comunications (1985) *The Community Museum and the Disabled Visitor*, Ontario Museum Notes, 12, Heritage Branch Ministry of Citizenship and Culture.

Pearson, A. (1985) Museums, art galleries, exhibition centres and visitor centres, *Arts for everyone*, Carnegie United Kingdom Trust and Centre for Environment for the Handicapped, 22-36.

Pearson, A. (1989) Museum education and disability', in Hooper-Greenhill, E. (ed.), *Initiatives in Museum Education*, Department of Museum Studies, University of Leicester, 22-3.

Pearson, A. (1991) Touch exhibitions in the United Kingdom', in Fondation de France and ICOM, *Museums Without Barriers*, Routledge, London, 122-126.

Pearson, F. (1981) Sculpture for the blind: National Museum of Wales, *Museums Journal*, 81(1).

Redfield, A. (1969) Mutual assistance: handicapped workers and the museum, *Museum News*, 47(10), 19.

Ricards, G.T. (1951) Exhibition for the blind and partially blind, *Museums Journal*, 50(12), 284-86.

Rowland, W. (1973) Museums and the blind, *ICOM (International Council of Museums) News*, 26(3), 117-21.

Royal National Institute for the Blind (1988) *Talking Touch: Report of a Seminar on the Use of Touch in Museums and Galleries Held at the Rnib on 29th February, 1988.*

Royal National Institute for the Blind (nd) *Planning for Your Visually-Impaired Public - Museums Information Pack*, RNIB leisure service information pack.

Royal Ontario Museum (1980) *The Museum and the Visually Impaired*, Royal Ontario Museum, Toronto.

Saley, M. (1976) Action to help the blind and physically handicapped, Niger National Museum, Niamey, *Museum*, 28(4), 210-11.

Smith, P.S. (1977) Against segregating the blind, *Museum News*, 55(3), 10-11.

Smithsonian Institution (1977) *Museums and the Handicapped: Guidelines for Educators*, Smithsonian Institution, Washington, DC.

Sorrell, D. (ed.) (1975) *Museums and the Handicapped*, Group for Educational Services in Museums, Departments of Museum Studies and Adult Education, University of Leicester.

South African National Gallery (1969) Sculpture for the blind, *SAMAB: Southern African Museums Association Bulletin*, 9(5), 314.

Steiner, C.K. (1978) Reaching the mentally handicapped, *Museum News*,

56(6), 19-23.

Steiner, C.K. (1979) *Museum Education for Retarded Adults - Reaching Out to a Neglected Audience*, Metropolitan Museum of Art, New York.

Steiner, C.K. (1979) *Museums and the Disabled*, The Metropolitan Museum of Art, New York.

Steiner, C.K. (1991) Museum programmes designed for mentally disabled visitors, in Fondation de France and ICOM, *Museums Without Barriers*, Routledge, London, 172-176.

Sullivan, R. (1990.) *Sculpture for Visually Handicapped People: The Art and the Craft*, Centre for Disability and the Arts, University of Leicester.

Sunderland, J.T. (1977) Museums and older Americans, *Museum News*, 55(3), 21-3.

Swanton, E.W. (1947) *A Country Museum; the Rise and Progress of Sir Jonathon Hutchinsons Museum at Haslemere*, Haslemere Educational Museum, Surrey.

Thorpe, S. (1987) Physical access, in Museums and Galleries Disability Association, *Museums-Opening the Door to Disabled People*, Report of a seminar held at the Merseyside Maritime Museum, 7 -13.

UNESCO (1981) Museums and the disabled, *Museum*, 33(3).

Voight, E. (1972) The extra-mural museum, *SAMAB: Southern African Museums Association Bulletin*, 10(6), 162-69.

Watkins, M. (1975) A small handling table for blind visitors, *Museums Journal*, 75(1), 29-30.

Weison, M. (1991) Art and the visual handicap. a role for the associations for the blind, the museums and art associations, and the official cultural authorities, in Fondation de France and ICOM, *Museums Without Barriers*, Routledge, London, 107-113.

Weison, M. (1991) Museums and the visually handicapped, in Fondation de France and ICOM, *Museums Without Barriers*, Routledge, London, 83-85.

Whittaker, J.H. McD. (1966) Geology for the blind, *Museums Journal*, 68(4), 298-299.

8.4 Science & Discovery Centres

Anderson, P. & Alexander, B. (1991) *Before the Blueprint: Science Center Buildings*, Association of Science - Technology Centers, Washington, DC.

Bagchi, S.K., Yahya, I. & Coles, P.R. (1992) The Piagetian children's science gallery, *Curator*, 35(2), 95-101.

Borun, M. *et al.* (1983) *Planets and Pulleys: Studies of School Visits to Science Museums*, Association of Science - Technology Centers, Washington, DC.

Bruman, R. & Hipschman, R. (1987) *Exploratorium Cookbook I, II, III: Construction Manuals for Exploratorium Exhibits*, Exploratorium, San Francisco.

Bryden, M. & Thompson, E. (1987) The Discovery Room: a three week experiment in the National Museums of Scotland, *Museum Design: Newsletter of the Group of Designers & Interpretors in Museums*, 3, 2-3.

Butler, S. (1992) *Science and Technology Museums*, Leicester University Press, Leicester, London and New York.

Carnes, A. (1986) Showplace, playground or forum?, *Museum News*, April, 28-35.

Committee on the Public Understanding of Science (1989) *Sharing Science: Issues in the Development of Interactive Science & Technology Centres*, Nuffield Foundation & COPUS.

Csikszentmihalyi, M. (1988) Human behaviour and the science center, in Heltne, P. & Marquardt, L. (eds.), *Science Learning in the Informal Setting*, Chicago Academy of Sciences, Chicago.

Danilov, V.J. (1980) *Towards the Year 2000: International Perspectives on Museums of Science & Technology*, Association of Science - Technology Centers, Washington DC.

Danilov, V.J. (1982) *Science and Technology Centers*, MIT press, Mass..

Danilov, V.J. (1984) Early childhood exhibits at science centers, *Curator*, 27, 173-188.

Danilov, V.J. (1984) Science centres in the Far East, *Museum Studies Journal*, 1(4), 24-30.

Danilov, V.J. (1986) Science exhibits and the young, *International J. of Museum Management and Curatorship*, 5, 241-257.

Decrosse, A. (1987) Explora - the permanent exhibition of the Centre for Science and Industry at La Villette, Paris, *Museum*, 39(3), 176-191.

Diamond, J., Smith, A. & Bond, A. (1988) California Academy of Sciences Discovery Room, *Curator*, 31(3), 157-166.

Druger, M. (1988) *Science for the Fun of It: A Guide to Informal Science Education*, National Science Teachers Association, Washington, DC.

Durant, J. (1992) *Museums & the Public Understanding of Science*, Science Museum, London.

Durant, J., Evans, G.A. & Thomas, G.P. (1989) The Public Understanding of Science, *Nature*, 340, 11-14.

Feher, E. & Rice, K. (1986) Development of scientific concepts through the use of interactive exhibits in a museum, *Curator*, 28(1), 35-46.

Fowles, J. (1991) Museums and Science Centres - collaboration for our environment, *Muse*, 8(4), 14-20.

Freeman, R. (1989) *The Discovery Gallery: Discovery Learning in the Museum*, Royal Ontario Museum, Toronto.

Greenwood, E.F., Phillips, P.W. & Wallace, I.D. (1989) The Natural History Centre at the Liverpool Museum, *International J. of Museum Management and Curatorship*, 8, 215-225.

Gregory, R. (1983) The Bristol Exploratory: a feeling for science, *New Scientist*, 17 November, 484-489.

Grinell, S. & Curtin, P. (1990) *Using Scientist Volunteers at Museums*, American Association for the Advancement of Science, Washington, DC.

Grinell, S. (ed.) (1992) *A New Place for Learning in Science: Starting and Running a Science Center*, Association of Science - Technology Centers, Washington, DC.

Hein, H. (1990) *The Exploratorium: The Museum as Laboratory*, Smithsonian Institution Press, Washington DC.

Hensley, J.R. (1990) Addressing public concerns at a science center, *Curator*, 33(2), 119-124.

Houlding, L.P. (1989) Pull-out drawers open windows, *Curator*, 32(4), 275-280.

Jones, T. (1992) Catalyst loses its modesty and comes of age, *New Scientist*, 15 August, 42.

Kennedy, J. (1990) *User Friendly: Hands-On Exhibits that Work*, Association of Science - Technology Centers, Washington, DC.

Kremer, K.B. & Mullins, G.W. (1992) Children's gender behaviour at Science museum exhibits, *Curator*, 35(1), 39-48.

Laetsch, W.M. *et al.* (1980) Children and family groups in science centres, *Science and Children*, 17(6), 14-19.

Levy, S. (1989) *Cogs, Cranks & Crates: Guidelines for Hands-On Traveling Exhibitions*, Association of Science - Technology Centers, Washington, DC.

Pettitt, C.W. & Phillips, D.A. (1984) The Buxton Micrarium, *Museums Journal*, 84(3), 123.

Phillips, D. (1986) Science centres: a lesson for art galleries?, *International J. of Museum Management and Curatorship*, 5, 259-266.

Pizzey, S. (ed.) (1987) *Interactive Science and Technology Centres*, Science Project Publications, London.

Royal Ontario Museum (1979) *Hands On: Setting Up a Discovery Room in Your Museum or School*, Royal Ontario Museum, Toronto.

Serrell, B. (ed.) (1990) *What Research Says about Learning in Science Museums, Volume 1*, Association of Science - Technology Centers, Washington, DC.

Serrell, B. (ed.) (1993) *What Research Says about Learning in Science Museums, Vol 2*, Association of Science - Technology Centers,

Washington, DC.

Tuckey, C.J. (1992) School children's reactions to the interactive science centre, *Curator*, 35(1), 28-38.

White, J. *et al* **(eds.)** (1991) *Snakes, Snails and History Tails: Building Discovery Rooms and Learning Labs at the Smithsonian Institution*, Smithsonian Institution Press, Washington DC.

8.5 Site Interpretation

Addyman, P. & Gaynor, A. (1984) The Jorvik Viking Centre - an experiment in archaeological site interpretation, *International J. of Museum Management and Curatorship*, 3(1), 7-18.

Alderson, W.T. & Low, S.P. (1976) *Interpretation of Historic Sites*, American Association for State and Local History, Nashville, Tennessee.

Aldridge, D. (1973) Regional and interpretive plans, *Museums Journal*, 73, 110-12.

Alfrey, J. & Putnam, T. (1992) *The Industrial Heritage: Managing Resources and Uses*, Routledge, London.

Allan, D.A. (1955) Site museums in Scotland, *Museum*, 8, 107-08.

American Association of Museums (1971) *Museums and Environment: A Handbook for Education*, American Association of Museums, Washington DC.

Anderson, J. (1985) *Time Machines*, American Association for State and Local History (AASLH), Nashville, Tennessee.

Anderson, J. (1986) *The Living History Sourcebook*, American Association for State and Local History (AASLH), Nashville, Tennessee.

Anon. (1973) Symposium - museum and environment, *Museum*, 25, 119-20.

Anon. (1975) Museums and interpretive techniques, *Museums Journal*, 75(2), 71-4.

Anon. (1984) Jorvik, *Heritage Interpretation*, 26, 3-4.

Ashbaugh, B.L. (1963) *Planning a Nature Center*, National Audubon Society, New York.

Barkley, B. (ed.) (1981) *Heritage Interpretation: Making Heritage Relevant*, British Columbia Provincial Museum, Victoria.

Beazley, E. (1971) *Countryside on View*, Constable, London.

Bellaigue, M.S. (1981) Industrial archaeology in industrial anthropology: the eco-museum of the community of Le Creusot-Montceau-Les-Mines, France, *Industrial Archaeology Review*, 5(3), 228-231.

Binks, G. (1981) Interpretation of Historic Monuments - some current issues, in Hughes and Rowley (eds.), *The Management and Presentation of Field Monuments*, Oxford University, 30-42.

Blatti, J. (ed) (1987) *Past Meets Present - Essays on Historic Interpretation*, American Association of Museums, Washington DC.

Carnegie UK Trust (1985) *Interpretation of the Environment - A Bibliography*, Carnegie UK Trust, Dunfermline.

Centre for Environmental Interpretation (1981) *Evaluation of Interpretation*, Centre for Environmental Interpretation, Manchester.

Centre for Environmental Interpretation (1981) Focus on audio-visual media, *Environmental Interpretation*, June.

Centre for Environmental Interpretation (1985) Focus on heritage centres, *Environmental Interpretation*, March.

Centre for Environmental Interpretation (1985) Focus on outdoor panels, *Environmental Interpretation*, June.

Centre for Environmental Interpretation (1986) Focus on funding, *Environmental Interpretation*, September.

Centre for Environmental Interpretation (1986) Focus on self-guided trails, *Environmental Interpretation*, November.

Civic Trust (1981) *Caring for the Visitor - The Calderdale Interpretation Strategy Study*, Oxford University, Department of External Studies.

Civic Trust & Centre for Environmental Interpretation (1983) *Up Greenhill and Down the Dale an Interpretive Plan for Wirksworth*, Derbyshire.

Connor, P. & Pearson, K. (1968) The birth of the Roman Palace Museum at Fishbourne, *Museums Journal*, 68(3), 115-17.

Countryside Commission (1975) *Guide to Countryside Interpretation, Part 1, Principles of Countryside Interpretation; Part 2, Interpretive Media and Facilities.*

Countryside Commission (1975) *Shipley Park Farm Interpretation Plan*, Cheltenham.

Countryside Commission (1975) *Tatton Park Interpretive Study*, Cheltenham.

Countryside Commission (1976) *Clumber Park - An Interpretive Study*, Cheltenham.

Countryside Commission (1976) *Hadrians Wall, a Strategy for Conservation and Visitor Services*, Cheltenham.

Countryside Commission (1976) *Interpretation in Visitor Centres*, Cheltenham.

Countryside Commission (1977) *Farm Open Days*, Advisory Series No 3, Cheltenham.

Countryside Commission (1977) *Interpretive Planning*, Advisory Series No 2, Cheltenham.

Countryside Commission (1978) *Guided Walks*, Advisory Series No 4, Cheltenham.

Countryside Commission (1978) *Interpretation in Visitor Centres*, Cheltenham.

Countryside Commission (1979) *Exmoor National Park Interpretive Plan Study*, Cheltenham.

Countryside Commission (1980) *Audio-Visual Media in Countryside Interpretation*, Cheltenham.

Countryside Commission (1980) *Self-Guided Trails*, Cheltenham.

Countryside Commission (1981) *Explore Your Local Countryside*, Cheltenham.

Countryside Commission (1981) *Information Signs in the Countryside*, Cheltenham.

Curry, D.A. (1969) Warleigh Wood Field Museum and Educational Nature Reserve, *Museums Journal*, 69(2), 70-1.

Dartington Amenity Research Trust (1979) *Interpreting the Derwent Valley*, DART.

Dartington Amenity Research Trust (1983) *Defence of the Realm - An Interpretive Strategy for Portsmouth and the Surrounding Region*, Centre for Environmental Interpretation, Manchester.

De Peyer, R. (1986) Re-interpreting the historic house, *Museums Journal*, 84(4), 221-30.

Deane, C.D. (1965) A field museum and nature trail in Northern Ireland, *Museums Journal*, 65, 97-9.

Deane, C.D. (1969) The Tollymore Park Trailside Museum, *Museums Journal*, 69, 68-9.

Dore, J.N. (1984) A new museum at Corbridge, Northumberland, *Museums Journal*, 83(4), 219-22.

English Tourist Board (1982) *Interpretive Techniques at Historic Buildings*, English Tourist Board, London.

Engstrom, K. (1973) Temporary and travelling exhibitions: a means of providing information on nature conservation, *Museum*, 25, 89-92.

Everard, M. (1980) Le Creusot-Montceau-les-Mines, the life of an eco-museum, assessment of ten years, *Museum*, 32, 226-34.

Fenton, A. (1973) Regional ethnology and environmental awareness, *Museums Journal*, 73, 107-10.

Fleming, D. (1986) From shepherds smock to EEC - interpretation in a rural museum, *Museums Journal*, 84(4), 179-86.

Gittins, J. (1986) Welsh Water splash out - with the help of others, *Heritage Interpretation*, 32, 4-6.

Goodey, B. (1974) *Urban Walks and Town Trails: Origins, Principles and Sources,*, Research memorandum 40, University of Birmingham.

Greenhough, M. (1986) On the waterfront: line interpretation in Liverpool, *Heritage Interpretation*, 32, 8-9.

Greenwood, E.F. (1976) Smithhills Hall Trailside Museum, Bolton, *Museums Journal*, 76(2), 66.

Hanna, J. (1977) *Interpretive Skills for Environmental Communicators*, Texas Art Galleries & Museums, Austin.

Hubendick, B. (1972) Museums and environment, *In the Museum in the Service of Man*, ICOM (International Council of Museums), Paris.

Hughes, M. & Rowley, C. (eds.) (1981) *The Management and Presentation of Field Monuments*, Oxford University, Department of External Studies.

Jenkins, J.G. (1984) Preserving - interpreting the heritage of Wales, *Heritage Interpretation*, 27, 8-10.

Johnels, A.G. (1973) Role of natural history museums, *Museum*, 25, 54-8.

Jorgenson, B. (1973) The New Zoological Museum, Copenhagen, *Museum*, 25, 63-8.

King, G.A.D. (1983) The relationship of museums with heritage organisations and their promotion, 4, *Museums Association Conference Proceedings*, 8.

Leone, M. (1983) Method as message: interpreting the past with the public, *Museum News*, 62(1), 34-41.

Lewis, R.H. (1945) Park museums - state and local, *Museum News*, 23(9), 7-11.

Lewis, R.H. (1959) Site museums in national parks, *Curator*, 2, 172.

Lewis, R.H. (1963) Selecting exhibit themes for park museums, *Park Practice Guideline*, 7, 14.

Lewis, R.H. (1973) Environmental education and research in Yellowstone National Park, *Museum*, 25, 85-8.

Lewis, W.J. (1981) *Interpreting for Park Visitors*, Eastern Acorn Press, Philadelphia.

Littledale, H. (1977) The Witley Common Information Centre, *AMSSEE Newsletter*, 30(Winter), 13.

Machlis, C.E. & Field, D.R. (1984) *On Interpretation - Sociology for Interpreters of Natural and Cultural History*, Oregon State University Press.

Marriot, F. (1973) The Ecomuseum of Marqueze, Sabres, *Museum*, 25, 79-84.

Marsh, J.J. (1986) *National and Cultural Heritage Interpretation Evaluation*, Interpretation Canada, Ottawa.

More, T.A. (1983) The non-user of an urban forest interpretive centre, *Journal of Interpretation*, 8(1), 1-10.

Murton, P.G. (1976) The Essex Naturalist Trust, Fingrinhoe Centre, *AMSSEE Newsletter*, 29(Summer), 4-5.

Orrom, M. (1978) The interpretive policy and visitor centres of the Forestry Commission, *Museums Journal*, 77, 171-73.

Orth, J. (1950) The Trailside Museum and Nature Trail at Bear Mountain, *Museum News*, 28(1), 6-8.

Parry, Lord (1983) The relationship of museums with heritage organisations and their promotion, 1, *Museums Association Conference Proceedings*, 4-5.

Percival, A. (1978) *Understanding Our Surroundings*, Civic Trust.

Pessino, C. (1975) City ecology for city children, *Curator*, 18, 47-55.

Pierssene, A. (1986) Can we do better than nature trails?, *Heritage Interpretation*, 32(Spring), 11-12.

Priestley, J. (1973) An American seminar on the open site museum, *Museums Journal*, 73(1), 7-10.

Prince, D.R. (1982) *Countryside Interpretation: A Cognitive Evaluation*, Centre for Environmental Interpretation, Manchester.

Prince, D.R. (1982) *Evaluating Interpretation: A Discussion*, Centre for Environmental Interpretation, Manchester.

Pritchard, T. (1983) Environmental conservation, *Museums Association Conference Proceedings*, 17-18.

Radcliffe, P.M. (1987) Period dress projects: considerations for administrators, *Curator*, 30(3), 193-8.

Ripley, S.D. (1973) Museums and the natural heritage, *Museum*, 25, 10-14.

Ripoll-Perello, E. & San Marti Greco, E. (1976) Ampurias: a history of the site, the excavation and the museum, *Museum*, 28, 85-99.

Rowell, C. (1983) The relationship of museums with heritage organisations and their promotion, 3, *Museums Association Conference Proceedings*, 6-7.

Rummens, D.M. (1984) Stott Park Bobbin Mill, *Heritage Interpretation*, 27, 3-4.

Schadla-Hall, R.T. (1984) Slightly looted - a review of the Jorvik Viking Centre, *Museums Journal*, 84(2), 62-4.

Sekers, D. (1984) Quarry Bank Mill: growth of a museum on a shoestring, *Museums Journal*, 84(2), 72-8.

Sharpe, T. & Howe, S.R. (1982) Family expeditions - the museum outdoors, *Museums Journal*, 82(3), 143-47.

Sharpe, W.G. (1976) *Interpreting the Environment*, Wiley, London.

Silvester, J.W.H. (1975) Exploiting site museums, *Museums Journal*, 75(1), 2-4.

Stansfield, G. (1967) Museums in the countryside, *Museums Journal*, 67, 212-18.

Stansfield, G. (1970) *Countryside Centres 1969 - Conference Report*, University of Leicester.

Stansfield, G. (1977) Information and interpretation in the countryside, *Journal of the Commons, Open Spaces and Footpaths Preservation Society*, 19(10), 7-13.

Stansfield, G. (1982) *Effective Interpretive Exhibitions*, Countryside Commission, Cheltenham.

Stansfield, G. (1983) Heritage and interpretation, *Museums Journal*, 83(1), 47-52.

Stansfield, G. (ed.) (1969) Conference on countryside centres, *Museums Journal*, 69, 63-77.

Stevens, T. (1983) *Interpretation: Who Does It, How and Why?*, Centre for Environmental Interpretation, Manchester.

Sultov, D. (1985) A site museum near Paulikeni, Bulgaria, *Museum*, 37(3), 136-9.

Taylor, G. (1977) Sherwood Forest Visitor Centre, *Countryside Recreation Review*, 2, 17-22.

Thom, V.M. (1980) Evaluating countryside interpretation: a critical look at the current situation, *Museums Journal*, 79(4), 179-84.

Tilden, F. (1957) *Interpreting Our Heritage*, University of North Carolina.

Tinniswood, A. (1981) *Guidebooks and Historic Buildings*, Department of Adult Education, University of Nottingham.

Tinniswood, A. (1982) *Guidelines: Some Problems Encountered in Writing Guide Books to Historic Buildings*, University of Nottingham, Nottingham.

Tomasevic-Buck, T. (1985) A Roman town and its presentation to the public, *Museum*, 37(3), 127-135.

Tynan, A.M. (1969) The Border Forest Park Museum, Northumberland, *Museums Journal*, 69, 69-70.

Varine-Bohan, H. De (1973) A fragmented museum - the Museum of Man and Industry, Le Creusot-Montceau-les-Mines, *Museum*, 25, 242-49.

Wallin, H.E. (1949) Educational opportunities in trailside museums, *Museum News*, 27(1), 7-8.

Watson, J.N.P. (1976) A floating mirror of wild Norfolk, *Country Life*, 160(30 September), 882-83.

Watson, M.S. (1983) The relationship of museums with heritage organisations and their promotion, 2, *Museums Association Conference Proceedings*, 5-6.

Wearing, M. (1977) Queen Elizabeth Country Park Centre, *AMSSEE Newsletter*, 30(Winter), 13.

8.6 Enquiries

Clarke, D.T.-D. (1992) Enquiries, in Thompson J.M.A. *et al. (eds.)*, *Manual of Curatorship*, Butterworth, London, 710-715.

Cooper, J.A. *et al.* (1980) *Geological Record Centre Handbook*, MDA, Duxford, 35-42.

Sharpe, T. & Rolfe, W.D (1979) Geological enquiries, *Museums Journal*, 79, 61-2.

Stapleton, C. (1982) How do you know what you've got?, *Connoisseur*, 212(849), 92-6.

Young, R.M.R. (1972) *Museum Enquiries*, Information Sheet No 11, Museums Association, London.

8.7 Publication

Anon. (1982) *World Museum Publications 1982 - A Directory*, Bowker.

Boorstein, D. (1975) Art book publishing in the 70s, *Museum News*, 53(5), 36-7 & 58.

Brown, G. (1983) When you care enough to send the very best, *Museum News*, 62(2), 22-33.

Burke, C. (1972) *Printing It: A Guide to Graphic Techniques for the Impecunious*, Ballantine Books, New York.

Council for British Archaeology (1979) *Signposts for Archaeological Publishing*, 2nd edition, CBA, London.

Cowan, A. (1993) Plan or perish: an integrated approach to museum and gallery publishing, *Muse*, 10(4), 39-41.

Degen, P.A. (1983) Quality design, *Museum News*, 62(2), 38-49.

Emmet, J. (1983) "Microfiche, the poor mans alternative to print, *International J. of Museum Management and Curatorship*, 2(1), 79.

Faul, R.H. (1975) Nothing succeeds like success, *Museum News*, 53(5), 32-5.

Felt, T.E. (1976) *Researching, Writing and Publishing Local History*, American Association for State and Local History (AASLH), Nashville, Tennessee.

Ferguson, M.D. (1978) Do-it-yourself design, *Museum News*, 56(4), 38-41.

Grote, A. (1982) Some observations on information sheets in museums, *International J. of Museum Management and Curatorship*, 1(2), 149-56.

Hosford, H. (1980) *Havent You Overlooked Something? on the Pitfalls of Printing*, British Columbia Provincial Museum, Victoria.

International Paper Company (1974) *Pocket Pal: A Graphic Arts Production Handbook*, 11th edition, International Paper Company, New York.

Jones, L.S. (1975) Where to publish, where to index?, *Museum News*, 53(5), 30-31 & 58.

Marcus, G.H. (1975) These catalogues don't stand on shelves, *Museum News*, 53(5), 25-9.

McPeake, W., Toy,S. & Fraser, M. (1993) Marketing and distributing museum publications, *Muse*, 10(4), 48-53.

Moore, E. (1975) The rocky road to publication, *Museum News*, 53(5), 21-4.

Pascal, N.B. (1979) Publishing within the museum, *Scholarly Publishing*, 10(2), 147-53.

Primary Communications Research Centre (1978) *Scholarly Publishers Guide: New Methods and Techniques*, PCRC, University of Leicester.

Publishers Association (1968) *Guide to Book Production Practice*, Publishers Association and British Federation of Master Printers, London.

Purcell, L.E. (1981) *Writing Printing Specifications: A Systematic Approach to Publications Managment*, American Association for State and Local History (AASLH), Nashville, Tennessee, Technical Leaflet No 142.

Putnam, J.B. (1975) An offer you shouldn't refuse, *Museum News*, 53(5), 42-3.

Quimby, I.M.G. (1983) Taking stock of the market, *Museum News*, 62(2), 34-7.

Rice, S. (1978) *Book Design: Systematic Aspects*, R.R. Bowker & Co., London.

Rudner, I. (1977) Consider you references, *SAMAB: Southern African Museums Association Bulletin*, 12(5), 194-96.

Smith, D.C. (1966) *Guide to Book Publishing*, R.R. Bowker & Co., London.

Society of Industrial Artists and Designers (1981) *Graphic Design for Printing - AChecklist*, Society of Industrial Artists and Designers (SIAD), London.

Society of Industrial Artists and Designers (1981) *Printing Knowledge for Designers - Checklist*, Society of Industrial Artists and Designers (SIAD), London.

Thom, I. & Brown, O. (1993) Why are we publishing: permanent record or vanity press?, *Muse*, 10(4), 18-21.

Tietz, R.M. (1981) Museum Publications, *SAMAB: Southern African Museums Association Bulletin*, 14(6), 227-39.

Tinniswood, A. (1981) *Guidebooks and Historic Buildings*, Department of Adult Education, University of Nottingham.

Tinniswood, A. (1982) *Guidelines: Some Problems Encountered in Writing Guide Books to Historic Buildings*, University of Nottingham, Nottingham.

Unwin, Sir S. (1960) *The Truth About Publishing*, Allen & Unwin, London.

White, A. (1973) Museum publications - a visitors view, *Museum News*, 51, 5-6.

8.8 Restaurants

Cheetham, F. (1972) Licensed bar and buttery at Norwich Castle Museum, *Museums Journal*, 71, 164.

Juttner, E. (1966) Gastronomia und Massenbesuch, *Naturschutz-Und Naturparks*, 51, 60-1.

King, C. (1975) Lets eat, *Museum News*, 53(9), 44-9.

Parkin, T. (1980) Interpreting and eating: a palatable pair?, *Interpretation Canada*, 18(2), 9-10.

Roth, E. (1990) Add meals to the menu of options you offer visitors, *Museum News*, November/December, 76-7.

Scroxton, J. (1988) Food service in museums, *Museums Journal*, 87(4), 187-190.

Seaby, W.A. (1963) Lecture halls, restaurants and cafeterias, *Museums Journal*, 63, 83-7.

8.9 Shops

Addison, W. (1967) Quality control in science museum merchandise - service to school children, *Museum News*, 46(4), 32-7.

Albers, H.R. (1973) And visions of royalties danced in their heads, *Museum News*, 52(1), 22-5.

Babbidge, I. (1972) *Beginning in Bookselling: A Handbook of Bookshop Practice*, Andre Deutsch, London.

Bain, I. (1984) Museum publishing and shops, in Thompson J.M.A. *et al. (eds.), Manual of Curatorship*, Butterworth, London, 460-466.

Barsook, B. (1982) A code of ethics for museum stores, *Museum News*, 60(3), 50-52.

Bassett, D.A. (1992) Museum publications: a descriptive and bibliographic guide, in Thompson J.M.A. *et al. (eds.), Manual of Curatorship*, Butterworth, London, 590-623.

Blume, H. (1981) *Charity Trading Handbook*, Charity Trading Advisory Group, London.

Blume, H. (1987) *The Museum Trading Handbook*, Charities Advisory Trust.

Booksellers Association (1977) *Opening a Bookshop - Some of Your Questions Answered*, Booksellers Association, London.

Brewster, D. (1993) Mail order catalogues: a guide to fulfilment, *Museum Development*, February, 18-22.

Brown, M.H. (1982) Keeping an eye on each other - the IRS and the museum store, *Museum News*, 61(1), 24-27.

Butler, D. (1993) The way ahead for museum retailing, *Museum Development*, May, 21-4.

Forester, C.T. (1981) The gift shop: tips on stocking museum stores, *History News*, 36(11), 34.

Gill, P. (1988) Relating the shop to the gallery, *Museum News*, January/February, 74-75.

Hewison, R. (1990) Sale of the century - Britain's museums are becoming shopping malls, *GQ: Gentlemen's Quarterly*, September, 166-171.

Hodripp, S. (1978) *The Shoppers Guide to Museum Stores*, Ash & Grant, London.

Krahel, D.H. (1971) Why a museum store?, *Curator*, 14, 200-204.

Long, M. & Sorrell, D. (eds.) (1978) *Museum Shops - A Powerful Force in Education*, Area Museum Service for the Midlands.

McHugh, B. (1979) Display and sales in gallery and museum shops, *Kalori*, 56, 30-33.

Munro, G. (1977) Museum shops from the outside, *Museums Journal*, 76, 143-145.

Murrey, G.G. (1983) Catalogue sales - mail order merchandising, *History News*, 38(2), 36-39.

Museums Association (1978) *Museum Shops*, Museums Association Information Sheet No 22.

Newcomb, K.K. (1977) *The Handbook for the Museum Store*, Museum Publications, Virginia.

Palmer, R. (1993) The Natural History Museum launches new retail strategy, *Museum Development*, February, 14-17.

Pemberton, M. (1986) Talking Shop, *Museums Journal*, 86(2), 89-95.

Rushton, B.N. (1968) Producing and selling slides, *Museum News*, 46(5), 27-32.

Sekers, D. (1976) The educational potential of museum shops, *Museums Journal*, 76, 146-147.

Thomas, L. (1967) The small store - quality service to the community, *Museum News*, 46(4), 37-9.

Williams, M. (1969) A museum sales system for the future, *Museum News*, 48(4), 22-.

Zurofsky, R. (1989) Sharp shop talk, *Museum News*, July/August, 45-7.

9 Professional & Institutional Context

9.1 Museums Profession

American Association of Museums (1989) *Staff Development: Innovative Techniques, Resources Report*, American Association of Museums, Washington DC.

American Association of Museums (1991) *1991 Survey of Compensation Practices among Museums, Reources Report*, American Association of Museums, Washington DC.

Association of Art Museum Directors (1992) *AAMD Salary Survey*, Assocation of Art Museum Directors, Washington DC.

Audience Concepts (1991) *Employee Benefits: A Museums's Most Valuable Investment - 1990 Survey of Art Museums.*

Boylan, P.J. (1993) Cross community curatorial competences, *Museums Journal*, 93(1), 26-29.

Cannon-Brookes, P. (1989) Management, professionalism and the archival function of museums, *International J. of Museum Management and Curatorship*, 8(2), 131-135.

Cossons, N. (1982) A new professionalism, *Museums Association Conference Proceedings.*

Cossons, N. (1991) Scholarship or self-indulgence?, *Royal Society of Arts (RSA) Journal*, 139(5415), 184-190.

Daneff, T. (1989) The experts' expert: Museum directors, *The Observer*, 23 July.

DiMaggio, P. (1983) The American art museum director as professional: results of a survey, *Bullet*, 24 June, 5-9.

Johnson, T. (1972) *Professions and Power*, MacMillan Press.

Kavanagh, G. (1992) The articulation of professional self-consciousness in Kavanagh, G. (Ed.), *The Museums Profession: Internal and External Relations*, Leicester University Press, Leicester, London and New York, 37-56.

Kavanagh, G. (ed.) (1992) *The Museums Profession: Internal and External Relations*, Leicester University Press, Leicester, London and New York.

Kavanagh G., et al. *(1*993) Curatorial identity, *Museums Journal*, 93(10), 27-33.

Leishman, M. (1993) Images and self-image, *Museums Journal*, 93(6), 30-32.

Murdoch, J. (1992) Defining curation, *Museums Journal*, 92(3), 18-19.

Museum Training Institute (1993) *Museum Sector Workforce Survey,: An analysis of the workforce in the museum gallery and heritage sector in the United Kingom,*, MTI, Bradford.

Museums Association (1993) Towards a new membership structure, *Museums Journal*, 93(12), iv.

Museums & Galleries Commission (1987) *Museum Professional Training and Career Structure*, HMSO, London.

New England Museum Association (1993) *1992/93 Salary Survey*, NEMA.

Perkin, H. (1989) *The Rise of the Professional Society*, Routledge, London.

Porter, G., et al. (1990) Are you sitting comfortably? Are equal opportunities a luxury?, *Museums Journal*, 90(11), 25-35.

Prince, D.R. (1988) Women and museums, *Museums Journal*, 88(2), 55-61.

Prince, D.R. & Higgins-McLoughlin B. (1986) *Museums UK: The Findings of the Museum Data Base Project.*, Museums Association, London.

Shaw, P. (1989) The state of pay, *Museums Journal*, 89(4), 26-28.

Southeastern Museums Conference (1992) *Southeastern Museum Conference Compensation and Benefits Practice Survey Results 1992*, SMC.

Teather, L.J. (1990) The museum keepers, the Museums Association and the growth of museum professionalism, *Museum Management & Curatorship*, 9, 25-41.

9.2 Museum Professionalism

American Association of Museums (1993) *Writing a Museum Code of Ethics: Resources Pack*, American Association of Museums, Washington DC.

Besterman, T. (1992) Disposals from museum collections, ethics and practicalities, *Museum Management & Curatorship*, 11, 29-44.

Blackmon, C.P., et al. (1988) *Open Strategies for Professional Development in Museums*, Field Museum of National History.

Cossons, N. (1982) A new professionalism, *Museums Association Conference Proceedings*.

Cossons, N. (1991) Scholarship or self-indulgence?, *Royal Society of Arts (RSA) Journal*, 139(5415), 184-190.

DiMaggio, P. (1983) The American art museum director as professional: results of a survey, *Bullet*, June 24, 5-9.

Kavanagh, G. (1992) The articulation of professional self-consciousness in Kavanagh, G. (Ed.), *The Museums Profession: Internal and External Relations*, Leicester University Press, Leicester, London and New York,

37-56.

MacDonald, R. (1992) Ethics: constructing a code, *Museum News*, May/June, 62-65.

MacGregor, N. (1990) Scholarship and the public, *Museum Management & Curatorship*, 9, 361-366.

Mauch, P. (ed.) (1989) *Ethics of Collecting Cultural Property*, University of New Mexico Press.

O'Neil, M. (1991) After the artefact: internal and external relations in museums, in Kavanagh, G. (ed.), *The Museums Profession*, Leciester University Press, 25-36.

Phillips, C. (1983) Museum director as manager, *History News*, 38 (3), 8-15.

Tucker, M. (1990) Common ground, *Museum News*, July/August, 44-46.

Ullberg, A.D. (1981) Recent developments in ethical codes and practices among museum staff in the United States, *Museum Professionals Group (MPG) Transactions*, 16, 57-69.

Ullberg, A.D. (1981) What happened in Greenville: the need for museum codes of ethics, *Museum News*, 60(2), 26-9.

Weil, S.E. (1988) The ongoing pursuit of professional status, *Museum News*, 67(2), 30-34.

9.3 Codes of Conduct

American Association of Museums (1991) *Code of Ethics for Museums*, American Association of Museums, Washington DC.

American Association of Museums (1993) *Professional Codes of Ethics (Reprint package from Museum News)*, American Association of Museums, Washington DC.

Art Gallery & Museums Association of New Zealand (1977) Art gallery and museums officers, *Code of Ethics*, AGMANZ.

Association of Art Museum Directors (1992) *Professional Practices in Art Museums*, Association of Art Museum Directors, Washington DC.

Canadian Museums Association (1979) *Statement of the Ethical Behaviour of Museum Professionals*, CMA.

International Council of Museums (1971) *Ethics of Acquisition*, ICOM (International Council of Museums), Paris.

International Council of Museums (1987) *Code of Professional Ethics*, ICOM (International Council of Museums), Paris.

Madison, H.L. (1925) Tentative code of ethics, published for the 20th annual meeting of the American Association of Museums, *Museums Journal*, 25, 19-23.

Museums Association (1991) *Code of Conduct for Museum Professionals,* Museums Association, London.

Museums Association of Australia (1982) *Museum Ethics and Practice,* MAA.

Royal Ontario Museum (1982) *Statement of Principles andf Policies on Ethics and Conduct,* ROM, Ontaria.

9.4 Institutional Standards

Accreditation Program, American Association of Museums (1989) *Accreditation: Self-Study and On-Site Evaluation and Questionnaire, Resources Report,* American Association of Museums, Washington DC.

Accreditation Program, American Association of Museums (1989) *Museum Accreditation: A Handbook for the Visiting Committee,* American Association of Museums, Washington DC.

Accreditation Program, American Association of Museums (1990) *Museum Accreditation: A Handbook for the Institution,* American Association of Museums, Washington DC.

Alderson, W.T. *et al.* (1981) Beyond the beginning: accreditation after 10 years, *Museum News,* 60(1), 34-49.

Ambrose, T.M. (1987) *New Museums: A Start-Up Guide,* Scottish Museums Council & HMSO.

Ambrose, T.M. (1988) Registration, *Scottish Museums Council News,* 4(2).

American Association of Museums (1970) *Museum Accreditation: A Report to the Professsion,* AAM, Washington, DC.

American Association of Museums (1981) *Small Museums and Accreditation,* AAM, Washington, DC.

American Association of Museums (1984) *Professional Standards for Museum Accreditation,* AAM, Washington, DC.

American Association of Museums (nd) *Museum Assessment Program,* American Association of Museums, Washington DC.

Ames, P J (1990) Breaking new ground: measuring museum merits, *International J. of Museum Management and Curatorship,* 9 (2), 137-147.

Anderson, R.G.W. (1991) Meeting the public needs?, *A New Museum for Scotland,* National Museum of Scotland, Edinburgh.

Audit Commission (1991) *The Road to Wigan Pier? Managing Local Authority Museums and Art Galleries,* HMSO, London.

Buchanan, J.E. (1981) A reading on MAP, *Museum News,* 60(2), 36-41.

Caton, J. (1991) Setting standards, *Museums Journal,* 91(1), 34-35.

Christison, M.B. (1980) Professional practices in university art museums, *Museum News*, 58(3), 30-40.

Cubbon, A.M. (1973) Accreditation, *Museums Journal*, 73(3), 97-8.

Dunning, F. (1993) No objects, no money, no venue, no problem, *Museums Journal*, 93(2), 22.

Findley, I. (1989) A blast for the past. Britain's heritage a policy for the future, *Museums Journal*, 89(8), 19-22.

Fitzgerald, M.H. (1973) *Museum Accreditation: Professional Standards*, American Association of Museums, Washington DC.

Graziano, S. (1984) The MAP team, *Museum News*, 62(5), 75-9.

Holt, R.J. (1980) Small museums and accreditation: Chesapeake Bay Maritime Museum, *Museum News*, 58(5), 60-2.

Igoe, K. (1986) How to put your museum on the map, *Museum News*, 65(2), 19-22.

Leavitt, T.W. (1981) Reaccreditation: learning from experience, *Museum News*, 60(1), 40-1.

Loughbrough, B. (1982) Professional standards and accreditation (1), *Museums Association Conference Proceedings*, 5-7.

Marsan, G.A. (1993) Measure the ecstasy, *Museums Journal*, 93(7), 27-28.

Morris, B. (1982) Professional standards and accreditation (2), *Museums Association Conference Proceedings*, 7-8.

Museums Association (1971) *Report of the Museums Association Working Party on Museum Accreditation*, Museums Association, London.

Museums Association (1987) *Code of Practice for Museum Authorities (amended)*, Museums Association, London.

Museums Association (1989) *Policy Statement on Museums*, Museums Association, London.

Museums Association (1990) *Guidelines for Museum Committee Members*, Museums Association, London.

Museums Association (1990) *Policy Initiatives: Performance Standards*, Museums Association, London.

Museums Association (1990) *Policy Initiatives: Privatisation*, Museums Association, London.

Museums Association (1991) *Guidelines on Policy Measurement*, Museums Association, London.

Museums & Galleries Commission (1988) *Guidelines for Registration*, MGC, London.

Museums & Galleries Commission (1992) *Guidelines on Disability for Museums and Galleries in the United Kingdom*, MGC, London.

Museums & Galleries Commission (1992) *Quality of Service in Museums and Galleries: Customer Care in Museums - Guidelines for Implementation*, Museums & Galleries Commission, London.

Museums & Galleries Commission (1992) *Standards in the Museum Care of Archaeological Collections*, MGC, London.

Museums & Galleries Commission (1992) *Standards in the Museum Care of Biologicial Collections*, MGC, London.

Museums & Galleries Commission (1993) *Registration Scheme for Museums and Galleries in the United Kingdom: Second Phase,*, MGC, London.

Museums & Galleries Commission (1993) *Standards in the Museum Care of Geologicial Collections*, MGC, London.

National Audit Office (1988) *Management of the Collections of the English National Museums and Galleries*, HMSO, London.

Newbery, C. (1988) MGC Registration Scheme, *Museums Bulletin*, April, 247-248.

Nicholson, T.D. (1981) Why accreditation doesn't work, *Museum News*, 60(1), 5-10.

Norman, J.Y. (1981) Accreditation: how museums benefit, *Museum News*, 60(1), 42-7.

Norman, J.Y. (1982) Reaccreditation. How it works and how its working, *Museum News*, 60(6), 63-8.

Office of Arts & Libraries (1991) *Report on the Development of Performance Indicators for the National Museums and Art Galleries*, OAL, London.

Ott, W. (1980) Small museums and accreditation: the Roswell Museum and Art Center, *Museum News*, 58(4), 46-9.

Paine, C. (1987) *The Local Museum*, Area Museum Service for South Eastern England, Milton Keynes.

Reardon-Tagore, K. (1991) Registration scheme milestone, *Museums Journal*, 91(1), 11.

Reger, L.L. (1982) Professional standards: keynote address, *Museums Association Conference Proceedings*, 2-5.

Schell, S. (1985) Taking a hard look, strategies for self-study in museums, *Museum News*, 63(3), 47-52.

Spencer, P. *et al.* (1993) Feel the width, *Museums Journal*, 93(7), 29-30.

Starr, K. (1982) In defense of accreditation: a response to Thomas D. Nicholson, *Museum News*, 60(3), 5-21.

Thompson, J.M.A. (1986) Accreditation, in Thompson, J.M.A. *et al.* (eds.), *Manual of Curatorship*, Butterworths, London, 105-113.

Timms, P. (1980) Small museums and accreditation: Fitchburg Art Museum, *Museum News*, 58(6), 54-7.

Wall, A.J. (1981) Demystifying the accreditation process, *Museum News*, 60(1), 48-53.

Weber, J. (1986) Accreditation and small museums, *Museum News*, 65(2), 13-17.

Weil, S.E. (1990) *Rethinking the Museum and Other Meditations*, Smithsonian Institution Press, Washington DC.

Williams, P.E. (1984) Value of accreditation, *Museum News*, 62(6), 55-67.

Williams, P.E. (1985) Promoting professional standards in Americas museums, *Museum*, 37(3), 150-155.

9.5 Governing Bodies

Ahmanson, C. (1971) Trustees and directors, *Museum News*, 50(1), 35-6.

Ames, P.J. & Spalding, H. (1988) Museum governance and trustee boards. a good engine that needs more oil, *International J. of Museum Management and Curatorship*, 33-36.

Association of Independent Museums (1980) *Setting Up and Running a New Museum*, AIM Guideline No 2.

Association of Independent Museums (1981) *Charitable Status for Museums*, AIM Guideline No 3.

Association of Independent Museums (1981) *Charitable Status for Museums - Scotland*, AIM Guideline No 3 in conjunction with CMGS.

Association of Independent Museums (1987) *The Role of Trustees in Independent Museums*, AIM Guideline No. 11, Association of Independent Museums.

Bowness, A. (1986) Relations between museums and employing authorities and governing bodies: national museums with special reference to museums with boards of trustees, in Thompson, J.M.A. *et al.* (eds.), *Manual of Curatorship*, Butterworth, London, 514-516.

Bradford, H. (1991) A new framework for museum marketing, in Kavanagh, G. (ed.), *The Museums Profession: Internal and External Relations*, Leicester University Press, Leicester, London and New York, 83-97.

Brown, D. (1982) The relationship between the governing body and the curatorial staff, *Museums Association Conference Proceedings*, 8-9.

Burus, W.A. (1962) Trustees: duties and responsibilities, *Museum News*, 41(4), 22-3.

Cheetham, F. (1986) Relations between museums and employing authorities and governing bodies: local authority museums with special reference to county museums, in Thompson, J.M.A.*et al.* (eds.), *Manual of Curatorship*, Butterworths, London, 518-22.

Cossons, N. (1976) The case of the cultural quango, *Museums Association Conference Proceedings*, 26-7.

Elcock, H. (1982) *Local Government, Politicians, Professionals and the Public in Local Authorities*, University Press, London.

Fenton, A. (1986) Administration of a national museum through a board of trustees, in Thompson, J.M.A. *et al.* (eds.), *Manual of Curatorship*, Butterworths, London, 516-18.

Hamilton, Sir D. (1977) The trustee and the national museums, *Museums Journal*, 77(3), 119-21.

Lister, Dame U. (1968) Curators and committee: a museum team, *Museums Journal*, 68(2), 82-4.

Mitchell, J. (1974) *How to Write Reports*, Fontana/Collins, Glasgow.

Museums Association (1991) Code of Practice for Museum Authorities, *Museums Yearbook*, Museums Association, London, 9-12.

Naumer, H.J. (1977) *Of Mutual Respect and Other Things: An Essay on Museum Trusteeship*, American Association of Museums, Washington DC.

Nelson, C.A. (1976) Trusteeship today, *Curator*, 19, 5-16.

North, I. (ed.) (1982) *On Trusteeship*, Art Galleries Association of Australia.

Norton, M. (1984) *A Guide to the Benefits of Charitable Status*, Directory of Social Change, London.

Norton, M. (1984) *How to Be a Good Trustee*, Directory of Social Change, London.

Paquet, M.A. *et al.* (1987) *A Handbook for Cultural Trustees*, University of Waterloo Press, Ontario.

Phillips, A. & Smith, K. (1982) *Charitable Status: A Practical Handbook*, Inter-action guides, London.

Selby, R.L. (1977) Byelaws for volunteer groups, *Museum News*, 56(), 21-3.

Sherrell-Leo, C. & Meyer, R.W. (1984) The buck stops here - and other trustee responsibilities, *History News*, 39(3), 28-30.

Smieton, Dame, M. (1977) The trustee and the national museums, *Museums Journal*, 77(3), 117-18.

Ullberg, A.D. (1984) Making boards work better, *Museum News*, 62(5), 45-6.

Ullberg, A.D. & Ullberg, P. (1981) *Museum Trusteeship*, American Association of Museums, Washington DC.

Unterman, I. & Davis, R.H. (1984) The strategy gap in not-for-profits, *Museum News*, 62(5), 38-44.

Waterson, M. (1982) Museum committees - allies or obstacles?, *Museums Association Conference Proceedings*, 9-10.

10   Museum Management

10.1 Management in Museums

Adair, J. (1987) *How to Manage Your Time*, Talbot Adair Press, Guildford.
Adair, J. (1988) *Effective Leadership*, Pan, London.
Alfrey, J. & Putnam, T. (1992) *The Industrial Heritage: Managing Resources and Uses*, Routledge, London.
Allden, A. & Ellis, A. (1990) Management: the flavour of the month, *Museum Development*, 90(11), 35-39.
Ambrose, T.M. (1993) *Managing New Museums: A Guide to Good Practice*, HMSO, London.
Ambrose, T. & Paine, C. (1993) *Museums Basics*, Routledge, London.
Audit Commission (1991) *The Road to Wigan Pier? Managing Local Authority Museums and Art Galleries*, HMSO, London.
Burrett, F.G. (1982) *Rayner Scrutiny of the Departmental Museums: Science Museum and Victoria & Albert Museum*, Office of Arts & Libraries, Department of Education & Science.
Cossons, N. (1970) McKinsey and the museum, *Museums Journal*, 70(3), 110-13.
Cossons, N., (ed) (1985) *Management for Change*, National Maritime Museum, London.
Drucker, P. (1978) *The Practice of Management*, Pan Books, London.
Fopp, M. (1986) The science of management, *Museums Journal*, 85(4), 187-89.
Gorr, L.F. (1980) A museum management bibliography: Part 1, *Museum News*, 58(5), 71-84.
Gorr, L.F. (1980) A museum management bibliography: Part 2, *Museum News*, 58(6), 67-77.
Greenhill, B. (1984) Three problems of museum management, *International J. of Museum Management and Curatorship*, 3(1), 67-70.
Handy, C. (1989) *The Age of Unreason*, Business Books, London.
Handy, C. (1990) *Understanding Voluntary Organisations*, Penguin.
Handy, C. (1993) *Understanding Organisations*, Penguin, Harmondsworth.
Hebditch, M.(ed) (1986) *Museum Management and Administration*, Museum of London.
Kittleman, J.M. (1976) Museum mismanagement, *Museum News*, March/April, 44-46.
Lawrence, P. & Lee, R. (1986) *Insight into Management*, Oxford University

Press, Oxford.

Lord, G. D., Lord B. (eds.) (1992) *The Manual of Museum Planning*, Museum of Science and Industry, Manchester and HMSO, London.

McConkey, D.D. (1975) *MBO for Non-Profit Organizations*, American Management Association, New York.

Meek, J.(ed) (1992) *Marketing the Arts*, ICOM (International Council of Museums), Paris.

Middleton, V. (1990) Irresistible demand forces, *Museums Journal*, 90(2), 31-34..

Middleton, V. (1991) *New Visions for Independent Museums in the UK*, Association of Independent Museums, West Sussex.

Museums and Galleries Commission (1988) *The National Museums*, HMSO, London.

Museums and Galleries Commission (1991) *Local Authority Museums*, HMSO, London.

Nicholson, J. (1992) *How do you Manage?*, BBC, London.

Peters, T.J. & Waterman, R.A. (1984) *In Search of Excellence*, Harper & Row, New York.

Pugh, D.S. (ed) (1987) *Organisation Theory: Selected Readings*, Penguin.

Pugh, D.S. & Hickson, D.J. (1989) *Writers on Organisations*, Penguin.

Sukel, W.M. MBO for museums, *Museologist,139*, 3-9, 1976.

Sukel, W.M. (1974) Museums as organisations, *Curator*, 17(4), 299-301.

Thompson, J. (1993) Contractual obligations, *Museums Journal*, 93(6), 25-6.

Thompson, J.M.A. et al. (eds.) (1992) *Manual of Curatorship: A guide to Museum Practice*, Butterworth, London.

Walford, N. (1985) Managing museums, *Museums Quarterly*, Spring.

Weil, S.E. (1985) M G R: a conspectus of museum management, *Beauty and the Beasts: On Museums, Art, the Law and the Market*, Smithsonian Institution Press, Washington DC, 69-80.

Weil, S.E. & Cheit, E.F. (1985) The well-managed museum, *Rethinking the Museum and other Meditations*, Smithsonian Institution Press, Washington DC, 69-72.

Woroncow, B. (1992) Public palaces or private places, *Museums Journal*, 92(12), 27-29.

10.2 Policy, Planning & Performance

Ahmanson, C. (1971) Trustees and directors, *Museum News*, 50(1), 35-6.

Allden, A. & Ellis, A. (1990) Management - naming the parts, *Museum*

Development, December, 11-13.

Allden, A. & Ellis, A. (1991) Back to the future, *Museum Development*, January, 38-40.

Ambrose, T.M. & Runyard, S. (eds.) (1991) *Forward Planning*, Routledge, London.

Ames, P.J. (1991) Measuring a museum's merits, in Kavanagh, G., (ed.), *The Museums Profession: Internal and External Relations*, Leicester University Press, Leicester, London and New York, 59-68.

Anon. (1991) Neil Chalmers, *Museum Development*, March, 35-40.

Audit Commission (1991) *The Road to Wigan Pier? Managing Local Authority Museums and Art Galleries*, HMSO, London, 29-38.

Beer, V. (1990) The problem and promise of museum goals, *Curator*, 33(1), 5-18.

Brown, D. (1982) The relationship between the governing body and the curatorial staff, *Museums Association Conference Proceedings*, 8-9.

Bud, R. *et al.* (1991) Measuring a museum's output, *Museums Journal*, 91(1), 29-31.

Chalmers, N. (1989) Defining our mission, *Museums Journal*, 88(4), 186-87..

Davies, S. (1992) Citizens, customers and curators, *Museums Journal*, 92(9), 20-21.

Davies, S. (1993) *Strategic planning in local authority museums*, Leeds Research Paper, School of Business and Economic Studies, University of Leeds.

Davies, S. (1993) Planning in a crisis, *Museums Journal*, 93(7), 31-33.

Dickenson, V. (1991) An inquiry into the relationship between museum boards and management, *Curator*, 34(4), 291-303.

Drucker, P.F. (1977) The university art museum: defining purpose and mission, in Drucker, P.F. (ed.), *Management Cases*, Heinemann, London, 28-35.

Ela, P. (1980) One museum's planning experience, *Museum News*, 58(6), 33-7.

Farnell, G. (1985) Setting targets for museums, in Cossons, N., (ed.), *Management for Change*, National Maritime Museum, London, 39-40.

George, R. & Sherell-Leo, C. (1986) *Starting Right: A Basic Guide to Museum Planning*, American Association for State and Local History, Nashville, Tennessee.

Greene, J.P. & Scott, R.L. (1991) A step by step guide approach to key areas, in Ambrose, T.M. & Runyard, S., (eds.), *Forward Planning*, Routledge, London, 42-51.

Hardy, J.M. (1972) *Corporate Planning for Non-Profit Organizations*, Association Press, New York.

Hatton, A. (1992) Museum planning and museum plans, *Museum Development*, January, 32-39.

Jackson, P. (1991) Performance Indicators: promises and pitfalls, in Pearce, S., (ed.), *Museum Economics and the Community*, New Research in Museum Studies, Vol. 2, Athlone, London, 41-64.

Johnson, P. & Thomas, B. (1990) The development of Beamish: an assessment, *Museum Management & Curatorship*, 9, 5-24.

Jowett, P. & Rothwell, M. (1988) *Performance Indicators in the Public Sector*, Macmillan Press, London.

Kovach, C. (1989) Strategic management for museum, *International J. of Museum Management and Curatorship*, 8(2), 137-148.

Lister, Dame U. (1968) Curators and committee: a museum team, *Museums Journal*, 68(2), 82-4.

Lord, B. & Lord, G.D. (1988) The museum planning process, *Museums Journal*, 88(4), 175-179.

Lord, G.D. & Lord, B. (1991) *The Manual of Museum Planning*, Museum of Science and Industry, Manchester and HMSO, London.

Marsan, G.A. (1993) Measure the ecstasy, *Museums Journal*, 93(7), 27-8.

McHugh, A. (1980) Strategic planning for museums, *Museum News*, 58(6), 23-29.

Morris, G. (1991) *Marketing Planning for Museums and.Galleries*, North West Museums Service.

Murdin, L. (1989) BM(NH) repositions, *Museums Journal*, December, 8-9..

Murdin, L. (1990) Director's gone Disney claims South Ken Union, *Museums Journal*, 90(6), 8.

Murdin, L. (1990) Natural History Museum faces summer of protest, *Museums Journal*, 90(7), 9.

Murdin, L. (1990) NHM in chaos over sackings, *Museums Journal*, 90(11), 9.

Murdin, L. (1990) The Chalmers view, *Museums Journal*, 90(8), 8.

Museum Assessment Program (1990) *Shaping the Museum: The MAP Institutional Planning Guide*, American Association of Museums, Washington DC.

Museums Association (1993) Guidelines on Performance Measurement, *Museums Yearbook*, Museums Association, London, 409-12.

Office of Arts & Libraries (1991) *Report on the Development of Performance Indicators for the National Museums and Galleries*, OAL, London.

Phillips, C. (1985) The politics of state history, *History News*, September, 17-20.

Simerly, R. (1982) Strategic long-range planning, *Museum News*, 60(6), 28-31.

Spencer, P. et al. (1993) Feel the width, *Museums Journal*, 93(7), 29-30.

Thompson, J. (1992) The role of the director, in Thompson, J.M.A., et al (eds.), *Manual of Curatorship: A guide to Museum Practice*, Butterworth, London.

Ullberg, A.D. (1984) Making boards work better, *Museum News*, 62(5), 45-6.

Unterman, I. & Davis, R.H. (1984) The strategy gap in not-for-profits, *Museum News*, 62(5), 38-44.

Walden, I. (1991) Qualities and quantities, *Museums Journal*, 91(1), 27- 28.

Weil, S.E. (1985) The more effective director; specialist or generalist?, *Rethinking the Museum and Other Meditations*, Smithsonian Institution Press, Washington DC, 95-103.

Wilkinson, P. (1993) Speaking with authority, *Museums Journal*, 93(2), 20.

10.3 Managing People

Adair, J. (1985) *Effective Teambuilding*, Pan Books, London.

Adair, J. (1987) *How to Manage Your time*, Talbot Adair Press, Guildford.

Adair, J. (1988) *Effective Leadership*, Pan, London.

Adsett, V. (1988) Job sharing: the Cheltenham experience, *Museums Journal*, 88(2), 71-2.

Armstrong, M. (1988) *A Handbook of Personnel Management Practice*, Kogan Page, London.

Arth, M. (1982) The changing role of the mid-level manager, *Museum News*, July/August, 32-35.

Babbidge, A. (1991) Working on your own with limited resources, in Ambrose, T., Runyard, S., (eds.), *Forward Planning*, Routledge, London, 60-64.

Bandes, S.J. & Holo, S. (1989) Intern ins and outs, *Museum News*, 68(4), 54-6.

Black, C.C. (1984) The nature of leadership, *Museum News*, 62(5), 28-30.

Bower, S. (1986) At the sharp end, *Museums Australia*, 1-3.

Cooper, C. L. & Davidson, M.J. (1984) *Women in Management*, Heinemann, London.

Davies, M. (1990) Glasgow belongs to..., *Museums Journal*, 90(7), 27-29.

Davies, M. (1991) Lifting the fog on the Tyne, *Museums Journal*, 91(7), 29-32.

De Borhegyi, S. (1978) Museum brainstorming: a creative approach to exhibit planning, *Curator*, 21(3), 217-224.

Diamond, M. (1992) Personnel Management, Thompson, J.M.A. *et al. (eds)*, *Manual of Curatorship*, Butterworths, London, 159-166.

Dressel, B. (1990) Make the right move, *Museum News*, November/December, 61-4.

Dressel, B. (1991) Best foot forward, *Museum News*, July/August, 46-49.

Emery, A.R. (1990) Museum Staff: Defining Expectation, *International J. of Museum Management and Curatorship*, 9(3), 265-272.

Everett, J. (1988) Taking your staff with you, *Museums Journal*, 88(3), 157-8.

Farnell, G. (1984) Team briefing: a means of improving communication within the museum, *International Journal of Museum Management and Curatorship*, 3, 153-157.

Farnell, G. (1985) Setting targets for museums, in Cossons, N., (ed.), *Management for Change*, National Maritime Museum, London, 39-40.

Fox, M.J. (1983) Directors as communicators, *Museum Studies Journal*, Spring, 12-15.

Friedman, A.J. (1991) Mix and match, *Museum News*, July/August, 38-42.

Friedman, R. (1982) Museum people. The special problems of personnel management in museums and historical agencies, *History News*, 37(3), 14-18.

Gaiber, M. (1984) Co-operation within museum walls: the team approach to exhibition development, *Museum Studies Journal*, Spring, 20-22.

Greene, J.P. (1985) Changing gear, in Cossons, N., (ed.), *The Management of Change in Museums*, National Maritime Museum, London, 24-25.

Greene, J.P. (1989) A cause for professional concern?, *Museums Journal*, April, 26-27.

Greene, J.P. (1989) Museums for the Year 2000: a case for continuous revolution, *Museums Journal*, 88(4), 179-80.

Greene, J.P. (1992) The management of volunteers, in Thompson, J.M.A., *et al. (eds.)*, *The Manual of Curatorship*, Butterworth, London, 167-171.

Griffin, D.J.G. (1987) Management for people, *Museums Australia 1987*, 219-235.

Griffin, D.J.G. (1987) Managing in the museum organisation: I Leadership and Communication, *International J. of Museum Management and Curatorship*, 6(4), 387-398.

Griffin, D.J.G. (1988) Managing in the museum organisation: II Conflicts, tasks, responsibilities, *International J. of Museum Management and Curatorship*, 7(1), 11-23.

Handy, C. (1985) *Understanding Organisations*, Penguin.

Handy, C. (1989) *The Age of Unreason*, Business Books, London.

Handy, C. (1990) *Understanding Voluntary Organisations*, Penguin.

Hardiman, R. (1990) Some more equal than others, *Museums Journal*, November, 28-30.

Hatton, A. (1989) Current issues in museum training in the United Kingdom, *International J. of Museum Management and Curatorship*, 8, 149-156.

Hatton, A. (1992) Management training: finding the right balance, *Museum Development*, October, 30-33.

Howie, F.M.P. (ed.) (1987) *Safety in Museums and Galleries*, Butterworths, London.

James, E. (1988) Career break - or career development?, *Museums Journal*, 88(2), 69-70.

Kahn, H. & Garden, S. (1993) Job attitudes and occupational stress in the United Kingdom museum sector. A pilot study, *Museum Management & Curatorship*, 12, 285-302.

Knowles, L. (1991) No more heroes, *Museums Journal*, 91(10), 21.

Lagercrantz, K. (1992) Making friends at a museum, in Meek, J., (ed.), *Marketing the Arts*, ICOM (International Council of Museums), Paris, 109-114.

Leishman, M. (1992) Accessibility: training to understand, *Museum Development*, November, 34-5.

Leishman, M. (1993) Image and self image, *Museums Journal*, 93(6), 30-32.

Locke, S., et al (1992) The county team, *Museums Journal*, 92(10), 29-31.

Mattingly, J. (1984) *Volunteers in museums and galleries*, The Volunteer Centre.

McIntyre, R. (1991) In praise of appraisal, *Museum Development*, June, 15-17.

Mead, E. M. (1985) Museum training and the small museum, *Curator*, 28(3), 183-201.

Meltzer, P.J. (1989) Help them help you, *Museum News*, March/April, 60-62.

Miller, R.L. (1979) Developing a personnel policy manual, *Museum News*, July/August, 29-32.

Miller, R.L. (1980) *Personnel Policies for Museums: A Handbook for Management*, American Association of Museums, Washington DC.

Museum Training Institute (1991) *A new qualification framework for Museums: A consultative document - Draft Standards: Management and Administration*, MTI, Bradford.

Museums Association (1988) *Salary Survey for the Museums Association, 1988-1989*, Reward Group, Stone.

Museums & Galleries Commission (1987) *Museum Professional Training and Career Structure*, HMSO, London.

Museums & Galleries Commission (1992) *Guidelines on Disability for Museums and Galleries in the United Kingdom*, MGC, London, 1-7.

Musgrove, S.W. (1989) Keeping your guard up, *Museums Journal*, 89(1), 28-9.

Naumer, H. (1987) Evaluating the museum director, *Museum News*, 66(4), 62-64.

Nicholson, J. (1992) *How do you Manage?*, BBC, London.

Noble, D.R. (1988) Turnover among museum directors, *International J. of Museum Management and Curatorship*, 7(1), 25-32.

Noble, D.R. (1989) Turnover among museum directors and some implications for innovation, *International J. of Museum Management and Curatorship*, 8, 163-174.

O'Neil, M. (1991) Museums and their communities, in Lord, G., Lord, D., (eds.), *The Manual of Museum Planning*, Museum of Science and Industry, Manchester and HMSO, London, 19-34.

Office of Arts and Libraries (1991) *Volunteers in Museums and Heritage Organisations: Policy, Planning and Management*, HMSO, London.

Ohren, M. (1988) Flexible working arrangements, *Museums Journal*, 88(2), 67-8.

Pedler, M., *et al.* (1986) *A Manager's Guide to Self-Development*, McGraw Hill, 190-202.

Phillips, C. (1983) The museum director as manager, *History News*, March, 9-15.

Phillips, D. (1989) Opinion, *Museums Journal*, 89(1), 15.

Phillips, D. (1990) On course for the next century, *Museums Journal*, 90(1), 34-5.

Porter, G., *et al.* (1990) Are you sitting comfortably? Are equal opportunities a luxury?, *Museums Journal*, 90(11), 25-35.

Prince, D.R. (1988) Women and museums, *Museums Journal*, 88(2), 55-61.

Rookledge, D. (1985) *Employment Practice and Law for the Independent Museums*, Association of Independent Museums (AIM), Guideline no. 9.

Scott, *et al.* (1993) *Museum Sector Workforce Survey*, Museum Training Institute, Bradford.

Scott, J. & Rochester, A. (1984) *Managing People*, Sphere/British Institute of Management.

Shaw, P. (1989) The state of pay, *Museums Journal*, 89(4), 26-8.

Singleton, R. (1983) Is training really necessary?, *Museum Studies Journal*, Fall, 25-28.

Tanner, K. (nd) *Museum Projects: A Handbook for Volunteers, Work Experience and Temporary Staff*, Area Museum Council for the South West.

Taylor, F.J. & Lundell, D. (1987) What is your job worth? How one organisation developed an appropriate pay scale, *Museum News*, 66(4), 55-59.

Taylor, K. (1985) Risking it: women as museum leaders, *Museum News*, February, 20-36.

Taylor, K. (ed.) (1984) Room at the top, *Museum News*, 62(5), 31-37.

Tolles, B.F. (ed.) (1991) *Leadership for the Future: Changing Directorial Roles in American History Museums and Historical Societies*, American Association for State and Local History, Nashville, Tennessee.

Torrington, D. & .Hall, L. (1987) *Personnel Management: A New Approach*, Prentice Hall.

Tucker, M. (1990) Common ground, *Museum News*, July/August, 45-46.

Van Mensch, P. (1984) *The Management Needs of Museum Personnel,*, Reinwardt Academie,Studies in Museology no. 5.

Wolf, R.L. (1984) Enhancing museum leadership through evaluation, *Museum Studies Journal*, Spring, 31-33.

Woodcock, M. (1989) *Team Development Manual*, Gower Publishing, Aldershot.

10.4 Financial Management

Aageson, T.H. (1986) *Financial Analysis for Museum Stores*, Museum Store Association, Doylestown, PA., USA.

Ambrose, T.M. (ed) (1991) *Money, Money, Money and Museums*, Scottish Museums Council & HMSO.

Anon. (1991) Guilty as charged: Neil Cossons, *Museum Development*, November, 32-39.

Arts Council & Museums & Galleries Commission (1989) *The Impact of Tax Incentives on Arts and Musem Fund Raising: A Summary*, National Campaign for the Arts, London.

Bertram, S. (1983) Hard times, *Museum News*, 61(3), 26-35.

Besterman, T. & Bott, V. (1982) To pay or not to pay?, *Museums Journal*, 82(2), 118-9.

Breuer, D. (1990) Licensing and retailing in Brighton, *Museum Development*, October, 21-25.

Burgess, S. (1990) Funding the redevelopment of the Imperial War Museum, *Museum Development*, December, 28-31.

Burke, M. (1990) Looking into licensing, *Museum News*, November/December, 57-9.

Cargo, R.A. (1987) The Denver Art Museum's admission fee: barrier or benefit?, *Museum Studies J.*, 3(1), 22-30.

Chapman, S. (1993) Winning sponsorship that fits the bill, *Museum Development*, September, 18-21.

Clarke, S. (1993) *The Complete Fund Raising Handbook*, 2nd edition, Directory of Social Change.

Committee of Area Museums Councils (1992) *Museum Factsheet: Grants, Tax Incentives and Concessions - A checklist for museums*, 1-9.

Cossons, N. (1985) The Greenwich experiment, *Admissions charges at National Museums: Museum Professionals Group Transactions*, 21, 18-20.

Danilov, V. J. (1988) Retaining control. Exhibit sponsorship at science centres, *Museum News*, January/February, 54-6.

Davies, M. (1989) Sponsorship threatens museum role, *Museums Journal*, December, 13-14.

De La Torre, M. & Monreal, L. (1982) *Museums: An Investment for Development*, ICOM (International Council of Museums), Paris.

Dickenson, V. (1993) The economics of museum admission charges, *Curator*, (36:3), 220-234.

Doulton, A.-M. (1991) *The Arts Funding Guide*, Directory of Social Change, London.

Doulton, A.-M. (ed.) (1992) *The Central Government Grants Guide*, 2nd edition, Directory of Social Change.

Eastwood, M., Casson, D. & Brown, P. (eds.) (1993) *A Guide to the Major Trusts Volume 2*, Directory of Social Change.

Eastwood, M. (ed.) (1992) *Guide to Company Giving*, 5th edition, Directory of Social Change.

Eckstein, J. (ed) (1993) *Cultural Trends 14 - Museums and Galleries: Funding and Finance*, Policy Studies Institute, London.

Farnell, G. & Heath, M. (1993) *Handbook of Grants: The Guide to sources of public funding for museums, galleries, heritage and visual arts organisations*, Museum Development Company.

Farrow, A. & Fitzherbert, L. (eds.) (1992) *A Guide to the Major Trusts Volume 1*, 5th edition, Directory of Social Change.

Fauntleroy, C.C. & Bentsen, W. (1983) Planned giving: fund raising for the future, *Museum News*, 62(2), 63-74.

Fishel, D. (1993) *The Arts Sponsorship Handbook*, Directory of Social Change, London.

Ganz, P. (1984) To charge or not to charge, *Museum News*, 62(4), 41-5.

Glennon, L. (1988) The museum and the corporation: new realities, *Museum News*, January/February, 36-43.

Greene, J.P. (1986) The museum as a small business, in Hebditch, M., (ed.), *Museum Management and Administration*, Museum of London, 20-22.

Grove, M. *et al.* (1983) The use of adversity, *Museum News*, 61(3), 26-35.

Harney, A.L. (1992) Money changers in the temple? Museums and the financial mission, *Museum News*, November/December, 38-43 & 62-3.

Hoffman, M. (1980) Writing realistic grant budgets, *Museum News*, 58(3), 48-53.

House of Commons Education, Science and Arts Committee (1990) *Should Museums Charge? Some Case Studies*, HMSO, London.

Institute of Charity Fundraising Managers (1993) *Who's Who in Fundraising*, Museum Development Company.

Jahnke, A. (1993) Losing the win-win game?, *Museum News*, September/October, 34-35 & 50-52.

Jammot, D. (1984) Cost-effectiveness and efficiency in a small museum, *Museum*, 36(1), 25-9.

Jedlicka, J. (1988) Corporate fundraising: a primer, *Museum News*, January/February, 78-9.

Johnson, P. & Thomas, B. (1991) Museums: an economic perspective, in

Pearce, S.M., (ed.), *Museum Economics and the Community*, New Research in Museum Studies, Vol. 2, Athlone, London.

Johnson, P. & Thomas, B. (1992) *Tourism, Museums and the Local Economy: the economic impact of the North of England Open Air Museum at Beamish*, Edward Elgar Ltd, Aldershot.

Johnston, D. (1988) Get it in writing - the corporate/museum partnership, *Museum News*, January/February, 20-23.

Leavitt, T. (1991) Permanent problem?, *Museum News*, May/June, 58-59.

Merrin Ltd (1990) *Tax Effective Giving to the Arts and Museums: A Guide for Fundraisers*, Arts Council/ MGC.

Middleton, F. & Lloyd, S. (1992) *Charities: The New Law*, Jordan & Sons.

Museum Professionals Group (1991) *Where's the Party? Functions in Museums and Galleries*, MPG.

Museums & Galleries Commission (1993) *Grants for Museums: The Principal Sources 1993/4*, HMSO, London.

Myerscough, J. (1988) *The Economic Importance of the Arts in Britain*, Policy Studies Institute, London.

Norton, M. (1991) *Raising Money from Industry*, Directory of Social Change, London.

Norton, M. (1991) *Raising Money from Trusts*, Directory of Social Change, London.

Peacock, A. & Godfrey, C. (1974) The economics of museums and galleries, *Museums Journal*, 74(2), 55-8.

Shiner, M. & Moore, N. (1993) *Fundraising: Sources & Skills for Voluntary Organisations*, Policy Studies Institute, London.

Storrar, J. (1993) Fundraising - the basics, *Scottish Museum News*, 9(1), 6-7.

Touche Ross (1990) Income generation: the first steps, *Museum Development*, February, 28-31.

Touche Ross Management Consultants (1989) *Museum Funding and Services: The Visitor's perspective*, Touche Ross.

Viner, D. (1985) Museum trading as a source of income, *Museums Journal*, 85(2), 91-94.

Ware, M. (1988) *Fund Raising for Museums*, AIM Guidelines No. 4, Association of Independent Museums.

Wicks, M. (1992) Sponsorship: a beginner's guide, *Museum Development*, August, 26-29.

Winterbotham, N. (1992) Counting the Tullie tally, *Museums Journal*, 92(4), 19.

10.5 Managing Museum Sites

Delaney, J. (1991) Managing with the visitor in mind, *Museum Development*, September, 22-26.

L & R Leisure (1990) Caring about quality, *Museum Development*, May, 26-30.

McGriffin, R.F. (1985) Health and safety in the museum workplace, *Museum News*, 64(2), 36-43.

Museum Assistants Group (1977) Health and safety in museums symposium, *MAG Transactions*, 13.

Museums & Galleries Commission (1992) *Quality of Service in Museums and Galleries: Customer Care in Museums - Guidelines for Implementation*, 1-7.

National Audit Office (1993) *Department of National Heritage, National Museums and Galleries: Quality of Service to the Public*, Report by the Comptroller Auditor General, House of Commons Papers 841, HMSO, London.

Scottish Museums Council (1985) *Museums are for People*, Scottish Museums Council &HMSO, Edinburgh.

Sudbury, P.V. (1984) Health and safety at work, in Thompson, J.M.A. *et al.* (eds.), *Manual of Curatorship*, Butterworths, London, 522-528.

Sweet, et al, (eds) (1992) *Customer Care: Peripheral or Essential?*, Carnegie UK Trust.

Tate, J. (1993) COSHH- a life preserver?, *Scottish Museum News*, 9(1), 8-9.

Winterbotham, N. (1991) Old pitfalls and new sidesteps - the Tullie House project, *Museum Professionals Group (MPG) Transactions*, 27, 22-4.

10.6 Project Management

Friedman, A.J. (1991) Mix and match, *Museum News*, July/August, 38-42.

Gaiber, M. (1984) Co-operation within museum walls: the team approach to exhibition development, *Museum Studies Journal*, Spring, 20-22.

Harrison, R. (1991) Project management, in Lord, G.D. & Lord, B. (eds.), *The Manual of Museum Planning*, Museum of Science and Industry, Manchester and HMSO, London, 247-2554.

Lehmbruck, M. (1979) Programming, *Museum*, 31(2), 92-95.

Lock, D. (1988) *Project Management*, Gower Publishing/Open University.

Lord, G. D., Lord B. (eds.) (1992) *The Manual of Museum Planning*, Museum of Science and Industry, Manchester and HMSO, London.

Martin, D. (1990) Working with designers: 1 - getting started, *Museums Journal*, 90(4), 31-38.

Martin, D. (1990) Working with designers: 2 - keeping control, *Museums Journal*, 90(6), 29-36.

Martin, D. (1990) Working with designers: 3 - constructive roles, *Museums Journal*, 90(8), 33-40.

Miles, R.S. (1985) Exhibitions: management, for a change, in Cossons, N., (ed.), *Management for Change*, National Maritime Museum, London, 31-34.

Morrison, B. (1978) Project management in art galleries and museums, *Gazette*, 11(1), 12-20.

Museums Association (1993) Guidelines on security when using outside contractors, *Museums Yearbook*, Museums Association, London, 415-6.

Pecquet, C. & Obryne, P. (1979) Programming: a tool at the service of the curator commissioning authority and the architect, *Museum*, 31(2), 74-91.

Toppin, G. (1991) Project management: how to keep major projects under control, *Museum Development*, March, 20-24.

10.7 Marketing Museums

Adams, G.D. (1983) *Museum Public Relations*, American Association for State and Local History, Nashville, Tennessee.

Adams, G.D. (1992) Listening to the audience, in Meek, J. (ed.), *Marketing the Arts*, ICOM (International Council of Museums), Paris, 117-124.

Addison, E. (1986) Is marketing a threat... or is it the greatest challenge that museums have ever faced?, *Muse*, Summer, 28-31.

**Addison, E., *et al.* (1993) Marketing for survival, *Muse*, 11(2).

Ames, P.J. (1988) A challenge to modern museum management: meshing missions and market, *International J. of Museum Management and Curatorship*, 7(2), 151.

Baker, N. (1990) Worlds Apart?, *Museums Journal*, 90(2), 27.

Baker, N. (1991) Communicating the character, *Museums Journal*, 91(3), 23-25.

Bellow, C. (ed.) (1980) *Public View - Musees Et Relations Publiques*, ICOM (International Council of Museums)/International Committee for Museums and Public Relations, Paris.

Bigley, J. (1987) Marketing in museums: background and theoretical foundations, *Museum Studies Journal*, Fall/Winter, 14-21.

Bradford, H. (1991) A new framework for museum marketing, in Kavanagh,

G. (ed.), *The Museums Profession: Internal and External Relations*, Leicester University Press, Leicester, London and New York, 83-97.

Bryant, J. (1988) *The Principles of Marketing - a Guide for Museums*, AIM Guideline no. 16, Association of Independent Museums.

Budd, M. (1987) Pilot visitor survey at Perth, *Scottish Museum News*, 3(2), 16-17.

Cameron, D.F. (1961) Putting public relations in its place, *Curator*, 4, 103-107.

Clemmow, S. (1991) Building audiences: advertising the Science Museum, *Museum Development*, December, 31-4.

Collins, M. (1991) Marketing partnerships, *Museum Development*, June, 18-21.

Collins, M. (1991) Profiling, *Museum Development*, August, 22-25.

Collins, M. (1991) The direct message for museums, *Museum Development*, April, 25-29.

Cossons, N. (1985) Making museums market oriented in Ambrose, T. (ed.), *Museums Are for People*, HMSO/ Scottish Museums Council.

Davis, R. & Lovelock, C.H. (1984) Museum Wharf, in Lovelock, C.H. & Weinberg, C.B, (eds.), *Public and Nonprofit Marketing: Cases and Readings*, Scientific Press and John Wiley and Sons, Palo Alto, California, USA, 215-229.

Delaney, J. (1991) Managing with the visitor in mind, *Museum Development*, September, 22-26.

Faber, M. (1992) Museums for everyone, in Meek, J., (ed.), *Marketing the Arts*, ICOM (International Council of Museums), Paris, 99-107.

French, Y. (1991) *The Handbook of Public Relations: For Museums, Galleries, Historic Houses, the Visual Arts and Heritage Attractions*, The Museum Development Company, Milton Keynes.

French, Y. (1991) Getting your image right, *Museum Development*, August, 12-15.

Fronville, C.L. (1985) Marketing for museum: profit techniques in a non-profit world, *Curator*, 28(3), 175-179.

Gerritson, S.L. (1989) Is the boom over?, *Museum News*, September/October, 62-4.

Hannagan, T.J. (1992) *Marketing for the Non-Profit Sector*, Macmillan Professional Masters Series.

Harney, A.L. (1992) Money changes in the temple? Museums and the financial mission, *Museum News*, November/December, 38-43, 62-63.

Hay, B. (1987) Who needs research? Part 1, *Scottish Museum News*, 3(2), 12-13.

Hay, B. (1987) Who needs research? Part 2, *Scottish Museum News*, 3(3), 12-15.

Hay, B. (1987) Who needs research? Part 3, *Scottish Museum News*, 3(4), 4-7.

Hood, M.G. (1983) Staying away - why people choose not to visit museums, *Museum News*, 61(4), 50-57.

James, R. (1991) "Could do Better" Marketing Museums in a Multi-Ethnic Community, *West Midlands Area Museum Service*.

Jones, A. (1990) No surprises, please, *Museum News*, May/June, 64-6.

Koe, F. (1991) Small museum, big plans, *Museum News*, January/February, 61-4.

Krudwig, K. (1991) Marketing 'Aztec', *Museum News*, November/December, 28-30.

L & R Leisure (1990) Caring about quality, *Museum Development*, May, 26-30.

Lagercrantz, K. (1992) Making friends at a museum, in Meek, J., (ed.), *Marketing the Arts*, ICOM (International Council of Museums), Paris, 109-114.

Lewis, J. (1990) Change in the museum industry in the 1990s, *Museum Development*, October, 26-31.

Lewis, P. (1992) Museums and marketing, in Thompson, J.M.A. *et al. (eds.)*, *Manual of Curatorship*, Butterworths, London, 148-158.

Martin, B. & Mason, S. (1990) Museums as Attractions, *Museum Development*, October, 32-40.

McLean, F.C. (1993) Marketing in museums: a contextual analysis, *Museum Management &Curatorship*, 12, 11-27.

Meek, J. (ed.) (1992) *Marketing the Arts: Every Vital Aspect of Museum Management*, ICOM (International Council of Museums), London.

Middleton, V. (1991) The future demand for museums 1990-2001, in Kavanagh, G., (ed.), *The Museums Profession: Internal and External Relations*, Leicester University Press, Leicester, London and New York, 139-160.

Museum Professionals Group (1987) Tourism. Museum Dream or Nightmare?, *Museum Professionals Group Transactions*, 23.

Museums & Galleries Commission (1993) *Museums and Tourism: Mutual Benefit*, HMSO, London.

Museums & Galleries Commission (1992) *Quality of Service in Museums and Galleries: Customer Care in Museums - Guidelines for Implementation*, MGC, London, 1-7.

Schiebel, J. (1989) Penchant for pizzazz, *Museum News*, March/April, 55-58.

Strickland-Eales, D. (1990) Direct marketing: the risks and rewards, *Museum Development*, September, 30-37.

Thorson, S. (1989) Consortia: creating a new P.R. panorama, *Museum News*, July/August, 36-42.

Trevelyan, V. (1991) Non-visitors with attitude, *Museums Journal*, 91(3), 20.

Veal, F.R. (1983) *Museum Public Relations*, Association of Independent

Museums, Guideline No.5.

Villner, K. (1992) Marketing a disaster, in Meek, J., (ed.), *Marketing the Arts*, ICOM (International Council of Museums), Paris, 73-80.

Williams, D. (1986) Send in the clowns..., *Scottish Museum News*, 2(4), 11-12.

Yorke, D.A. & Jones, R.R. (1984) Marketing and museums, *European Journal of Marketing*, 2(18), 90-99.

See also (1986) Museum marketing, *Muse*, 4(2), 17-40.

11 Museum Buildings

Ahrens, D. (1986) The transformation of a Romanesque Monastery into a public museum, *Curator*, 29(3), 173-182.

Aloi, R. (1962) *Musei: Architettura*, Telnica, Milan, Hoepli, Milan.

Alsford, S. (1985) The use of people-mover systems in museums and associated cultural institutions, *International J. of Museum Management and Curatorship*, 4(4), 329-44.

Amery, C. (1991) *A Celebration of Art and Architecture: The National Gallery Sainsbury Wing*, National Gallery, London.

Anon. (1978) East Anglia Arts - the Sainsbury Centre, *Architectural Review*, 164(982), 347-62.

Anon. (1983) *The Plan for the Development of the Museum of Australia*, Report of the interim Council, Commonwealth of Australia.

Anon. (1983) The Burrell Collection, *Architects Journal*, 19, 57-98.

Anon. (1983) The plan for the development of the Museum of Australia, *Commonwealth of Australia*.

Anon. (1984) The Burrell: art and nature, *Architectural Review*, 175(1044), 28-37.

Anon. (1985) Editorial, *International J. of Museum Management and Curatorship*, 4(1), 5-8.

Anon. (1985) Editorial: Buildings vs. collections: the Kunstgewerbemuseum in Berlin, *International J. of Museum Management and Curatorship*, 4(4), 307-16.

Anon. (1985) Tate in the north - a gallery of modern art for Liverpool, *North West Museum and Gallery Service Newsletter*, Autumn/Winter, 12-13.

Anon. (1986) The Picasso Museum in Paris, *Museum*, 38(3), 176-182.

Anon. (1986) Two adaptations of Mediaeval churches, *International J. of Museum Management and Curatorship*, 5(1), 89-91.

Anon. (1987) Note and comment: National Gallery Extension, *International J. of Museum Management and Curatorship*, 6(2), 211-7.

Arbeit, A.A. (1964) The architect and the museum, *Museum News*, 43(2), 11-17.

Bank, G.G. (1988) Determining the cost: architect George Hartman's formula, *Museum News*, 66(5), 74-5.

Bartz, D. et al. (1990) Adapting to adaptive use, *Museum News*, 69(1), 54-57.

Beattie, A. (1984) Structural engineering aspects of planning for new works, refurbishment and maintenance, *International J. of Museum Management and Curatorship*, 3 (4), 363-6.

Bell, J.A.M. (1972) *Museum and Gallery Building: A Guide to Building and*

Design Procedure, Museums Association Sheet No. 14.

Bell, J.A.M. (1979) The Museum of London, *Museum*, 31(2), 120-5.

Boylan, P.J. (1980) Seven years hard labour, *Area Museum and Art Gallery Service for the Midlands*.

Brawne, M. (1965) *The New Museum*, Praeger, New York.

Brawne, M. (1983) Some recent trends in museum design and the new National Archaeological Museum of Jordan, *International J. of Museum Management and Curatorship*, 2(2), 257-64.

Brawne, M. (1984) Museums: mirrors of their time, *Architectural Review*, 175(1044), 17-19.

Bruno, A. (1986) Rivoli - a castle for contemporary art, *Museum*, 38(1), 4-8.

Burgard, R. (1986) The Dom-Romerberg Quarter: revitalisation of the city, *International J. of Museum Management and Curatorship*, 5(1), 14-18.

Caldwell, I. (1984) Building strategy for museums and galleries, *International J. of Museum Management and Curatorship*, 3(4), 327-336.

Cannon-Brookes, P. (1983) Old lamps instead of new? The rehabilitation and adaptation of historic buildings as museums and art galleries, *International J. of Museum Management and Curatorship*, 2(1), 27-52.

Cannon-Brookes, P. (1986) Frankfurt and Atlanta: Richard Mieir as a designer of museums, *International J. of Museum Management and Curatorship*, 5(1), 39-64.

Cannon-Brookes, P. (1986) James Stirling's Arthur M. Sackler Museum, *International J. of Museum Management and Curatorship*, 5(4), 319-327.

Catapano, F.T. (1986) The invisible problem: building management in museum operations, *Museum News*, 64(5), 9-16.

Clifford, T. (1984) Interior design and restoration of Manchester City Art Gallery, *Architectural Review*, 175(1047), 68-73.

Coleman, L.V. (1927) *Manual for Small Museums*, New York/London.

Coleman, L.V. (1948) Recent museum building in the USA, *Museums Journal*, 47, 221.

Coleman, L.V. (1950) *Museum Buildings*, American Association of Museums, Washington DC.

Davis, D. (1990) *The Museum Transformed: Design and Culture in the Post-Pompidou Age*, Abberville Press, New York.

Dhargalkar, J. (1984) The role of the conservation architect, *International J. of Museum Management and Curatorship*, 3 (4), 343-50.

Dornberg, J. (1988) Germany's museum building boom: lavish spending architecture, *Museum News*, 66(5), 12-16.

Fischer, V. (1986) The German Museum of Architecture, *International J. of Museum Management and Curatorship*, 5(1), 19-26.

Fradier, G. (1978) The Georges Pompidou National Center for Art and Culture Paris, *Museum*, 30(2), 77-87.

Fransen, H. (1978) The use of historic buildings as museums, *Museology*, 2.

Garfield, D. (1987) The Smithsonian's new museum under the Mall, *Museum News*, 66(1), 44-9.

Glaeser, L. (1972) Museum architecture: publish or perish, *Museum News*, 51(3), 39-42.

Glancey, J. (1984) Burrell Museum, Glasgow, *Architectural Review*, 175(1044), 28-37.

Glen, M. & Tillyard, R. (1984) Two views of the Burrell collection, *Heritage interpretation*, 27, 3-4.

Gordon, A. (1983) The rejuvenation of the Leeds City Art Gallery - flair and determination, *International J. of Museum Management and Curatorship*, 2(2), 159-70.

Gordon, A. & Cannon-Brookes, P. (1984) Housing the Burrell Collection - a forty year saga, *International J. of Museum Management and Curatorship*, 3(1), 19-60.

Grant, C.L. (1990) Construction Instruction, *Museum News*, 69(4), 55-57.

Gretton, R. (1966) Museum architecture: a primer, *Museum News*, 44(6), 13-17.

Guthe, E.C. (1957) *So You Want a Good Museum*, American Association of Museums, Washington DC.

Hamlyn, R. (1987) The Clore Gallery for the Turner Collection at the Tate Gallery - a brief history, *International J. of Museum Management and Curatorship*, 6(1), 19-36.

Harney, A.L. (1990) Adaptive use: new life for an old idea, *Museum News*, 69(1), 41-45.

Harrison, R.O. (1966) *Technical Requirements for Small Museums*, Canadian Museums Association, Ottawa.

Haverkampf, H.-E. (1986) The Frankfurt Museumsufer, *International J. of Museum Management and Curatorship*, 5(1), 13.

Hebditch, M. (1976) The Corinium Museum at Cirencester: an appraisal, *Museums Journal*, 76(7).

Hebditch, M. (1992) The management of buildings in Thompson, J.M.A. *et al. (eds.),, Manual of Curatorship*, Butterworth, London, 172-177.

Hilberry, J.D. (1990) Plan to expand, *Museum News*, 69(4), 51-54.

Hollein, H. (1986) The Museum of Modern Art, Frankfurt, *International J. of Museum Management and Curatorship*, 5(1), 31-8.

Hudson, K. (1977) *Museums for the 1980s: A Survey of World Trends*, London, MacMillan.

Hume, I. (1992) Floor loadings and historic buildings, *English Heritage Conservation Bulletin*, 18, 1-2.

Jaffe, M. (1976) The responsibilities of a museum to the character of its own building, *Museums Association Conference Proceedings*, 36-8.

Johnson, E.V. & Horgan, J.C. (1988) Becoming a good museum client, *Museum News*, 66(5), 72-3.

Jones, D.R. (1991) A stable future for Suffolk's archives, in Norman, M. & Todd, V. (eds.), *Storage*, United Kingdom Institute for Conservation, 27-32.

Jones, J. (1965) Museum and art gallery building in England 1845-1914 Part 1, *Museums Journal*, 65(3), 230-8.

Jones, J. (1966) Museum and art gallery building in England 1845-1914 Part 2, *Museums Journal*, 65(4), 271-80.

Kendall, W. (1961) Museums and architecture, *Museums Journal*, 61(6), 267-74.

Klotz, H., Krase, W. & Lupertz, M. (1985) *New Museum Building in the Federal Republic of Germany*, Klett-Cotta, Stuttgart.

Kruger, H. (1984) Planning and layout of museums: the central importance of the room, *International J. of Museum Management and Curatorship*, 3(4), 351-6.

Lord, B. & Lord, G.D. (1983) *Planning Our Museums*, Canadian Museums Association, Ottawa.

Marks, R. (1984) Building the Burrell, *Scottish Art Review*, 16(1), 3-8.

McDonald, E. & Cardinal, D.J. (1986) Building Canada's National Museum of Man: an interprofessional dialogue, *Museum*, 38(1), 9-16.

Mickenberg, D. (1990) Resplendent recycling, *Museum News*, 69(1), 46-49.

Montaner, J.M. (1990) *New Museums*, Architectural & Design Press.

Montaner, J. & Oliveras, J. (1986) *The Museums of the Last Generation*, Academy Editions/St. Martins Press, London.

Park, E. & Carlhian, J.P. (1987) *A New View from the Castle (Arthur M. Sackler Gallery, National Museum of American Art)*, Smithsonian Institution Press, Washington DC.

Parr, A.E. (1961) Problems of museum architecture: American Museum of Natural History, *Curator*, 4(4), 304-27.

Pearson, A. (1985) *Art for Everyone: Guidance for Disabled People*, Carnegie U.K. Trust and Centre on Environment for the Handicapped, Dumfries.

Pei, I.M. (1972) On museum architecture, *Museum News*, 51(1), 11-14.

Pelegrin, G. (1979) Programming and the Louvre, *Museum*, 31(2), 106-109.

Physick, K.J. (1982) *The Victoria and Albert Museum - The History of the Building*, Phaidon/Christie.

Reading, A. (1984) Building services, *International J. of Museum Management and Curatorship*, 3(4), 337-42.

Royal Commission on Historical Manuscripts (1993) *Archive Buildings in the United Kingdom 1977-1992*, HMSO, London.

Royal Institute of British Architects (1972) *Architecture Periodicals index*, RIBA, London.

Ruddel, D.T. (1985) Streetscape: dead end or signpost for the future, *Muse*, 2(4), 18-21.

Ruffle, J. (1985) A new gallery for the Oriental Museum, University of

Durham, *International J. of Museum Management and Curatorship*, 4(4), 383-8.

Scott, D.W. (1979) The new building of the National Gallery of Art, Washington, DC, *Museum*, 31(2), 110-15.

Searing, H. (1982) *New American Art Museums*, University of California Press, Berkeley.

Searing, H. (1987) The development of a museum typology, *Museum News*, 65(4), 20-31.

Seiling, H. (1967) The genesis of the museum, *Architectural Review*, 141, 103.

Shopsin, W.B. (1990) Pursuit of Suitability, *Museum News*, 69(1), 51-53.

Singer, T.J., Thomas, N.J. & Wilson, A. (1974) St. Nicholas Church and City Museum, Bristol, *Museums Journal*, 74(3).

Smith, M.A. (1985) Renewed museums revisited: how adaptive use really works, *Museum News*, 63(4), 13-29.

Staniforth, S. & Hayes, B. (1989) keep the old piles standing, *New Scientist*, 19 August, 37-41.

Stephens, S. (ed.) (1986) *Building the New Museum*, Architectural League of New York.

Stirling, J. (nd) *Die Neve Staatsgalerie Stuttgart*, Verlag Gerd Hatje.

Strike, J. (1993) *Architecture in Conservation: Managing Development at Historic Sites*, Routledge, London.

Summerson, J. (1985) The architecture of British museums and art galleries in, *The Fine and Decorative Art Collections of Britain and Ireland*, National Art Collections Fund, 17-25.

Tardito, R. (1986) The creation of the "Grand Brera", *International J. of Museum Management and Curatorship*, 5(4), 337-348.

Tomlinson, M. & Price, N. (1984) Museums and galleries: the planning and refurbishment of the Public Health and Engineering Services, *International J. of Museum Management and Curatorship*, 3(4), 367-72.

Tuve, R.L. (1980) The San Antonio Museum of Art: the adaptive re-use of the old Lone Star Brewery, *Technology and Conservation*, 5(4), 26-31 & 47.

UNESCO (1960) *The Organization of Museums: Practical Advice*, UNESCO Museums and Monuments Series No. 9, Paris.

UNESCO (1975) Historic buildings as museums, *Museum*, 27(3), 101-27.

Urban & Economic Development Ltd (1987) *Re-Using Redundant Buildings*, Department of the Environment.

Venturi, R. (1988) In the center of town: the museum as cathedral, *Museum News*, 66(5), 22-3.

Viner, D. (1976) The Corinium Museum at Cirencester: redevelopment and conservation, *Museums Journal*, 76(1), 5-6.

Viner, D. (1980) Museums and historic buildings (Special Issue), *Museum*, 32(3).

Voniier, T. (1988) Working together: the museum and the architect, *Museum News*, 66(5), 34-8.

Wilson, P. (1987) The Clore Gallery - lighting strategy & practice, *International J. of Museum Management and Curatorship*, 6(1), 37-42.

Wise, D. (1984) Specification for minimal maintenance, *International J. of Museum Management and Curatorship*, 3(4), 357-62.

Zuravleff, M.K. (1984) *Architectural Review*, 175(1044), Special issue.

Zuravleff, M.K. (1985) *Architectural Review*, 178(1065), Special issue.

Zuravleff, M.K. (1987) Expansion (Lila Acheson Wallace Wing - Metropolitan Museum of Art), *Museum News*, 65(4), 45-51.

12 Information Sources

12.1 Abstracts

Scottish Museum Council (1985-) *Museum Abstracts.*
Screven, C.G. & Shettel, H.H. (1993) *Visitor Studies Bibliography & Abstracts.*

12.2 Bibliographies

American Association for State and Local History (1985-87) *A Bibliography on Historical Organization State Practices: 1. Historic Preservation; 2. Care and Conservation of Collections; 3. Interpretation; 4. Documentation of Collections; 5. Administration.*
Bassett, D.A. (1986) Museums and museum publications in Britain, 1975-85, *British Book News*, British Council, London, 263-273.
Bassett, D.A. (1992) Museum publications: a descriptive and bibliographic guide, in Thompson, J.M.A., *et al. (eds.), Manual of Curatorship,* Butterworths, London, 623-649.
Bassett, D.A. (1992) Museums and education: a brief bibliographic guide, in Thompson, J.M.A. (ed.), *Manual of Curatorship,* Butterworth, London, 623-649.
Blackmore, S., Lee, T.R. & Turnbull, A.M. (1975) *Exhibitions: An Annotated Bibliography,* Department of Psychology, University of Surrey.
Bosdet, M. & Durbin, G. (1989) *Museum Education Bibliography 1978-1988,* Group for Education in Museums.
Canadian Museums Association (Various dates) *A Bibliography,* (With Supplements).
Carnegie UK Trust (1985) *Interpretation of the Environment - A Bibliography,* Carnegie UK Trust, Dunfermline.
Central Administration of Museums and Art Galleries, Bratislava (Annual) *Selected Bibliography of Museological Literature.*
De Torres, A.R. (ed.) (1990) *Collections Care: A Selected Bibliography,* National Institute for the Conservation of Cultural Property.
Elliott, P., & Loomis, R.J. (1975) *Studies of Visitor Behaviour in Museums*

and Exhibitions - An Annotated Bibliography, Office of Museum Programs, Smithsonian Institution, Washington, DC.

Gerhard, C. (1990) *Preventative Conservation in the Tropics: A Bibliography*, Institute of Fine Arts, New York.

Gorr, L.F. (1980) A museum management bibliography: Part 1, *Museum News*, 58(5), 71-84.

Gorr, L.F. (1980) A museum management bibliography: Part 2, *Museum News*, 58(6), 67-77.

International Council of Museums (1981) *Museums - Education - Cultural Action, Selective Bibliography*, UNESCO-ICOM Documentation Centre, ICOM (International Council of Museums), Paris.

International Council of Museums (Annual) *International Museological Bibliography*.

International Institute for Conservation (Bi-annual) *Art and Archaeology Technical Abstracts*.

Krist, G. *et al.* (1987) *Bibliography, Theses, Dissertations, Research Reports in Conservation*, ICOM Committee for Conservation, Budapest.

Roulstone, M. (ed.) (1980) *The Bibliography of Museum and Art Gallery Publications and Audio-Visual Aids in Great Britain and Ireland 1979/80*, Chadwick Healey.

Shapiro, M.S. & Kemp, L.W. (eds.) (1990) *The Museum: A Reference Guide*, Greenwood Press, London.

Sharpe, T. (1983) *Geology in Museums: A Bibliography and Index*, National Museum of Wales, Cardiff.

Smith, R.C. (1928) *A Bibliography of Museums and Museum Work*, American Association of Museums, Washington DC.

Stansfield, G. (1976) *Sources of Museological Literature*, Museums Association Information Sheet.

Wolf, R.L. *et al.* (1979) *New Perspectives in Evaluating Museum Environments: An Annotated Bibliography*, Office of Museum Programs, Smithsonian Institution, Washington DC.

Woodhead, P. & Stansfield, G. (1989) *Key Guide to Information Sources in Museum Studies*, Mansell, London.

12.3 Directories

American Association of Museums (1993) *The Official Museum Directory*, American Association of Museums, Washington DC.

Arnold-Forster, K. (1993) *Held in Trust: Museums and Collections of Universities in Northern England*, HMSO, London.

Barton, K. (1992) *Exploring Museums: Southern England Anf The Channel Islands*, HMSO, London.

Bartz, B. et al. (eds.) (1992) *Museums of the World*, 4th revision, K.G. Saur, Munich.

British Leisure Publications (1993) *Museums and Galleries in Great Britain and Ireland*, British Leisure Publications.

Canadian Museums Association (1992) *The Official Directory of Canadian Museums and Related Institutions 1993-94*, Canadian Museums Association, Ottawa.

Danilov, V.J. (1990) *America's Science Museums*, Greenwood Press, London.

Fleming, D. (1989) *Exploring Museums, North East England*, HMSO, London.

Hatton, A. (1993) *Exploring Museums: East Anglia*, HMSO, London.

Hudson, K. (1982) *Good Museums Guide*, 2nd edition, Macmillan, London.

Hudson, K. & Nicholls, A. (1982) *The Directory of Museums*, 2nd edition, MacMillan, London.

Hudson, K. & Nicholls, A. (1987) *The Cambridge Guide to the Museums of Britain and Ireland*, Cambridge University Press.

Hudson, K. & Nicholls, A. (1991) *The Cambridge Guide to the Museums of Europe*, Cambridge University Press.

International Council of Museums (1986) *Dictarium Museolicum*, Budapest.

Jackson, V. et al. (eds.) (1987) *Art Museums of the World*, Greenwood Press, London.

Jenkins, J. (1989) *Exploring Museums: Wales*, HMSO, London.

Johnstone, C. & Weston, W. (1981) *The Which? Heritage Guide*, Consumers Association and Hodder & Stoughton, 7-13.

London Museums Service (1990) *Museums in London,*, 4th edition, London Museums Service.

Marsh, G. (1990) *Exploring Museums: Home Counties*, HMSO, London.

Museums Association (1991) *Museums Yearbook*, Museums Association, London.

Olding, S. (1989) *Exploring Museums: London,*, HMSO, London.

Padwick, R. (ed.) (1993) *Directory of Exhibition Spaces*, 3rd edition, A.N.Publications.

Phillips, D. (1990) *Exploring Museums: North West England and Isle of Man*, HMSO, London.

Popplewell, S. (1990) *Exploring Museums: Northern Ireland and Eire*, HMSO, London.

Rogers, M. (1991) *Blue Guide to the Museums and Galleries of London*, 3rd edition, Black.

Rosovsky, N. et al. (1989) *The Museums of Israel*, Abrams, New York.

Suomen Museolitto (1990) *Finnish Museums*, Finnish Museums Association, Helsinki.

Thompson, C. (1990) *Exploring Museums: Scotland*, HMSO, London.

Wilson, A. (1989) *Exploring Museums: South West England*, HMSO, London.

12.4 Periodicals

AGMANZ Journal (formerly AGMANZ News) - Art Galleries & Museums Association of New Zealand (quarterly).

AIM - Bulletin of the Association of Independent Museums. (every 2 months).

Amgueddfa - National Museum of Wales, Cardiff (periodic).

AMSSEE News - Area Museum Service for South Eastern England (periodic).

ASC Newsletter - Association of Systematics Collections, Lawrence (every 2 months).

ASTC Newsletter - Association of Science - Technology Centers, Washington (Eevery 2 months).

Aviso - American Association of Museums, Washington DC (monthly).

Biology Curators Group Newsletter - Biology Curators Groupq (3 times a year).

British Association of Friends of Museums Newsletter - British Association of Friends of Museums Newsletter. (periodic).

British Museum Yearbook - British Museum, London (annual).

Conservation - Getty Conservation Institute, California (quarterly).

Conservation News - United Kingdom Institute for Conservation (3 times a year).

Conservation Notes - Canadian Conservation Institute (periodic).

Conservator - United Kingdom Institute for Conservation (Annual).

Curator - American Museum of Natural History (quarterly).

Designers/Interpreters Newsletter - Newsletter of the Group of Designers and Interpreters in Museums (periodic).

Geological Curator (formerly GCG Newsletter) - Geological Curators Group (2 times a year).

History News - American Association for State and Local History, Nashville (bimonthly).

ICCROM Newsletter - International Centre for the Study of the Preservation and the Restoration of Cultural Property, Rome (Annual).

ICOFOM Study Series - International Committee for Museology (International Council of Museums) (Occasional).

ICOM (International Council of Museums) Education - International Council of Museums, Paris (annual).

ICOM (International Council of Museums) News - International Council of

Museums (quarterly).

IIC News - International Institute for Conservation of Historic & Artistic Works (annual).

Interpretation - Bulletin of the Centre for Environmental Interpretation, Manchester (3 times per year).

Journal of Biological Curation - Biology Curators Group (annual).

Journal of Education in Museums - Group for Education in Museums (annual).

Journal of Museum Ethnography - Museum Ethnographers Group (Annual).

Journal of the American Institute for Conservation. - American Institute for Conservation .

Journal of the History of Collections - Oxford University Press (biannually from 1989).

Material History Bulletin - New Brunswick, Canada (annual).

MDA Information - Museum Documentation Association, Cambridge (periodic).

MPG News (formerly MAG News) - Museum Professionals Group (Periodic).

MPG Transactions (formerly MAG Transactions) - Museum Professionals Group (periodic).

MTI News - Museum Training Institute, Bradford (quarterly).

Muse (formerly Gazette) - Canadian Museums Association, Ottawa (quarterly).

Muse News (formerly Kalori Quarterly Newsletter) - Council of Australian Museum Associations (quarterly).

Musees Et Collections Publiques De France - Association Generale des Conservateurs des Collections Publiques de France (quarterly).

Musei e Gallerie D'Italia - Italian Museums Association (2 times a year).

Museogramme (formerly AMC Gazette) - Canadian Museums Association, Ottawa (monthly).

Museological Working Papers - MuWop - ICOM (International Council of Museums) International Committee for Museology, Stockholm (periodic).

Museologist - North-East Conference of the American Association of Museums (annual).

Museology - University of Capetown, Capetown (periodic).

Museum Archaeologist - Society of Museum Archaeologists (periodic).

Museum Design (formerly GDIM Newsletter) - Newsletter of the Group of Designers and Interpreters in Museums (periodic).

Museum Development - The Museum Development Company (Monthly).

Museum Ethnographers Group Newsletter - Museum Ethnographers Group (annual).

Museum International (formerly Museum), United Nations Educational (Quarterly - 1948-1992).

Museum Management & Curatorship (formerly the International Journal of

Museum Management & Curatorship) - Butterworths (quarterly).

Museum News - American Association of Museums, Washington DC (every 2 months).

Museum News - National Heritage, London (2 times a year).

Museum Studies Journal - John F. Kennedy University, Center for Museum Studies (biannually).

Museum Trainers Forum Newsletter - Museum Trainers Forum, Leicester (biannually).

Museums Australia (formerly Kalori) - Council of Australian Museum Associations (annual from 1982).

Museums Journal - Museums Association, London (monthly).

New Research in Museum Studies - Athlone Press, London (annual).

North of England Museum Service News - North of England Museum Service (periodic).

North West Museum and Gallery Service Newsletter - North West Museum and Gallery Service (periodic).

SAMAB: Southern African Museums Association Bulletin - South African Museums Association Bulletin (annual).

Science Museum Review - Science Museum, London (annual).

Scottish Museum News - Scottish Museum Area Council (periodic).

Social History Curators Group Journal - Social History Curators Group (periodic).

Studies in Conservation - International Institute for Conservation of Historic and Artistic Works., , (biannually).

Visitor Behaviour - Psychology Institute, Jacksonville (quarterly).

Winterthur Portfolio - University Press of Virginia (annual).

Author Index